Arabic

3rd Edition

by Amine Bouchentouf

for dummies®
A Wiley Brand

Arabic For Dummies®, 3rd Edition

Published by: **John Wiley & Sons, Inc.**, 111 River Street, Hoboken, NJ 07030-5774, www.wiley.com

For general information on our other products and services, please contact our Customer Care Department within the U.S. at 877-762-2974, outside the U.S. at 317-572-3993, or fax 317-572-4002. For technical support, please visit https://hub.wiley.com/community/support/dummies.

Wiley publishes in a variety of print and electronic formats and by print-on-demand. Some material included with standard print versions of this book may not be included in e-books or in print-on-demand. If this book refers to media such as a CD or DVD that is not included in the version you purchased, you may download this material at http://booksupport.wiley.com. For more information about Wiley products, visit www.wiley.com.

Library of Congress Control Number: 2018949880

ISBN 978-1-119-47539-2 (pbk); ISBN 978-1-119-47556-9 (ebk); ISBN 978-1-119-47548-4 (ebk)

Manufactured in the United States of America

C10004064_082818

Contents at a Glance

Table of Contents

Introduction

Arabic, the official language of more than 27 countries, is the mother tongue of more than 420 million people. It's spoken throughout the Middle East, from Morocco to Iraq. Additionally, because Arabic is the language of the Koran and Islam, more than 1.3 billion people across the world understand it.

Due to recent geopolitical events, Arabic has catapulted to the top of the list of important world languages. Even in countries where Arabic isn't the official language, people are scrambling to master this important and vital global language.

For people in North America and Europe, at first glance Arabic seems like a difficult language to master; after all, it isn't a Romance language and doesn't use the Latin alphabet. However, like any other language, Arabic is governed by a set of rules, and when you master these rules, you're able to speak Arabic like a native speaker!

Arabic For Dummies, 3rd Edition, is designed to identify and explain the rules that govern the Arabic language in the easiest and most interactive way possible. I organize each chapter in a straightforward and coherent manner and present the material in an interactive and engaging way.

About This Book

Unlike most books on the Arabic language, I have written *Arabic For Dummies,* 3rd Edition, in a way that gives you the most accurate and in-depth information available to help you develop and improve your conversational skills. The book is modular in nature, which means every chapter is organized in such a way that you don't have to read the whole book in order to understand the topic that's discussed. Feel free to jump to chapters and sections to suit your specific needs. Also, I explain every grammatical and linguistic point in plain English so that you can incorporate the concept immediately. I take great care to explain every concept clearly and succinctly.

To provide the best foundation and the widest usage for students of Arabic, *Arabic For Dummies*, 3rd Edition, focuses on Modern Standard Arabic (MSA), which is the most widely used form of Arabic in the world. Arabic basically has three different types:

- **Koranic Arabic:** This is the Arabic used to write the Koran, the holy book for Muslims. This form of Arabic is very rigid and hasn't changed much since the Koran was written approximately 1,500 years ago. Koranic Arabic is widely used in religious circles for prayer, discussions of Islamic issues, and serious deliberations. Its usage is limited primarily to a strict religious context. It's the equivalent of Biblical English.
- **The regional dialects:** They're the most informal type of Arabic. They tend to fall into four geographical categories:
  - North African dialect (Morocco, Algeria, Tunisia, and Libya)
  - Egyptian dialect (Egypt)
  - Gulf Arabic (Saudi Arabia, Kuwait, Iraq, Qatar, and the United Arab Emirates)
  - Levantine dialect (parts of Syria, Palestine, and Jordan)

  Even though the words are pronounced differently and some of the everyday expressions differ dramatically from region to region, speakers from different regions can understand each other. The common denominator for the regional dialects is that they're all based on MSA.
- **Modern Standard Arabic (MSA):** This is the most widely used and understood form of Arabic in the world. MSA is the language that Arabic anchors use to present the news, and professionals use to discuss business and technical issues.

Throughout the book, each new Arabic word appears in Arabic script and **boldface,** followed by the transliteration system used by the Library of Congress, which is how you properly pronounce it (with the stressed syllables italicized), and its English equivalent in parentheses.

Because this is a language book, I include some sections to help you master the linguistic concepts with greater ease. Here's a description of the specialty sections you find in each chapter:

- **Talkin' the Talk dialogues:** Here's where you get to see Arabic in action. These common Arabic dialogues show you how to use important vocabulary words and terms you should be aware of.

- **Words to Know blackboards:** An important part of mastering a new language is becoming familiar with important words and phrases. Key terms that I recommend you memorize are included in these sections, which present the transcription of the Arabic word in Arabic script, the transliteration (the pronunciation; stressed syllables are underlined), and the translation.
- **Fun & Games activities:** The aim of *Arabic For Dummies*, 3rd Edition, is to help you master the Arabic language in an interactive and engaging way. With that in mind, each chapter ends with a Fun & Games section that lets you review the key concept covered in the chapter in a fun but effective way.

Foolish Assumptions

In writing *Arabic For Dummies*, 3rd Edition, I made the following assumptions about you:

- You've had very little exposure (or none at all) to the Arabic language. Or maybe you've been exposed to Arabic but are interested in brushing up on your language skills.
- You're interested in mastering Arabic for either personal or professional reasons.
- You want to be able to speak a few words and phrases so that you can communicate basic information in Arabic.
- You're not looking for a dry book on Arabic grammar; you want to discover Arabic in a fun and engaging manner.
- You're looking for a practical course that will have you speaking basic Arabic in no time!

Icons Used in This Book

In order to help you get in and get out of this book easily and efficiently, I use icons (little pictures) that identify important pieces of information by category. The following icons appear in this book:

TIP

When you see this icon, make sure you read carefully. It points to information that will directly improve your Arabic language skills.

REMEMBER

I use this icon to bring to your attention information that you definitely want to keep in mind when studying and practicing Arabic.

WARNING

Discovering a new language can be a wonderful experience. However, there are always potential pitfalls to avoid, whether grammatical, linguistic, or cultural. This icon points out important notions about Arabic that may trip you up.

GRAMMATICALLY SPEAKING

Grammar is the glue that binds a language together. Even though this isn't a grammar book, it does include important grammar lessons you need to be aware of. This icon is attached to major grammar points that will help you master the Arabic language.

CULTURAL WISDOM

This icon points out nonverbal methods of communication common in Arabic-speaking countries and among Arabic speakers. I use this icon to fill the gap between language and culture so that you know the cultural contexts in which you can use newly discovered words and phrases.

Beyond the Book

This book is full of useful information, but you can find even more online! Check out this book's Cheat Sheet, which contains useful questions, common greetings and expressions, days of the week, and a guide to numbers all in a handy portable format. Just go to `www.dummies.com` and search for "Arabic For Dummies Cheat Sheet."

You can also hear all the Talkin' the Talk dialogues provided in the book to get a better handle on correct pronunciation. Just go to `www.dummies.com/go/arabicfd` to access the online audio tracks.

Where to Go from Here

This book is organized so that you can jump around from topic to topic. You don't have to read the whole thing. Want to know how to ask for directions in Arabic? Jump to Chapter 8. Need to exchange money in an Arabic country? Check out Chapter 15. Want to figure out how to greet friends and family? Check out Chapter 4. Peruse the table of contents or index, find a topic that interests you, and start reading.

1 Getting Started with Arabic

IN THIS PART . . .

Get the lowdown on the basics of Arabic.

Familiarize yourself with Arabic script and the 28 letters of the Arabic alphabet.

Get an overview of Arabic grammatical and linguistic constructs and find out how nouns verbs, and adjectives interact with each other to create phrases and sentences.

Try out basic greetings and expressions.

Work on numbers, dates, and measurements.

Practice some useful Arabic at the office and around the house.

» Introducing the Arabic alphabet

» Talking Arabic like the locals

» Getting acquainted with everyday Arabic

Chapter 1
The Arabic You Already Know

Let me مرحبا (*mar.ḥah.ba*) (*welcome*) you to the wonderful world of Arabic! Arabic is the official language of 27 countries and is spoken by more than 420 million people across the globe. It's the language in which the Quran, the Holy Book in Islam, was revealed and written, and a large majority of the more than 1.3 billion Muslims across the world study Arabic in order to read the Quran and to fulfill their religious duties. By speaking Arabic, you get access to people and places from Morocco to Indonesia.

In this chapter, I ease you into Arabic by showing you some familiar English words that trace their roots to Arabic. You discover the Arabic alphabet and its beautiful letters, and I give you tips on how to pronounce those letters so that you can sound like a native speaker. Part of exploring a new language is discovering a new culture and a new way of looking at things, so in this first chapter of the third edition of *Arabic For Dummies*, you begin your discovery of Arabic and its unique characteristics, including the fact that it's written from right to left!

Taking Stock of What's Familiar

If English is your primary language, part of grasping a new لغة (*lu.*ghah) (*language*) is creating connections between the كلمات (ka.li.*māt*) (*words*) of the language, in this case Arabic and English. You may be surprised to hear that quite a few English words trace their origins to Arabic. For example, did you know that "magazine," "candy," and "coffee" are actually Arabic words? Table 1-1 lists some familiar English words with Arabic origins.

TABLE 1-1

Arabic Origins of English Words

English	Arabic Origin	Arabic Meaning
admiral	أمير البحر (*a*.mīr al-*baḥr*)	ruler of the sea
alcohol	الكحل (al.*kuḥul*)	a mixture of powdered antimony
alcove	القبة (al.*qub*.bah)	a dome or arch
algebra	الجبر (al.*jabr*)	to reduce or consolidate
almanac	المناخ (al.ma.*nākh*)	a calendar
arsenal	دار السلاح (dār as.si.*lāḥ*)	house of weapons
azure	اللازورد (al.lā.za.*ward*)	lapis lazuli
candy	سكر القصب (*suk*.kar al.*qa*.ṣab)	cane sugar
coffee	قهوة (*qah*.wah)	coffee
cotton	قطن (quṭn)	cotton
elixir	إكسير (ik.*sīr*)	philosopher's stone
gazelle	غزال (gha.*zāl*)	gazelle
hazard	زهر (zahr)	dice
magazine	المخزن (al.*makh*.zan)	a storehouse
saffron	زعفران (za'.fa.*rān*)	saffron
Sahara	الصحراء (aṣ.ṣaḥ.*rā'*)	Sahara (desert)
sherbet	شربات (shar.*bāt*)	dessert
sofa	صوفا (*ṣū*.fā)	a cushion
sugar	سكر (*suk*.kar)	sugar
zero	صفر (ṣifr)	zero

As you can see from the table, Arabic has had a major influence on the English language. Some English words such as "admiral" and "arsenal" have an indirect Arabic origin, whereas others, such as "coffee" and "cotton," are exact matches. The influence runs the other way, too, especially when it comes to relatively contemporary terms. For example, the word تلفزيون (ti.li.fiz.*yōn*) (*television*) comes straight from the word "television." As is often the case with languages, Arabic and English tend to influence each other, which is what makes studying them so much fun.

Discovering the Arabic Alphabet

Unlike English and other Romance languages, you write and read Arabic from right to left. Like English, Arabic has both vowels and consonants, but the main vowels in Arabic aren't actual letters. Rather, Arabic vowels are symbols that you place on top of or below consonants to create certain sounds. As for consonants, Arabic has 28 different consonants, and each one is represented by a letter. In order to vocalize these letters, you place a vowel above or below the particular consonant. For example, when you put a فتحة (*fat*.ḥah), a vowel representing the "ah" sound, above the consonant representing the letter "b," you get the sound "bah" as in "ball." When you take the same consonant and use a كسرة (*kas*.rah), which represents the short "i" sound, you get the sound "bih" as in "big."

To help you get a better grasp of the different letters in the alphabet, I explain vowels and consonants in the following sections.

All about vowels

Arabic has three main vowels. Luckily, they're very simple to pronounce because they're similar to English vowels. However, you need to realize that Arabic also has vowel derivatives that are as important as the main vowels. These vowel derivatives fall into three categories: *double vowels*, *long vowels*, and *diphthongs*. In this section, I walk you through all the different vowels, vowel derivatives, and vowel combinations.

Main vowels

The three main Arabic vowels are

- فتحة (***fat*.ḥah**): The first main vowel in Arabic is called a فتحة (*fat*.ḥah). A فتحة is the equivalent of the short "a" in "apple." Occasionally, a فتحة also sounds like the short "e" in "bet" or "set." Much like the other vowels, the way you pronounce a فتحة depends on what consonants come before or after it. In Arabic script, the فتحة is written as a small horizontal line above a consonant.

In English transcription, which I use in this book, it's simply represented by the letter "a," as in the words كلب (kalb) (*dog*) and ولد (*wa*.lad) (*boy*).

- **ضمة (*ḍam*.mah):** The second main Arabic vowel is the ضمة (*ḍam*.mah). This vowel sounds like the "uh" in "foot" or "book." In Arabic script, it's written like a tiny backward "e" above a particular consonant. In English transcription, it's represented by the letter "u," as in فندق (*fun*.duq) (*hotel*) or سحب (*su*.ḥub) (*clouds*).
- **كسرة (*kas*.rah):** The third main vowel in Arabic is the كسرة (*kas*.rah), which sounds like the long "e" in "feet" or "treat." This vowel is written the same way as a فتحة — as a small horizontal line — except that it goes underneath the consonant. In English transcription, it's written as an "i," as in بنت (*bint*) (girl) or إسلام (is.*lām*) (*Islam*).

Double vowels

One type of vowel derivative is the double vowel, which is known in Arabic as تنوين (tan.*wīn*). The process of تنوين is a fairly simple one; basically, you take a main vowel and place the same vowel right next to it, thus creating two vowels, or a double vowel. The sound that the double vowel makes depends on the main vowel that's doubled. Here are all possible combinations of double vowels:

- **Double *fat.ḥah*:** تنوين with فتحة creates the "an" sound, as in أهلًا وسهلًا (*ah*.lan wa.*sah*.lan) (*Hi*).
- **Double *ḍam*.mah:** تنوين with ضمة creates the "un" sound. For example, كرةٌ (*ku*.ra.tun) (*ball*) contains a double ضمة.
- **Double *kas*.rah:** تنوين with كسرة makes the "in" sound, as in صفحةٍ (*ṣaf*.ḥa.tin) (*page*).

Long vowels

Long vowels are derivatives that elongate the main vowels. Arabic is a very poetic and musical language, so a musical metaphor is appropriate. Think of the difference between long vowels and short (main) vowels in terms of a musical beat, and you should be able to differentiate between them much easier. If a main vowel lasts for one beat, then its long vowel equivalent lasts for two beats. Whereas you create double vowels by writing two main vowels next to each other, you create long vowels by adding a letter to one of the main vowels. Each main vowel has a corresponding consonant that elongates it. Here are a few examples to help you get your head around this long vowel process:

- To create a long vowel form of a فتحة, you attach an ألف (*a*.lif) to the consonant that the فتحة is associated with. In English transcription, the long فتحة form is written as "ā," such as in كتاب (ki.*tāb*) (*book*) orباب (*bāb*) (*door*). The "ā" means that you hold the vowel sound for two beats as opposed to one.

- The long vowel form of ضمة is obtained by attaching a واو (*wāw*) to the consonant with the ضمة. This addition elongates the vowel "uh" into a more pronounced "ū," such as in نور (*nūr*) (*light*) or غول (*ghūl*) (*ghoul*). Make sure you hold the "ū" vowel for two beats and not one.
- To create a long vowel form of a كسرة, you attach a ياء (yā') to the consonant with the كسرة. Just as the ألف elongates فتح and the واو elongates the ضمة, the ياء elongates the كسرة. Some examples include the "ī" in words like كبير (ka.*bīr*) (*big*) and صغير (ṣa.*ghīr*) (*small*).

Table 1-2 shows the Arabic characters for the long vowels.

TABLE 1-2

Arabic Vowel Characters

Arabic Character	Character's Name	Explanation
fat.ḥah	ألف ('alif)	To create a long vowel form of a فتحة
ḍam.mah	واو (wāw)	To create a long vowel form of a ضمة
kas.rah	ياء (yaa')	To create a long vowel form of a كسرة

Diphthongs

Diphthongs in Arabic are a special category of vowels because, in essence, they're monosyllabic sounds that begin with one vowel and "glide" into another vowel. A common example in English is the sound at the end of the word "toy." Fortunately, Arabic has only two diphthong sounds used to distinguish between the ياء (yā') and the واو (wāw) forms of long vowels. In a nutshell, diphthongs in Arabic are used to elongate a vowel, which helps differentiate between certain words.

REMEMBER

When you come across either of these two letters, one of the first questions to ask yourself is: "Is this a long vowel or a diphthong?" Making this determination is easy: When either the ياء or the واو is a diphthong, you see a سكون (su.*kūn*) above the consonant. A سكون is similar to the main vowels in that it's a little symbol (a small circle) that you place above the consonant. However, unlike the vowels, you don't vocalize the سكون — it's almost like a silent vowel. So when a واو or ياء has a سكون over it, you know that the sound is a diphthong. Here are some examples:

- **واو diphthongs:** يوم (yawm) (*day*); نوم (nawm) (*sleep*); صوت (ṣawt) (*noise*)
- **ياء diphthongs:** بيت (bayt) (*house*); عين ('ayn) (*eye*);ليل (layl) (*night*)

All about consonants

Arabic uses 28 different consonants, and each consonant is represented by a different letter. Because the Arabic alphabet is written in cursive, most of the letters connect with each other. For this reason, every single letter that represents a consonant actually can be written four different ways depending on its position in a word — whether it's in the initial, medial, or final positions, or whether it stands alone. In English transcription of the Arabic script, all letters are case-sensitive.

The good news: Most of the consonants in Arabic have English equivalents. However, a few Arabic consonants are quite foreign to nonnative speakers. Table 1-3 shows all 28 Arabic consonants, how they're written in Arabic, how they're transcribed in English, and how they sound. This table can help you pronounce the letters so that you sound like a native speaker.

TABLE 1-3 Arabic Consonants

Arabic Character	Letter Name	Pronunciation	Sounds Like	Example
ا (a)	a-lif	Sounds like the "a" in "apple"	أب (ab)	father
ب (b)	ba'	Sounds like the "b" in "baby"	باب (bāb)	door
ت (t)	ta'	Sounds like the "t" in "table"	تلميذ (til.*mīdh*)	student
ث (th)	tha'	Sounds like the "th" in "think"	ثلاثة (tha.*lā*.thah)	three
ج (j)	jīm	Sounds like the "j" in "measure"	جميل (ja.*mīl*)	pretty
ح (ḥ)	ḥa'	No equivalent in English; imagine the sound you make when you want to blow on your reading glasses (the soft, raspy noise)	حار (ḥar)	hot
خ (kh)	kha'	Sounds a lot like "Bach" in German or "Baruch" in Hebrew	خوخ (khawkh)	peach
د (d)	dāl	Sounds like the "d" in "dog"	دار (dār)	house
ذ (dh)	dhāl	Sounds like the "th" in "those"	ذهب (*dha*.hab)	gold
ر (r)	rā'	Like the Spanish "r," rolled fast	رجل (*ra*.jul)	man
ز (za')	zāy	Sounds like the "z" in "zebra"	زوجة (*zaw*.jah)	wife
س (s)	sīn	Sounds like the "s" in "snake"	سمك (*sa*.mak)	fish

Arabic Character	Letter Name	Pronunciation	Sounds Like	Example
ش (sh)	shin	Sounds like "sh" in "ship"	شمس (shams)	sun
ص (ṣ)	ṣād	A very deep "s" sound you can make if you open your mouth really wide and lower your jaw	صديق (ṣa.*dīq*)	friend
ض (ḍ)	ḍād	A very deep "d"sound; the exact sound as a dād except that you use a "D" instead of an "d"	ضباب (ḍa.*bāb*)	fog
ط (ṭ)	ṭā'	A deep "t" sound; start off by saying a regular "t" and then lower your mouth to round with your tongue on your teeth	طبيب (ṭa.*bīb*)	doctor
ظ (ẓ)	ẓā'	Take the "th" as in "those" and draw it to the back of your throat	ظهر (ẓahr)	back
ع (')	'āyn	No equivalent; breathe heavily and consistently through your esophagus and then intermittently choke off the airflow to create staccato sound	عراق ('i.*rāq*)	Iraq
غ (gh)	ghāyn	Sounds like the French "r" in "rendezvous"	غريب (gha.*rīb*)	strange
ل (l)	Lām	Sounds like the "L" in "Larry"	لبنان (lub-*nān*)	Lebanon
ق (q)	qāf	Similar to "k," but produced farther at the back of the throat; you should feel airflow being constricted	قهوة (*qah*.wah)	coffee
ك (k)	kāf	Sounds like the "k" in "keeper"	كتب (*ku*.tub)	books
ف (f)	fā'	Sounds like the "f" in "father"	فهمتُ (fa-ham-tu)	understood
م (m)	mīm	Sounds like the "m" in "Mary"	مخزن (*makh*.zan)	storehouse
ن (n)	nūn	Sounds like the "n" in "no"	نظيف (na.*ẓīf*)	clean
ه (h)	hā'	Create by exhaling deeply; think of yourself as a marathoner who just finished a race and is breathing heavily	هو (*hu*.wa)	he
و (w)	wāw	Sounds like the "w" in "winner"	وزير (wa.*zīr*)	minister
ي (y)	yā'	Sounds like the "y" in "yes"	يمين (ya.*mīn*)	right

To sound as fluent as possible, memorize as many of the letters as you can and try to associate each letter with the Arabic words in which it appears. The trick to getting the pronunciation of some of these more exotic Arabic sounds is repetition, repetition, and even more repetition! That old saying, "Practice makes perfect" certainly applies to Arabic.

Speaking Arabic like a Native

In this section, I share a couple of tricks to help you focus on pronunciation of difficult letters that, if you can master, are sure to make you sound like a native speaker. Here are some difficult letters and some related words you should familiarize yourself with:

- ح: أحمر (*aḥ*.mar) (*red*); حسن (*ḥa*.san) (*a man's name*); حوار (ḥi.*wār*) (*conversation*); حزين (ḥa.*zīn*) (*sad*)
- ع: عجيب ('a.*jīb*) (*amazing*); عزيمة ('a.*zī*.mah) (*determination*); عريض ('a.*rīḍ*) (*wide*)
- ق: قف (qif) (*stop*); قرد (qird) (*monkey*); قوس (qaws) (*bow*)
- غ: غضبان (ghaḍ.*bān*) (*angry*); غرفة (*ghur*.fah) (*room*); غداً (*gha*.dan) (*tomorrow*)

TIP

The difference between native Arabic speakers and nonnatives is enunciation. If you can enunciate your letters clearly — particularly the more difficult ones — you'll sound like you're fluent. Practice these words over and over until you feel comfortable repeating them really quickly and very distinctly. With practice, you can sound more like a native and less like someone who's just trying to pick up the language. Plus, memorizing these words not only helps with your pronunciation but also helps build your vocabulary.

» Deciphering the transliteration

» Getting more comfortable with the Arabic script

Chapter 2
Taking a Closer Look at the Arabic Alphabet

As you start studying Arabic and increasing your knowledge of vocabulary words, the obvious difference between Arabic and English is noticeable. It's the script. Unlike English and many of the western European languages that use Romanized letters (think a, b, c, d, and so on), Arabic uses script. To someone who doesn't have any understanding of the language, Arabic may look like a secret code of squiggles, lines, and dots.

Because you're reading this book and are making an effort to improve your Arabic-speaking skills, you know that they're actually individual letters that make the words and sentences of the poetic Arabic language.

Chapter 1 introduces the Arabic alphabet to you, what each of the 28 letters looks like, and how they correspond to the English letters. This chapter examines the alphabet a tad closer. I explain what abjad is, which is the specific writing system used in this book. I explain the Library of Congress transliteration system, so you can figure out how to pronounce the Arabic script. I also delve into the script more closely and provide you several Arabic words as examples that start with the different Arabic letters. When you finish this chapter, you should have a stronger knowledge of the Arabic alphabet and the script.

Getting a Grasp on أبجد

The term أبجد (*ab*.jad) refers to a specific writing system whereby the letters are used exclusively to denote the consonants while the vowels are excluded from the writing system entirely. Abjad is the writing system used in this book, and it's also the writing system used throughout the Arabic world. For instance, most newspapers you pick up in the Middle East use the abjad writing system, whereby the consonants are included but not the vowels. Even if you're watching Arabic TV, the Arabic subtitles are in abjad.

Does abjad help Arabic speakers or does it offer more difficulty? The fact of the matter is abjad is the most common writing system used in Arabic. There's unfortunately no way around this conventional system, so it's up to you, a student of Arabic, to fully dedicate yourself to become a good user of abjad.

Figuring Out the Transcription

This book uses the Library of Congress transcription system, which is a widely used and approved transcription and transliteration system. Officially known as the *ALA-LC Romanization Scheme*, this system was jointly developed and approved by the American Library Association (ALA) and the Library of Congress (LC).

THE ORIGINS OF ABJAD

The term *abjad* actually gets its origin from the pronunciation of the first letters in the Arabic alphabet: ا, ب, ج, د. The Phoenicians were the first to use an abjad writing system prominently, and it has been used in Semitic languages ever since its first use around 1000 B.C. In addition to Arabic, abjad's ancestral use was applied in such languages as Aramaic, Greek, and Hebrew. This writing form is rich with history, especially considering that it gets its origins from the Phoenicians, who sought to simplify an earlier writing system that was common at the time: Egyptian hieroglyphs. When you're looking at the Arabic script and abjad, don't forget that you're looking at a complex and elegant writing system that dates back to man's first recorded attempt at creating a uniform writing system that everyone can access.

Both the Library of Congress and the American Library Association have a vested interest in having an accurate and widely recognized transcription system for their users. The Library of Congress houses many foreign language texts that need to be archived, shelved, circulated, and used as references by thousands if not millions of users. The transcription essentially allows English speakers access to millions of texts without actually learning the original language script.

In the transliteration in this book, you see letters in the transliteration text that are italicized. The italicized portion of the text should be emphasized during pronunciation; in other words, you have to stress this syllable when speaking the word.

Another common symbol that you see is a small horizontal line over certain vowels, such as the vowel *a* or the vowel *i*. In this case, you have to extend the pronunciation of the vowel so that it's longer than the other vowels. Here's an example of a word where you would extend the pronunciation: mī.*lād* (*birth*). In this case, you have to extend both the vowel *i* and the vowel *a*.

Finally, whenever you come across an apostrophe, that means you have to make the *'ayn* sound. The transliteration system is straightforward, and you can pick it up very quickly with a little practice.

The Library of Congress system uses Arabic script for the following languages: Arabic, Kurdish, Farsi Persian, Urdu, and even Pashto. As such, the script that I use in this book can also be applied to several different languages as well. In addition to Arabic, the Library of Congress also uses Romanization for Cyrillic languages such as Russian and Serbian, Hebrew, and even Classical Greek languages and dialects.

Because this system is so widespread and covers a wide range of languages, you can rest assured that you're getting exposed to the most widely accepted transliteration scheme out there. In mastering this system, you can easily apply it to other languages as well.

Getting Better Acquainted with the Script

You may be surprised to find out that the Arabic script isn't used exclusively for the Arabic language. Rather, the Arabic script is used to depict other important world languages, such as Urdu and Farsi.

Urdu is the official language of Pakistan and is also widely used in parts of India. In total, there are approximately 100 million Urdu speakers worldwide. Farsi, on the other hand, is the official language of Iran, but it's also widely spoken in Iraq, Afghanistan, Uzbekistan, and even Tajikistan — more than 110 million people speak Farsi worldwide. So when you unlock the Arabic script, you get access to other key world languages.

Many folks are daunted by the Arabic script because the letters seem unfamiliar. A common phrase I often hear from students is that the script isn't relatable to the traditional Roman script used in English and other Romance languages. However, Arabic and Roman scripts share a common history. In many parts of Spain, the Arabic script was used alongside Roman script for centuries. In fact, Arabic script is the second most widely used in the world right after Latin.

REMEMBER

Another key difference is that Arabic is written from right to left, which is challenging at first. However, with a little patience and practice you can get used to it very quickly and won't even realize that you're reading from right to left! In Chapter 1, I include a word that is associated with each consonant in Arabic. In this section, I expand on that discussion so you can familiarize yourself with the script. Table 2-1 can help you to develop a faster understanding of the script, the words, and their usage in a sentence.

TABLE 2-1 **Examples of Arabic Script in Action**

Arabic Letter English Equivalent	Arabic Script	Transliteration	English
ا a			
	أسرة	*us*.rah	family
	أسنان	as.*nān*	teeth
	أذنين	u.dhu.*nayn*	two ears
	أكل	*a*.ka.la	he ate
	أين	*ay*.na	where
ب b			
	باب	bāb	door
	بعد	ba'd	after
	بنت	bint	girl
	بيت	bayt	house
	بطاطا	ba.*ṭā*.ṭā	potato

Arabic Letter English Equivalent	Arabic Script	Transliteration	English
ت t			
	تلك	*til*.ka	that (F)
	تاريخ الميلاد	tā.*rīkh* al.mī.*lād*	date of birth
	تكلم	ta.*kal*.la.ma	he spoke
	توتة	*tū*.tah	a berry
	توازن	ta.*wā*.zun	balance
ث th			
	ثلاجة	thal.*lā*.jah	refrigerator
	ثلج	thalj	snow
	ثمن	*tha*.man	price
	ثانية	*thā*.ni.yah	second
ج j			
	جامعة	*jā*.mi.'ah	university
	جملة	*jum*.lah	sentence
	جواهري	ja.*wā*.hi.rī	jeweler
	جريدة	ja.*rī*.dah	newspaper
	جسد	*ja*.sad	body
ح ḥ			
	حذاء	ḥi.*dhā'*	shoe
	حساء	ḥa.*sā'*	soup
	حليب	ḥa.*līb*	milk
	حافلة	*ḥā*.fi.lah	bus
	حرارة	ḥa.*rā*.rah	temperature

(continued)

TABLE 2-1 ***(continued)***

Arabic Letter English Equivalent	Arabic Script	Transliteration	English
خ kh			
	خس	khas	lettuce
	خوخة	*khaw*.khah	a peach
	خزانة	khi.*zā*.nah	cupboard
	الخميس	al.kha.*mīs*	Thursday
	خرشوف	khar.*shūf*	artichokes
د d			
	دجاج	da.*jāj*	chicken
	ديسمبر	dī.*sam*.bir	December
	دقيقة	da.*qī*.qah	minute
	دواء	da.*wā'*	medicine
	درجة	*da*.ra.jah	degree
ذ dh			
	ذلك	*dhā*.li.ka	that (M)
	ذهب	*dha*.ha.ba	he went
	ذرة	*dhu*.rah	corn
	ذراع	dhi.*rā'*	arm
ر r			
	رحلة	*riḥ*.lah	trip
	رعد	ra'd	thunder
	ركبة	*ruk*.bah	knee
	ريح	rīḥ	wind
	ربيع	ra.*bī'*	spring

Arabic Letter English Equivalent	Arabic Script	Transliteration	English
ز **z**			
	زيتونة	zay.*tū*.nah	an olive
	زيت	zayt	cooking oil
	زيت الزيتون	zayt az.zay.*tūn*	olive oil
	زيارة	zi.*yā*.rah	a visit
	زبون	zu.*būn*	client
س **s**			
	ساعة	*sā*.'ah	hour
	سحب	sa.*ḥāb*	clouds
	سرير	sa.*rīr*	bed
	سكر	*suk*.kar	sugar
	سينما	*sī*.ni.mā	movie theater
ش **sh**			
	شمس	shams	sun
	شوكة	*shaw*.kah	fork
	شيك	shīk	check
	شركة	*sha*.ri.kah	company
	شتاء	shi.*tā'*	winter
ص **ṣ**			
	صباح	ṣa.*bāḥ*	morning
	صيف	ṣayf	summer
	صغير	ṣa.*ghīr*	small
	صابون	*ṣā*.*būn*	soap
	صيدلية	ṣay.da.*liy*.yah	pharmacy

(continued)

TABLE 2-1 ***(continued)***

Arabic Letter English Equivalent	Arabic Script	Transliteration	English
ض **ḍ**			
	ضحك	ḍuḥk	laughter
	ضغط	ḍaghṭ	pressure
	ضفدع	*ḍuf*.da'	frog
	ضفاف	ḍi.*fāf*	river banks
	ضعيف	ḍa.*'īf*	weak
ط **ṭ**			
	طعام	ṭa.*'ām*	food
	طقس	ṭaqs	weather
	طماطم	ṭa.*mā*.ṭim	tomatoes
	طابق	*ṭā*.biq	floor
ظ **ẓ**			
	ظهر	ẓahr	back
	ظرف	ẓarf	circumstance
	ظروف	ẓu.*rūf*	circumstances
	ظنّ	*ẓan*.na	he thought
ع **'**			
	عاصفة	*'ā*.ṣi.fah	storm
	عدس	'ads	lentils
	عسل	*'a*.sal	honey
	عشاء	'a.*shā'*	dinner
	عيادة	'i.*yā*.dah	clinic

Arabic Letter English Equivalent	Arabic Script	Transliteration	English
غ gh			
	غداً	*gha*.dan	tomorrow
	غناء	ghi.*nā'*	singing
	غرفة	*ghur*.fah	room
	غول	ghūl	ghoul
	غسول الشعر	gha.*sūl* ash.*sha'r*	shampoo
ف f			
	فطور	fu.*ṭūr*	breakfast
	فندق	*fun*.duq	hotel
	فروسية	fu.rū.*siy*.yah	horseback riding
	فم	famm	mouth
ق q			
	قطار	qi.*ṭār*	train
	قراءة	qi.*rā*.'ah	reading
	قميص	qa.*mīṣ*	shirt
	قهوة	*qah*.wah	coffee
	قاموس	qā.*mūs*	dictionary
ك **k**			
	كتب	*ka*.ta.ba	he wrote
	كرسي	*kur*.sī	chair
	كلمة	*ka*.li.mah	word
	كؤوس	ku.*'ūs*	cups
	كسوة	*kis*.wah	clothes

(continued)

TABLE 2-1 *(continued)*

Arabic Letter English Equivalent	Arabic Script	Transliteration	English
ل l			
	لغة	*lu*.ghah	language
	لحم	laḥm	meat
	لحم الغنم	laḥm al.*gha*.nam	lamb
	لصاق	li.*ṣāq*	glue
	ليمون	lay.*mūn*	lemon
م m			
	مارس	*mā*.ris	March
	مدرسة	*mad*.ra.sah	school
	المال	al.*māl*	money
	مسبح	*mas*.baḥ	swimming pool
ن n			
	نور	nūr	light
	نقل	naql	transportation
	نوفمبر	nū.*fam*.bir	November
	نوم	nawm	sleep
	نتيجة	na.*tī*.jah	score
ه **h**			
	هواية	hu.*wā*.yah	hobby
	هاتف	*hā*.tif	telephone
	هذا	*hā*.dhā	this (M)
	هذه	*hā*.dhi.hi	this (F)
	هليون	hil.*yūn*	asparagus

Arabic Letter English Equivalent	Arabic Script	Transliteration	English
و w			
	ورق اللعب	wa.raq al.*la*.'ib	playing cards
	ولد	*wa*.lad	boy
	وديعة	wa.*dī*.'ah	deposit
	ورقة	*wa*.ra.qah	paper
	واحد	*wā*.ḥid	one
ي y			
	يد	yad	hand
	يوم	yawm	day
	يناير	ya.*nā*.yir	January
	يأكل	*ya'*.kul	he eats
	يكتب	*yak*.tub	he writes

The Arabic script and language may seem daunting at first. But remember that the language is structured in a highly efficient and organized manner, following consistent rules, which I cover in the first chapters of the book, and throughout later chapters as well. After you master these language rules, you can see just how simple and friendly the language actually is!

FUN & GAMES

Match the Arabic letters in the first column with the English letters they correspond to in the second column. You can find the answers in Appendix C.

1. ي	**a.** f
2. ب	**b.** n
3. ل	**c.** y
4. ف	**d.** sh
5. ث	**e.** kh
6. ن	**f.** b
7. ش	**g.** gh
8. خ	**h.** j
9. ج	**i.** th
10. غ	**j.** l

» Getting specific with definite and indefinite articles

» Forming simple sentences

» Getting to know Arabic verbs

Chapter 3
Tackling Basic Arabic Grammar

Grammar is the foundation of any language. It's the glue that binds all the different elements of language together and allows us to communicate using a defined set of rules. Because grammar is so important, this chapter gives you an overview of the major grammatical concepts in the Arabic language, from the basic parts of speech (nouns, adjectives, articles, and verbs) to instructions on how to build both simple and descriptive sentences using common regular and irregular verbs. In addition, I introduce prepositions, demonstratives, and other parts of speech that will help you create phrases and sentences and, in general, express yourself in Arabic.

TIP

As you work through different chapters and sections of *Arabic For Dummies*, 3rd Edition, if you're ever unsure of how to proceed with a sentence formation, simply flip back to this chapter and review the grammar details that apply to your question. You'll be all set!

Introducing Nouns, Adjectives, and Articles

Nouns and adjectives are two of the most essential elements in any language. Nouns in Arabic, much like in English and other Romance languages, are the parts of speech used to name a person, place, thing, quality, or action. Adjectives, on the other hand, are the parts of speech that modify nouns. Although nouns and adjectives go hand in hand, the best way to understand how they work in Arabic is to address each one separately.

Getting a grip on nouns

In Arabic, every noun has a masculine, feminine, singular, and plural form. Table 3-1 lists some common Arabic أسماء (as.*mā'*) (*nouns*). You'll notice that I've listed both singular and plural forms of some nouns as well as masculine (M) and feminine (F) forms of others.

TABLE 3-1 Common Nouns in Arabic

Arabic	Pronunciation	English
ولد	*wa*.lad	boy
أولاد	aw.*lād*	boys
بنت	bint	girl
بنات	ba.*nāt*	girls
رجل	*ra*.jul	man
رجال	ri.*jāl*	men
امرأة	im.*ra*.'ah	woman
نساء	ni.*sā'*	women
تلميذ	til.*mīdh*	Pre-college student (M)

Arabic	Pronunciation	English
تلميذة	til.*mī*.dhah	Pre-college student (F)
مدرّس	mu.*dar*.ris	teacher (M)
مدرّسة	mu.dar.*ri*.sah	teacher (F)
طالب	*ṭā*.lib	student (M)
طالبة	*ṭā*.li.bah	student (F)
أستاذ	us.*tādh*	professor (M)
أستاذة	us.*tā*.dhah	professor (F)
مدرسة	*mad*.ra.sah	school
جامعة	*jā*.mi.'ah	university
كلية	kul.*liy*.yah	college
كتاب	ki.*tāb*	book
طاولة	*ṭā*.wi.lah	table
سيارة	say.*yā*.rah	car

Identifying adjectives

In Arabic, an نعت (*na't*) (*adjective*) must be in agreement with the noun it modifies in both gender and plurality. Table 3-2 presents some common adjectives in both the feminine and masculine forms.

Notice that the masculine forms of the adjectives in Table 3-2 are manipulated slightly to achieve the feminine adjective forms; essentially, all you do is add the suffix **-a** to the masculine adjective to obtain its feminine form. This rule applies to all regular adjective forms.

TABLE 3-2 Common Adjectives in Arabic

Arabic	Pronunciation	English
كبير	ka.*bīr*	big (M)
كبيرة	ka.*bī*.rah	big (F)
صغير	ṣa.*ghīr*	small (M)
صغيرة	ṣa.*ghī*.rah	small (F)
طويل	ṭa.*wīl*	tall (M)
طويلة	ṭa.*wī*.lah	tall (F)
قصير	qa.ṣīr	short (M)
قصيرة	qa.*ṣī*.rah	short (F)
جميل	ja.*mīl*	beautiful/handsome (M)
جميلة	ja.*mī*.lah	beautiful/pretty (F)
قبيح	qa.*bīḥ*	ugly (M)
قبيحة	qa.*bī*.ḥah	ugly (F)
قوي	qa.*wiyy*	strong (M)
قوية	qa.*wiy*.yah	strong (F)
ضعيف	ḍa.*'īf*	weak (M)
ضعيفة	ḍa.*'ī*.fah	weak (F)
صحيح	ṣa.*ḥiḥ*	healthy (M)
صحيحة	ṣa.*ḥī*.ḥah	healthy (F)
مريض	ma.*rīḍ*	sick (M)
مريضة	ma.*rī*. ḍah	sick (F)
ذكي	*dha*.kī	smart (M)

Arabic	Pronunciation	English
ذكية	dha.*kiy*.yah	smart (F)
غبي	*gha*.bī	dumb (M)
غبية	gha.*biy*.yah	dumb (F)
سريع	sa.*rī'*	fast (M)
سريعة	sa.*rī*.'ah	fast (F)
بطيء	ba.*ṭī'*	slow (M)
بطيئة	ba.*ṭī*.'ah	slow (F)
ثقيل	tha.*qīl*	heavy (M)
ثقيلة	tha.*qī*.lah	heavy (F)
خفيف	kha.*fīf*	light (M)
خفيفة	kha.*fī*.fah	light (F)
صعب	*ṣa'b*	difficult (M)
صعبة	*ṣa'*.bah	difficult (F)
سهل	sahl	easy (M)
سهلة	*sah*.lah	easy (F)
لطيف	la.*ṭīf*	nice/kind (M)
لطيفة	la.*ṭī*.fah	nice/kind (F)
عجيب	'a.*jīb*	amazing (M)
عجيبة	'a.*jī*.bah	amazing (F)
لذيذ	la.*dhīdh*	delicious (M)
لذيذة	la.*dhī*.dhah	delicious (F)

REMEMBER

However, in addition to the regular adjective forms, another category of adjectives exists in which the masculine and feminine forms are completely different from each other. This is the *irregular adjective form.*

Fortunately, all irregular adjectives fall in the same category: colors; and every color is an irregular adjective. Put simply, ألوان (al.*wān*) (*colors*) in Arabic are all irregular adjectives because the masculine color form is radically different than its feminine version. Table 3-3 lists the most common irregular adjectives.

Every لون (lawn) (*color*) in Table 3-3 (as well as the colors I didn't have space to list) must agree in gender with the noun it describes.

TABLE 3-3

Irregular Adjectives: Colors

Arabic	Pronunciation	English
أبيض	*ab*.yaḍ	white (M)
بيضاء	bay.*ḍā'*	white (F)
أسود	*as*.wad	black (M)
سوداء	saw.*dā'*	black (F)
أزرق	*az*.raq	blue (M)
زرقاء	zar.*qā'*	blue (F)
أخضر	*akh*.ḍar	green (M)
خضراء	khaḍ.*rā'*	green (F)
أحمر	*aḥ*.mar	red (M)
حمراء	ḥam.*rā'*	red (F)
أصفر	*aṣ*.far	yellow (M)
صفراء	ṣaf.*rā'*	yellow (F)
أسمر	*as*.mar	brown (M)
سمراء	sam.*rā'*	brown (F)
أرجواني	ur.ju.*wā*.nī	purple (M)
أرجوانية	ur.ju.wā.*niy*.yah	purple (F)

GRAMMATICALLY SPEAKING

One of the biggest differences between adjective and noun interactions in the English and Arabic languages is that nouns in Arabic come *before* the adjectives. In English, nouns always come *after* their adjectives.

Discovering definite and indefinite articles

A common trait that nouns and adjectives share in the Arabic language is that both can be modified using definite article prefixes. To refresh your memory, an *article* is a part of speech that you use to indicate nouns or adjectives and specify their applications. In English, there are two types of articles: indefinite and definite articles. The indefinite articles in English are "a" and "an," such as in "a book" or "an umbrella." The definite article is the word "the," as in "the book" or "the umbrella."

Unlike English, Arabic has no outright indefinite article; instead, the indefinite article in Arabic is always implied. For example, when you say كتاب (ki.*tāb*) (*book*), you mean both "book" and "a book." Similarly, مدرسة (*mad*.ra.sah) (*school*) means both "school" and "a school." However, Arabic does employ a definite article, which is the prefix you attach to either the noun or the adjective you want to define.

The rule

REMEMBER

The definite article in Arabic is the prefix ال "*al-*". When you want to define a noun or adjective, you simply attach this prefix to the word. For example, "the book" is الكتاب, and "the school" is المدرسة.

The inevitable exceptions

GRAMMATICALLY SPEAKING

In the examples الكتاب and المدرسة, the prefix ال "*al-*" retains its original form. However, there are exceptions to this rule. Sometimes, the "l" in the prefix ال "*al-*" drops off and is replaced by a letter similar to the first letter of the word being definite. For example, the word نور (nūr) means "light" in Arabic. If you want to say "the light," you may assume that you simply attach the prefix ال "*al-*" and get النور. However, that's not quite right. Instead, the appropriate way of saying "the light" in Arabic is النور (an.*nūr*), where you replace the "l" in ال "*al-*" with the first letter of the definite word, which in this case is "n." Another example of this definite article exception is the word صباح (ṣa.*bāḥ*) (*morning*). When you define it, the resulting word is الصباح (aṣ.ṣa.*bāḥ*) (*the morning*) and not (al.ṣa.*bāḥ*).

So how do you know whether to use ال "*al-*" or another definite article prefix format? The answer is actually quite simple and has something to do with a really cool concept. Every single letter in Arabic falls into one of two categories: sun letters and moon letters. Put simply, every word that begins with a moon letter gets the prefix *al-*, and every word that begins with a sun letter gets the prefix **a-** followed by its sun letter. Table 3-4 lists all the sun letters. Every other letter in Arabic is automatically a moon letter.

TABLE 3-4

The Sun Letters

Arabic	Pronunciation	English
تاء	tā'	t
ثاء	thā'	th
دال	dāl	d
ذال	dhāl	dh
ر	rā	r
ز	zāy	z
س	sīn	s
ش	shin	sh
ص	ṣād	ṣ
ض	ḍād	ḍ
ط	ṭā'	ṭ
ظ	ẓā'	ẓ
ل	lām	l
ن	nūn	n

Table 3-5 lists some common nouns and adjectives that are definite. Notice the difference between the words that begin with sun letters and moon letters.

TABLE 3-5

Common Definite Nouns and Articles

Arabic	Pronunciation	English
الكتاب	al.ki.*tāb*	the book
المدرسة	al.*mad*.ra.sah	the school
الولد	al.*wa*.lad	the boy
البنت	al.*bint*	the girl
الرجل	ar.*ra*.jul	the man

Arabic	Pronunciation	English
المرأة	al.*mar*.'ah	the woman
الصباح	aṣ.ṣa.*bāḥ*	the morning
الشمس	ash.*shams*	the sun
القمر	al.*qa*.mar	the moon
الكبير	al.ka.*bīr*	the big (one) (M)
الصغير	aṣ.ṣa.*ghīr*	the small (one) (M)
السريع	as.sa.*rī'*	the fast (one) (M)
الأزرق	al.*'az*.raq	the blue (one) (M)
الزرقاء	az.zar.*qā'*	the blue (one) (F)
الصفراء	aṣ.ṣaf.*rā'*	the yellow (one) (F)
السمراء	as.sam.*rā'*	the brown/brunette (one) (F)
اللذيذ	al.la.*dhīdh*	the delicious (one) (M)

Understanding the interaction between nouns and adjectives

Nouns and adjectives go hand in hand. In this section, I show you how you can manipulate nouns and adjectives to create little phrases. Recall that unlike in the English language, nouns in Arabic always come *before* the adjective.

You can create three types of phrases by manipulating nouns and adjectives. This section examines the ways you can pair up nouns and adjectives to create definite and indefinite phrases. (Later in the chapter, I show you how to create a complete sentence by simply using a noun and an adjective.)

Indefinite phrases

One of the most important things to remember about nouns and adjectives in Arabic is that they can be both definite and indefinite using the definite article prefix ال "*al-*". Hence, to create an indefinite phrase, all you do is take an indefinite noun and add to it an indefinite adjective. For example, to say "a big book" or "big book," you add the adjective كبير (ka.*bīr*) (*big*) to the noun كتاب (ki.*tāb*) (*book*). So the phrase كتاب كبير means "a big book" in Arabic. Here are some other examples of indefinite phrases featuring indefinite nouns and adjectives:

- ولد طويل (*wa*.lad ṭa.*wīl*) (*a tall boy*)
- بنت جميلة (bint ja.*mī*.lah) (*a pretty girl*)
- رجل قوي (*ra*.jul *qa*.wī) (*a strong man*)
- امرأة لطيفة (im.*ra*.'ah la.*ṭī*.fah) (*a nice woman*)
- مدرسة صغيرة (*mad*.ra.sah ṣa.*ghī*.rah) (*a small school*)
- طاولة حمراء (*ṭā*.wi.lah ḥam.*rā'*) (*a red table*)

Notice that the adjectives agree with their corresponding nouns in gender. For example, you say بنت جميلة and *not* بنت جميل.

Adding more descriptive words to the noun is very simple: Because adjectives follow the noun in Arabic, you just add an extra adjective and you're done! But don't forget to add the conjunction و (*wa*) (*and*) between the adjectives. Check out some examples:

- ولد طويل وكبير (*wa*.lad ṭa.*wīl* wa.ka.*bīr*) (*a tall and big boy*)
- بنت طويلة وجميلة (bint ṭa.*wī*.lah wa.ja.*mī*.lah) (*a tall and pretty girl*)
- رجل قوي وسريع (*ra*.jul *qa*.wī wa.sa.*rī'*) (*a strong and fast man*)
- امرأة لطيفة وقوية (im.*ra*.'ah la.*ṭī*.fah wa.qa.*wiy*.yah) (*a nice and strong woman*)
- مدرسة صغيرة وبيضاء (*mad*.ra.sah ṣa.*ghī*.rah wa.bay.*ḍā'*) (*a small and white school*)
- طاولة حمراء وقصيرة (*ṭā*.wi.lah ḥam.*rā'* wa.qa.*ṣī*.*rah*) (*a red and short table*)

Definite phrases

The biggest difference between creating an indefinite phrase and a definite phrase is the use of the definite article prefix ال "*al-*." Both noun and adjective must be definite using the definite article prefix. For example, to say "the big book," you say الكتاب الكبير. Here are some examples of definite phrases:

- الولد الطويل (al.*wa*.lad aṭ.ṭa.*wīl*) (*the tall boy*)
- البنت الجميلة (al.*bint* al.ja.*mī*.lah) (*the pretty girl*)
- الرجل القوي (ar.*ra*.jul al.*qa*.wī) (*the strong man*)

- الامرأة اللطيفة (al.im.*ra*.'ah al.la.*ṭī*.fah) (*the nice woman*)
- المدرسة الصغيرة (al.*mad*.ra.sah aṣ.ṣa.*ghī*.rah) (*the small school*)
- الطاولة الحمراء (aṭ.*ṭā*.wi.lah' al.ḥam.*rā'*) (*the red table*)

Using similar patterns, you can create a definite phrase using multiple adjectives. Just like in indefinite phrases, make sure you use the conjunction و (wa) in between adjectives:

- الولد الطويل والكبير (al.*wa*.lad aṭ.ṭa.*wīl* wal.ka.*bīr*) (*the tall and big boy*)
- البنت الطويلة والجميلة (al.*bint* aṭ.ṭa.*wī*.lah wal.ja.*mī*.lah) (*the tall and pretty girl*)
- الرجل القوي والسريع (ar.*ra*.jul al.*qa*.wī was.sa.*rī'*) (*the strong and fast man*)
- المرأة اللطيفة والقوية (al.*mar*.'ah al.la.*ṭī*.fah wal.qa.*wiy*.yah) (*the nice and strong woman*)
- المدرسة الصغيرة والبيضاء (al.*mad*.ra.sah aṣ.ṣa.*ghī*.rah wal.bay.*ḍā'*) (*the small and white school*)
- الطاولة الحمراء والقصيرة (aṭ.*ṭā*.wi.lah al.ḥam.*rā'* wal.qa.*ṣī*.rah) (*the red and short table*)

Creating Simple, Verb-Free Sentences

You can form sentences in two ways in Arabic: You can manipulate definite and indefinite nouns and adjectives, or you can pull together nouns, adjectives, and verbs. In Arabic, you can actually create a complete sentence with a subject and a predicate without actually using a verb! This concept may seem a little strange at first, but this section helps you quickly see the logic and reasoning behind such a structure.

To be or not to be: Sentences without verbs

Before you can construct verb-free sentences, you need to know that there is actually no "to be" verb in the Arabic language. The verb "is/are" as a proper verb simply doesn't exist. That's not to say that you can't create an "is/are" sentence in Arabic — you can. "Is/are" sentences are created without the use of an actual verb. In other words, you create "to be" sentences by manipulating indefinite and definite nouns and adjectives, similar to what I cover in the section "Understanding the interaction between nouns and adjectives" earlier in this chapter.

When you put an indefinite noun with an indefinite adjective, you create an indefinite phrase. Similarly, when you add a definite adjective to a definite noun, you end up with a definite phrase. So what happens when you combine a definite noun with an indefinite adjective? This combination — definite noun and indefinite adjective — produces an "is/are" sentence similar to what you get when you use the verb "to be" in English.

For example, take the definite noun الكتاب (*the book*) and add to it the indefinite adjective كبير (*big*). The resulting phrase is الكتاب كبير, which means "The book is big." Here are some more examples to illustrate the construction of "is/are" sentences:

- الولد مريض (al.*wa*.lad ma.*riḍ*) (*The boy is sick.*)
- البنت صغيرة (al.*bint* ṣa.*ghī*.rah) (*The girl is young.*)
- السيارة خضراء (as.say.*yā*.rah khaḍ.*rā'*) (*The car is green.*)
- الطالبة ذكية (aṭ.*ṭā*.li.bah dha.*kiy*.yah) (*The student is smart.*) (F)
- المدرّس قصير (al.mu.*dar*.ris qa.*ṣīr*) (*The teacher is short.*) (M)
- الأستاذ طويل (al.'us.*tādh* ṭa.*wīl*) (*The professor is tall.*) (M)

If you want to use additional adjectives in these verb-free sentences, you simply add the conjunction **wa**. Here are some examples of "is/are" sentences with multiple adjectives:

- الولد مريض وضعيف (al.*wa*.lad ma.*rīḍ* wa.*ḍa*.'*īf*) (*The boy is sick and weak.*)
- البنت صحيحة وقوية (al.*bint* ṣa.*ḥī*.ḥah wa.qa.*wiy*.yah) (*The girl is healthy and strong.*)
- السيارة خضراء وسريعة (as.say.*yā*.rah khaḍ.*rā'* wa.sa.*rī*.'ah) (*The car is green and fast.*)
- الطالبة ذكية ولطيفة (aṭ.*ṭā*.li.bah dha.*kiy*.yah wa.la.*ṭī*.fah) (*The student is smart and nice.*) (F)
- المدرّس قصير وذكي (al.mu.*dar*.ris qa.*ṣīr* wa.*dha*.kī) (*The teacher is short and smart.*) (M)
- الكتاب طويل وصعب (al.ki.*tāb* ṭa.*wīl* wa.*ṣa'b*) (*The book is long and difficult.*) (M)

This construct is fairly flexible, and if you change the nature of one of the adjectives, you radically alter the meaning of the جملة (*jum*.lah) (*sentence*). For instance, the examples all show a definite noun with two indefinite adjectives. What happens when you mix things up and add an indefinite noun to an indefinite adjective and a definite adjective?

Consider the example البنت صحيحة وقوية (*The girl is healthy and strong*). Keep البنت as a definite noun but change the indefinite adjective صحيحة into its definite version, الصحيحة; also, drop the و, and keep قوية as an indefinite adjective. The resulting phrase is البنت الصحيحة قوية, which means "The healthy girl is strong."

You can grasp what's going on here by dividing the terms into clauses: The first phrase is the definite noun/definite adjective combination البنت الصحيحة (*the healthy girl*); the second phrase is the indefinite adjective قوية (*strong*). Combining these phrases is the same as combining a definite noun with an indefinite adjective — the result is an "is/are" sentence. Here are more examples to help clear up any confusion you may have regarding this concept:

- الولد المريض ضعيف (al.*wa*.lad al.ma.*rīḍ* ḍa.*'īf*) (*The sick boy is weak.*)
- السيارة الخضراء سريعة (as.say.*yā*.rah al.khaḍ.*rā'* sa.*rī*.'ah) (*The green car is fast.*)
- الطالبة الذكية لطيفة (aṭ.*ṭā*.li.bah adh.dha.*kiy*.yah la.*ṭī*.fah) (*The smart student is nice.*) (F)
- المدرّس القصير ذكي (al.mu.*dar*.ris al.qa.*ṣīr dha*.kī) (*The short teacher is smart.*) (M)
- الكتاب الطويل صعب (al.ki.*tāb* aṭ.ṭa.*wīl* ṣa'b) (*The long book is difficult.*) (M)

Notice that a simple change in the definite article changes the meaning of the phrase or sentence. For example, when the noun is definite and both adjectives are indefinite, you create an "is" sentence, as in "The boy is big." On the other hand, when both noun and adjective are definite, the adjective affects the noun directly, and you get "the big boy."

Building sentences with common prepositions

In grammatical terms, حروف الجرّ (ḥu.*rūf* al.*jarr*) (*prepositions*) are words or small phrases that indicate a relationship between substantive and other types of words, such as adjectives, verbs, nouns, or other substantives. In both English and Arabic, prepositions are parts of speech that are essential in the formation of sentences. You can add them to "is/are" sentences to give them more specificity. Table 3-6 lists the most common prepositions you're likely to use in Arabic.

TABLE 3-6

Common Prepositions

Arabic	Pronunciation	English
من	min	from
في	fī	in
إلى	*i*.lá	to
مع	*ma*.'a	with
على	*'a*.lá	on
قريب من	qa.*rīb* min	close to
بعيد عن	ba.*'īd* 'an	far from
أمام	a.*mām*	in front of
وراء	wa.*rā'*	behind
تحت	*taḥt*	underneath
فوق	*fawq*	above
بجانب	bi.*jā*.nib	next to

You can use these prepositions to construct clauses and phrases using both indefinite and definite nouns and adjectives. Here are some examples:

- البنت أمام المدرسة (al.*bint* a.*mām* al.*mad*.ra.sah) (*The girl is in front of the school.*)
- الطاولة في الغرفة (aṭ.*ṭā*.wi.lah fī al.*ghur*.fah) (*The table is in the room.*)
- الأستاذة في الجامعة (al.'us.*tā*.dhah fī al.*jā*.mi.'ah) (*The professor is at the university.*) (F)
- المطعم بجانب الفندق (al.*maṭ*.'am bi.*jā*.nib al.*fun*.duq) (*The restaurant is next to the hotel.*)
- الرجل من أمريكا (ar.*ra*.jul min am.*rī*.kā) (*The man is from America.*)
- المدينة قريبة من الشاطئ (al.ma.*dī*.nah qa.*rī*.bah min ash.*shā*.ṭi') (*The city is close to the beach.*)
- السيارة البيضاء وراء المنزل (as.say.*yā*.rah al.bay.*ḍā'* wa.*rā'* al.*man*.zil) (*The white car is behind the house.*)
- الولد اللطيف مع المدرّس (al.*wa*.lad al.la.*ṭīf* *ma'* al.mu.*dar*.ris) (*The nice boy is with the teacher.*)

In addition, you can use multiple adjectives with both the subject and object nouns:

- الامرأة الجميلة في السيارة السريعة (al.im.*ra*.'ah al.ja.*mī*.lah fī as.say.*yā*.rah as.sa.*rī*.'ah) (*The beautiful woman is in the fast car.*)
- المدرّسة الذكية أمام المدرسة البيضاء (al.mu.dar.*ri*.sah adh.dha.*kiy*.yah a.*mām* al.*mad*.ra.sah al.bay.*ḍā'*) (*The smart teacher is in front of the white school.*) (F)
- الكرسي الصغير وراء الطاولة الكبيرة (al.*kur*.sī aṣ.ṣa.*ghīr* wa.*rā'* aṭ.*ṭā*.wi.lah al.ka.*bī*.rah) (*The small chair is behind the big table.*)

Using demonstratives and forming sentences

A *demonstrative* is the part of speech that you use to indicate or specify a noun that you're referring to. Common demonstratives in English are the words "this" and "that." In English, demonstratives are gender-neutral, meaning that they can refer to nouns that are both feminine and masculine. In Arabic, however, some demonstratives are gender-neutral whereas others are gender-specific.

REMEMBER

How do you know whether a demonstrative is gender-neutral or gender-specific? Here's the short answer: If a demonstrative refers to a number of objects (such as "those" or "these"), it's gender-neutral and may be used for both masculine and feminine objects. If, on the other hand, you're using a singular demonstrative ("this" or "that"), it must be in agreement with the gender of the object being singled out.

Following are demonstratives in the singular format:

- هذا (*hā*.dhā) (*this*) (M)
- هذه (*hā*.dhi.hi) (*this*) (F)
- ذلك (*dhā*.li.ka) (*that*) (M)
- تلك (*til*.ka) (*that*) (F)

Here are the plural demonstratives, which are gender-neutral:

- هؤلاء (hā.'u.*lā*.'i) (*these*)
- أولئك (u.*lā*.'i.ka) (*those*)

You can combine demonstratives with both definite and indefinite nouns and adjectives. For example, to say "this boy," add the definite noun الولد (*boy*) to the demonstrative هذا (*this*; M); because demonstratives always come before the nouns they identify, the resulting phrase is هذا الولد. Here are more examples of this construct:

» هذه البنت (*hā*.dhi.hi al.*bint*) (*this girl*)
» أولئك البنات (u.*lā*.'i.ka al.ba.*nāt*) (*those girls*)
» هؤلاء الأولاد (hā.'u.*lā*.'i al.'aw.*lād*) (*these boys*)
» تلك الأستاذة (*til*.ka al.'us.*tā*.dhah) (*that professor*) (F)
» ذلك الكتاب (*dhā*.li.ka al.ki.*tāb*) (*that book*)

When you use a demonstrative, which is, in essence, a definite article, the meaning of the phrase changes depending on whether the object is definite or indefinite. When a demonstrative is followed by a defined noun, you get a definite phrase, as in the examples in the preceding list. However, when you attach an indefinite noun to a demonstrative, the result is an "is/are" sentence. For instance, if you add the demonstrative هذا to the indefinite subject noun ولد, you get هذا ولد (*hā*.dhā *wa*.lad) (*This is a boy*). Using the examples from the preceding list, I show you what happens when you drop the definite article from the subject noun in a demonstrative clause:

» هذه بنت (*hā*.dhi.hi bint) (*This is a girl.*)
» أولئك بنات (u.*lā*.'i.ka ba.*nāt*) (*Those are girls.*)
» هؤلاء أولاد (hā.'u.*lā*.'i aw.*lād*) (*These are boys.*)
» تلك أستاذة (*til*.ka us.*tā*.dha) (*That is a professor.*) (F)
» ذلك كتاب (*dhā*.li.ka ki.*tāb*) (*That is a book.*)

When you combine a demonstrative clause with a definite subject noun and an indefinite adjective, the resulting phrase is a more descriptive "is/are" sentence:

» هذه البنت جميلة (*hā*.dhi.hi al.*bint* ja.*mī*.lah) (*This girl is pretty.*)
» أولئك البنات طويلات (u.*lā*.'i.ka al.ba.*nāt* ṭa.wī.*lāt*) (*Those girls are tall.*)
» تلك المدرسة كبيرة (*til*.ka al.*mad*.ra.sah ka.*bī*.rah) (*That school is big.*)

Conversely, when you combine a demonstrative clause with a definite subject noun and a definite adjective, you get a regular demonstrative phrase:

» هذا الرجل الطويل (*hā*.dhā ar.*ra*.jul aṭ.ṭa.*wīl*) (*that tall man*)
» ذلك الكتاب العجيب (*dhā*.li.ka al.ki.*tāb* al.'a.*jīb*) (*that amazing book*)
» تلك المدينة الصغيرة (*til*.ka al.ma.*dī*.nah aṣ.ṣa.*ghī*.rah) (*that small city*)

Forming "to be" sentences using personal pronouns

Every language has *personal pronouns*, the parts of speech that stand in for people, places, things, or ideas. Arabic is no different, except that personal pronouns in Arabic are a lot more comprehensive and specific than personal pronoun structures in other languages, such as English. Table 3-7 presents all the major personal pronouns in the Arabic language.

TABLE 3-7 Personal Pronouns

Arabic	Pronunciation	English
أنا	*a*.nā	I
أنتَ	*an*.ta	you (MS)
أنتِ	*an*.ti	you (FS)
هو	*hu*.wa	he/it
هي	*hi*.ya	she/it
نحن	*naḥ*.nu	we
أنتم	*an*.tum	you (MP)
أنتنّ	an.*tun*.na	you (FP)
هم	hum	they (MP)
هنّ	*hun*.na	they (FP)
أنتما	an.*tu*.mā	you (dual)
هما	*hu*.mā	they (M/dual)
هما	*hu*.mā	they (F/dual)

REMEMBER

In the translation and conjugation tables in this section and throughout *Arabic For Dummies*, 3rd Edition, in addition to singular and plural denotations, you see a form labeled *dual*. This number form, which describes a pair or two of an item, doesn't exist in English.

In addition to the personal pronouns common in English and other languages, Arabic makes a gender distinction with "you" in the singular and masculine forms. Furthermore, Arabic includes special pronouns reserved for describing two items (no more, no less). So all in all, personal pronouns in Arabic may describe one thing, two things, and three or more things.

The personal pronoun always comes before the predicate noun that it designates, and it also creates an "is/are" sentence. For instance, when you say هي بنت (*hi*.ya bint), you mean "She is a girl." Similarly, هو ولد (*hu*.wa *wa*.lad) means "He is a boy." The meaning changes slightly when the subject noun is definite. For example, هي البنت means "She is the girl," and هو الولد means "He is the boy." Here are some more examples to familiarize you with this concept:

- أنا رجل (*a*.nā *ra*.jul) (*I am a man.*)
- أنا الرجل (*a*.nā ar.*ra*.jul) (*I am the man.*)
- هم أولاد (hum aw.*lād*) (*They are boys.*)
- امرأة (*hi*.ya al.*mar*.'ah) (*She is the woman.*)
- أنتَ كبير (*an*.ta ka.*bīr*) (*You are big.*) (MS)
- أنتِ جميلة (*an*.ti ja.*mī*.lah) (*You are beautiful.*) (FS)
- أنتم سعداء (*an*.tum su.'a.*dā'*) (*You are happy.*) (MP)
- أنتِ بنت جميلة(*an*.ti bint ja.*mī*.lah) (*You are a pretty girl.*)
- أنتَ الولد الكبير (*an*.ta al.*wa*.lad al.ka.*bīr*) (*You are the big boy.*)
- هنّ النساء اللطيفات (*hun*.na an.ni.*sā'* al.la.ṭī.*fāt*) (*They are the nice women.*)
- هنّ نساء لطيفات (*hun*.na ni.*sā'* la.ṭī.*fāt*) (*They are nice women.*)
- هو رجل قوي (*hu*.wa *ra*.jul *qa*.wī) (*He is a strong man.*)
- هو الرجل القوي (*hu*.wa ar.*ra*.jul al.*qa*.wī) (*He is the strong man.*)

Creating negative "to be" sentences

Although Arabic doesn't have a "to be" regular verb to create "I am" or "you are" phrases, it does have a verb you use to say "I am not" or "you are not." This special irregular verb ليس (*lay*.sa) creates negative "to be" sentences. The following table shows ليس conjugated using all the personal pronouns.

Form	Pronunciation	English
أنا لستُ	*a*.nā *las*.tu	I am not
أنتَ لستَ	*an*.ta *las*.ta	You are not (MS)
أنتِ لستِ	*an*.ti *las*.ti	You are not (FS)
هو ليس	*hu*.wa *lay*.sa	He is not
هي ليست	*hi*.ya *lay*.sat	She is not
نحن لسنا	*naḥ*.nu *las*.nā	We are not
أنتم لستم	*an*.tum *las*.tum	You are not (MP)
أنتنّ لستنّ	an.*tun*.na las.*tun*.na	You are not (FP)
هم ليسوا	hum *lay*.sū	They are not (MP)
هنّ لسنّ	*hun*.na *las*.na	They are not (FP)
أنتما لستما	an.*tu*.mā las.*tu*.mā	You are not (dual/MP/FP)
هما ليسا	*hu*.mā *lay*.sā	They are not (dual/MP)
هما ليستا	*hu*.mā lay.*sa*.tā	They are not (dual/FP)

Following are some examples of negative "to be" sentences using the verb ليس.

- » أنا لستُ طالباً (*a*.nā *las*.tu *ṭā*.li.ban) (*I am not a student.*)
- » أنتَ لستَ مريضاً (*an*.ta *las*.ta ma.*rī*.ḍan) (*You are not sick.*) (M)
- » نحن لسنا في المدرسة (*naḥ*.nu *las*.nā fī al.*mad*.ra.sah) (*We are not at school.*)
- » الكرة ليست تحت السيارة (al.*ku*.rah *lay*.sat *taḥt* as.say.*yā*.rah) (*The ball is not under the car.*)
- » المطعم ليس بجانب الفندق (al.*maṭ*.'am *lay*.sa bi.*jā*.nib al.*fun*.duq) (*The restaurant is not next to the hotel.*)
- » المدرسة ليست كبيرة (al.*mad*.ra.sah *lay*.sat ka.*bī*.rah) (*The school is not big.*)

» أنت لست الولد الصغير (*an*.ta *las*.ta al.*wa*.lad aṣ.ṣa.*ghīr*) (*You are not the small boy.*) (MS)

» البنت الطويلة ليست ضعيفة (al.*bint* aṭ.ṭa.*wī*.lah *lay*.sat ḍa.*ʿī*.fah) (*The tall girl is not weak.*)

"To be" in the past tense

The Arabic verb for "was/were" (in other words, "to be" in the past tense) is كان (*kā*.na) (*was/were*). Similar to the negative form of "to be," the past form is an irregular verb form conjugated using all the personal pronouns.

Form	Pronunciation	English
أنا كنتُ	*a*.nā *kun*.tu	I was
أنتَ كنتَ	*an*.ta *kun*.ta	You were (MS)
أنتِ كنتِ	*an*.ti *kun*.ti	You were (FS)
هو كان	*hu*.wa *kā*.na	He was
هي كانت	*hi*.ya *kā*.nat	She was
نحن كنّا	*nah*.nu *kun*.nā	We were
أنتم كنتم	*an*.tum *kun*.tum	You were (MP)
أنتنّ كنتنّ	an.*tun*.na kun.*tun*.na	You were (FP)
هم كانوا	hum *kā*.nū	They were (MP)
هنّ كنّ	*hun*.na *kun*.na	They were (FP)
أنتما كنتما	an.*tu*.mā kun.*tu*.mā	You were (dual MP/FP)
هما كانا	*hu*.mā *kā*.nā	They were (dual/MP)
هما كانتا	*hu*.mā kā.*na*.tā	They were (dual/FP)

Here are some sentences featuring كان:

» أنا كنتُ مريضاً (*a*.nā *kun*.tu ma.*rī*.ḍan) (*I was sick.*)

» أنتَ كنتَ في المكتبة (*an*.ta *kun*.ta fī al.*mak*.ta.bah) (*You were in the library.*)

» هي كانت قريبة من المنزل (*hi*.ya *kā*.nat qa.*rī*.bah min al.*man*.zil) (*She was close to the house.*)

» نحن كنّا في المسبح (*naḥ*.nu *kun*.nā fīl.*mas*.baḥ) (*We were at the swimming pool.*)

» المدرسة كانت أمام المطعم (al.*mad*.ra.sah *kā*.nat a.*mā*.ma al.*maṭ*.'am) (*The school was in front of the restaurant.*)

» الكتاب الأزرق كان فوق الطاولة الصغيرة (al.ki.*tāb* al.*'az*.raq *kā*.na *fawq* aṭ.*ṭā*.wi.lah aṣ.ṣa.*ghī*.rah) (*The blue book was on the small table.*)

» المرأة والرجل كانا في البيت (al.*mar*.'ah war.*ra*.jul *kā*.nā fī al.*bayt*) (*The woman and the man were at home.*)

» الأولاد كانوا قريبين من البنات (al.'aw.*lād kā*.nū qa.rī.*bīn* min al.ba.*nāt*) (*The boys were close to the girls.*)

» الطعام كان لذيذاً (aṭ.ṭa.*'ām kā*.na la.*dhī*.dhan) (*The food was delicious.*)

Working with Verbs

You'll be very pleased to know that verb tenses in Arabic, when compared to other languages, are fairly straightforward. Basically, you only need to be concerned with two proper verb forms: the past and the present. A future verb tense exists, but it's a derivative of the present tense that you achieve by attaching a prefix to the present tense of the verb.

In this section, I tell you everything you need to know about أفعال (af.*'āl*) (*verbs*) in Arabic. I examine the past tense followed by the present and future tenses, and then I show you irregular verb forms for all three tenses.

Digging up the past tense

The structural form of the past tense is one of the easiest grammatical structures in the Arabic language. Basically, every regular verb that is conjugated in the past tense follows a very strict pattern. First, you refer to all regular verbs in the past tense using the هو (*hu*.wa) (*he*) personal pronoun. Second, the overwhelming majority of verbs in this form in the past tense have three consonants that are accompanied by the same vowel: the فتحة (*fat*.ḥah). The فتحة creates the "ah" sound.

For example, the verb "wrote" in the past tense is كتب (*ka*.ta.ba); its three consonants are "k," "t," and "b." Here are some common verbs you may use while speaking Arabic:

- » أكل (*a*.ka.la) (*ate*)
- » فعل (*fa*.'a.la) (*did*)
- » ذهب (*dha*.ha.ba) (*went*)
- » قرأ (*qa*.ra.'a) (*read*)

The following table shows the verb كتب (*ka*.ta.ba) (*wrote*) conjugated using all the personal pronouns. Note that the first part of the verb remains constant; only its suffix changes depending on the personal pronoun used.

Form	Pronunciation	English
أنا كتبتُ	*a*.nā ka.*tab*.tu	I wrote
أنتَ كتبتَ	*an*.ta ka.*tab*.ta	You wrote (MS)
أنتِ كتبتِ	*an*.ti ka.*tab*.ti	You wrote (FS)
هو كتب	*hu*.wa *ka*.ta.ba	He wrote
هي كتبت	*hi*.ya *ka*.ta.bat	She wrote
نحن كتبنا	*naḥ*.nu ka.*tab*.nā	We wrote
أنتم كتبتم	*an*.tum ka.*tab*.tum	You wrote (MP)
أنتنّ كتبتنّ	an.*tun*.na ka.tab.*tun*.na	You wrote (FP)
هم كتبوا	hum *ka*.ta.bū	They wrote (MP)
هنّ كتبنّ	*hun*.na ka.*tab*.na	They wrote (FP)
أنتما كتبتما	an.*tu*.mā ka.tab.*tu*.mā	You wrote (dual/M/F)
هما كتبا	*hu*.mā *ka*.ta.bā	They wrote (dual/M)
هما كتبتا	*hu*.mā ka.ta.ba.*tā*	They wrote (dual/F)

Now here's the verb درس (*da*.ra.sa) (studied) conjugated using all the personal pronouns.

Form	Pronunciation	English
أنا درستُ	*a*.na da.*ras*.tu	I studied
أنتَ درستَ	*an*.ta da.*ras*.ta	You studied (MS)
أنتِ درستِ	*an*.ti da.*ras*.ti	You studied (FS)
هو درس	*hu*.wa *da*.ra.sa	He studied
هي درست	*hi*.ya *da*.ra.sat	She studied
نحن درسن	*naḥ*.nu da.*ras*.nā	We studied
أنتم درستم	*an*.tum da.*ras*.tum	You studied (MP)
أنتنّ درستنّ	an.*tun*.na da.ras.*tun*.na	You studied (FP)
هم درسوا	hum *da*.ra.sū	They studied (MP)
هنّ درسنّ	*hun*.na da.*ras*.na	They studied (FP)
أنتما درستما	an.*tu*.mā da.ras.*tu*.mā	You studied (dual/M/F)
هما درسا	*hu*.mā *da*.ra.sā	They studied (dual/M)
هما درستا	*hu*.mā da.ra.*sa*.tā	They studied (dual/F)

Compare the conjugations of درس and كتب and you probably see a clear pattern emerge: Every personal pronoun has a corresponding suffix used to conjugate and identify the verb form in its specific tense. Table 3-8 outlines these specific suffixes.

Anytime you come across a regular verb you want to conjugate in the past tense, use these verb suffixes with the corresponding personal pronouns.

At this stage, you should know that not all regular verbs in the past tense have three consonants. Some regular verbs have more than three consonants, such as:

- تفرّج (ta.*far*.ra.ja) (*watched*)
- تكلّم (ta.*kal*.la.ma) (*talked*)

TABLE 3-8 **Personal Pronoun Suffixes for Verbs in the Past Tense**

Arabic Pronoun	Pronunciation	Translation	Verb Suffix
أنا	*a*.nā	I	-tu
أنتَ	*an*.ta	you (MS)	-ta
أنتِ	*an*.ti	you (FS)	-ti
هو	*hu*.wa	he/it	-a
هي	*hi*.ya	she/it	-at
نحن	*naḥ*.nu	we	-nā
أنتم	*an*.tum	you (MP)	-tum
أنتنّ	an.*tun*.na	you (FP)	-tun.na
هم	hum	they (MP)	-ū
هنّ	*hun*.na	they (FP)	-na
أنتما	an.*tu*.mā	you (dual)	-tu.mā
هما	*hu*.mā	they (M/dual)	-ā
هما	*hu*.mā	they (F/dual)	-a.tā

Even though these verbs have more than three consonants, they're still considered regular verbs. To conjugate them, you keep the first part of the word constant and only change the last consonant of the word using the corresponding suffixes to match the personal pronouns. To get a better sense of this conversion, take a look at the verb تكلّم (*talked*) conjugated in the past tense. Notice that the first part of the word stays the same; only the ending changes.

Form	Pronunciation	English
أنا تكلّمتُ	*a*.nā ta.kal.*lam*.tu	I talked
نتَ أتكلّمتَ	*an*.ta ta.kal.*lam*.ta	You talked (MS)
أنتِ أتكلّمتِ	*an*.ti ta.kal.*lam*.ti	You talked (FS)
هو تكلّم	*hu*.wa ta.*kal*.lam.a	He talked

Form	Pronunciation	English
هي تكلّمت	*hi*.ya ta.kal.*la*.mat	She talked
نحن تكلّمنا	*naḥ*.nu ta.kal.*lam*.nā	We talked
أنتم تكلّمتم	*an*.tum ta.kal.*lam*.tum	You talked (MP)
أنتنّ تكلّمتنّ	an.*tun*.na ta.kal.lam.*tun*.na	You talked (FP)
هم تكلّموا	hum ta.kal.*la*.mū	They talked (MP)
هنّ تكلّمنّ	*hun*.na ta.kal.*lam*.na	They talked (FP)
أنتما تكلّمتما	an.*tu*.mā ta.kal.lam.*tu*.mā	You talked (dual/MP/FP)
تكلّما	*hu*.mā ta.kal.*la*.mā	They talked (dual/M)
هما تكلّمتا	*hu*.mā ta.kal.la.*ma*.tā	They talked (dual/F)

When you know how to conjugate verbs in the past tense, your sentence-building options are endless. Here are some simple sentences that combine nouns, adjectives, and verbs in the past tense:

- الولد ذهب إلى المدرسة (al.*wa*.lad *dha*.ha.ba *i*.lá al.*mad*.ra.sah) (*The boy went to school.*)
- البنت تكلّمت في الصف (al.*bint* ta.kal.*la*.mat fī aṣ.*ṣaff*) (*The girl talked in the classroom.*)
- أكلنا طعاماً لذيذاً (a.*kal*.nā ṭa.*'ā*.man la.*dhī*.dhan) (*We ate delicious food.*)
- ذهب الرجل إلى الجامعة بالسيارة (*dha*.ha.ba ar.*ra*.jul *i*.lá al.*jā*.mi.'ah bis.say.*yā*.rah) (*The man went to the school by car.*)

Examining the present tense

Conjugating verbs in the past tense is relatively straightforward, but conjugating verbs in the present tense is a bit trickier. Instead of changing only the ending of the verb, you must also alter its beginning. In other words, you need to be familiar not only with the suffix but also the prefix that corresponds to each personal pronoun.

To illustrate the difference between past and present tense, the verb كتب (*wrote*) is conjugated as يكتب (*yak*.tub) (*to write*), whereas the verb درس (studied) is يدرس (*yad*.ru.su) (*to study*).

Here's the verb "to write" conjugated using all the personal pronouns. Notice how both the suffixes and prefixes change in the present tense.

Form	Pronunciation	English
أكتب	*a*.nā *ak*.tub	I am writing
أنتَ تكتب	*an*.ta *tak*.tub	You are writing (MS)
أنتِ تكتبين	*an*.ti tak.tu.*bīn*	You are writing (FS)
هو يكتب	*hu*.wa *yak*.tub	He is writing
هي تكتب	*hi*.ya *tak*.tub	She is writing
نحن نكتب	*naḥ*.nu *nak*.tub	We are writing
أنتم تكتبون	*an*.tum tak.tu.*būn*	You are writing (MP)
أنتنّ تكتبنّ	an.*tun*.na tak.*tub*.na	You are writing (FP)
هم يكتبون	hum yak.tu.*būn*	They are writing (MP)
هنّ يكتبنّ	*hun*.na yak.*tub*.na	They are writing (FP)
أنتما تكتبان	an.*tu*.mā tak.tu.*bān*	You are writing (dual/M/F)
هما يكتبان	*hu*.mā yak.tu.*bān*	They are writing (dual/M)
هما تكتبان	*hu*.mā tak.tu.*bān*	They are writing (dual/F)

As you can see, you need to be familiar with both the prefixes and suffixes to conjugate verbs in the present tense. Table 3-9 includes every personal pronoun with its corresponding prefix and suffix for the present tense.

Aside from prefixes and suffixes, another major difference between the past and present tenses in Arabic is that every verb in the present tense has a dominant vowel that's unique and distinctive. For example, the dominant vowel in يكتب is a ضمة (*ḍam*.mah) (*"u" sound*). However, in the verb يفعل (*yaf*.ʻal) (*to do*), the dominant vowel is the فتحة (*fat*.ḥah) (*"a" sound*). This means that when you conjugate the verb يفعل using the personal pronoun أنا, you say أنا أفعَل (*a*.nā *af*.ʻa.lu) and *not* أنا أفعُل (*a*.nā *af*.ʻu.lu). For complete coverage of Arabic vowels ضمة, فتحة, كسرة (*ḍam*.mah, *fat*.ḥah, and *kas*.rah), check out Chapter 1.

TABLE 3-9 **Personal Pronoun Prefixes and Suffixes for Verbs in the Present Tense**

Arabic Pronoun	Pronunciation	Translation	Verb Prefix	Verb Suffix
أنا	*a*.nā	I	'a-	-u
أنتَ	*an*.ta	you (MS)	ta-	-u
أنتِ	*an*.ti	you (FS)	ta-	-īna
هو	*hu*.wa	he/it	ya-	-u
هي	*hi*.ya	she/it	ta-	-u
نحن	*naḥ*.nu	we	na-	-u
أنتم	*an*.tum	you (MP)	ta-	-ū.na
أنتنّ	an.*tun*.na	you (FP)	ta-	-na
هم	hum	they (MP)	ya-	-ū.na
هنّ	*hun*.na	they (FP)	ya-	-na
أنتما	an.*tu*.mā	you (dual)	ta-	-ā.ni
هما	*hu*.mā	they (M/dual)	ya-	-ā.ni
هما	*hu*.mā	they (F/dual)	ta-	-ā.ni

The dominant vowel is always the middle vowel. Unfortunately, there's no hard rule you can use to determine which dominant vowel is associated with each verb. The best way to identify the dominant vowel is to look up the verb in the قاموس (qā.*mūs*) (*dictionary*).

In this list, I divide up some of the most common Arabic verbs according to their dominant vowels:

» ضمة (*ḍam*.mah)
  - يكتب (*yak*.tub) (*to write*)
  - يدرس (*yad*.rus) (*to study*)
  - يأكل (*ya'*.kul) (*to eat*)
  - يسكن (*yas*.kun) (*to live*)

- فتحة (*fat*.ḥah)
  - يفعل (*yaf*.'al) (*to do*)
  - يقرأ (*yaq*.ra') (*to read*)
  - يذهب (*yadh*.hab) (*to go*)
  - يفتح (*yaf*.taḥ) (*to open*)
- كسرة (*kas*.rah)
  - يرجع (*yar*.ji ') (*to return*)
  - يعرف (*ya'*.rif) (*to know*)

REMEMBER

When you conjugate a verb in the present tense, you must do two things:

1. **Identify the dominant vowel that will be used to conjugate the verb using all personal pronouns.**
2. **Isolate the prefix and suffix that correspond to the appropriate personal pronouns.**

Peeking into the future tense

Although Arabic grammar has a future tense, you'll be glad to know that the tense has no outright verb structure. Rather, you achieve the future tense by adding the prefix **sa-** to the existing present tense form of the verb. For example, يكتب means "to write." Add the prefix sa- to يكتب and you get سيكتب (sa.*yak*.tub) (*he will write*).

To illustrate the future tense, here's the verb يكتب (*yak*.tu.bu) conjugated in the future tense.

Form	Pronunciation	English
أنا سأكتب	*a*.nā sa.*'ak*.tub	I will write
أنت ستكتب	*an*.ta sa.*tak*.tub	You will write (MS)
أنت ستكتبين	*an*.ti sa.tak.tu.*bīn*	You will write (FS)
هو سيكتب	*hu*.wa sa.*yak*.tub	He will write
هي ستكتب	*hi*.ya sa.*tak*.tub	She will write
نحن سنكتب	*naḥ*.nu sa.*nak*.tub	We will write

Form	Pronunciation	English
أنتم ستكتبون	*an*.tum sa.tak.tu.*būn*	You will write (MP)
أنتن ستكتبنّ	an.*tun*.na sa.tak.*tub*.na	You will write (FP)
هم سيكتبون	hum sa.yak.tu.*būn*	They will write (MP)
هنّ سيكتبنّ	*hun*.na sa.yak.*tub*.na	They will write (FP)
أنتما ستكتبان	an.*tu*.mā sa.tak.tu.*bān*	You will write (dual/M/F)
هما سيكتبان	*hu*.mā sa.yak.tu.*bān*	They will write (dual/M)
هما ستكتبان	*hu*.mā sa.tak.tu.*bān*	They will write (dual/F)

Examining irregular verb forms

Arabic uses both regular and irregular verbs. Regular verbs have a specific pattern and follow a specific set of rules, but irregular verbs do not. Because these irregular forms include some of the most common verbs in the language (such as "to buy," "to sell," and "to give"), you should examine them separately. This section looks at some of the most common irregular verbs in the Arabic language.

The verb "to sell" is conjugated as باع (*bā*.ʻa) (*sold*) in the past tense. In the conjugation that follows, notice that unlike regular verbs, باع has only two consonants (the ب bā' and the ع ʻayn).

Form	Pronunciation	English
أنا بعتُ	*a*.nā *biʻ*.tu	I sold
أنتَ بعتَ	*an*.ta *biʻ*.ta	You sold (MS)
أنتِ بعتِ	*an*.ti *biʻ*.ti	You sold (FS)
هو باع	*hu*.wa *bā*.ʻa	He sold
هي باعت	*hi*.ya *bā*.ʻat	She sold
نحن بعنا	*naḥ*.nu *biʻ*.nā	We sold
أنتم بعتم	*an*.tum *biʻ*.tum	You sold (MP)
أنتنّ بعتنّ	an.*tun*.na biʻ.*tun*.na	You sold (FP)

Form	Pronunciation	English
هم باعوا	hum *bā*.'ū	They sold (MP)
هنّ بعنّ	*hun*.na *bi'*.na	They sold (FP)
أنتما بعتما	an.*tu*.mā bi'.*tu*.mā	You sold (dual/M/F)
هما باعا	*hu*.mā *bā*.'ā	They sold (dual/M)
هما باعتا	*hu*.mā bā.'*a*.tā	They sold (dual/F)

In order to conjugate the verb باع in the present tense, use the form يبيع (ya.*bī*.'u) (*to sell*).

Form	Pronunciation	English
أنا أبيع	*a*.nā a.*bī'*	I am selling
أنتَ تبيع	*an*.ta ta.*bī'*	You are selling (MS)
أنتِ تبيعين	*an*.ti ta.bī'*īn*	You are selling (FS)
هو يبيع	*hu*.wa ya.*bī'*	He is selling
هي تبيع	*hi*.ya ta.*bī'*	She is selling
نحن نبيع	*naḥ*.nu na.*bī'*	We are selling
أنتم تبيعون	*an*.tum ta.bī.'*ūn*	You are selling (MP)
أنتنّ تبعنّ	an.*tun*.na ta.*bi'*.na	You are selling (FP)
هم يبيعون	hum ya.bī.'*ūn*	They are selling (MP)
هنّ يبعنّ	*hun*.na ya.*bi'*.na	They are selling (FP)
أنتما تبيعان	an.*tu*.mā ta.bī.'*ān*	You are selling (dual/M/F)
هما يبيعان	*hu*.mā ya.bī.'*ān*	They are selling (dual/M)
هما تبيعان	*hu*.mā ta.bī.'*ān*	They are selling (dual/F)

For the future tense, simply add the prefix سـ (sa-) to the present form to get سيبيع (sa.ya.*bī'*) (*he will sell*).

Form	Pronunciation	English
أنا سأبيع	*a*.nā sa.'a.*bī'*	I will sell
أنتَ ستبيع	*an*.ta sa.ta.*bī'*	You will sell (MS)
أنتِ ستبيعين	*an*.ti sa.ta.bī'.*īn*	You will sell (FS)
هو سيبيع	*hu*.wa sa.ya.*bī'*	He will sell
هي ستبيع	*hi*.ya sa.ta.*bī'*	She will sell
نحن سنبيع	*naḥ*.nu sa.na.*bī'*	We will sell
أنتم ستبيعون	*an*.tum sa.ta.bī'.*ūn*	You will sell (MP)
أنتنّ ستبعنّ	an.*tun*.na sa.ta.*bi'*.na	You will sell (FP)
هم سيبيعون	hum sa.ya.bī.*'ūn*	They will sell (MP)
هنّ سيبعنّ	*hun*.na sa.ya.*bi'*.na	They will sell (FP)
أنتما ستبيعان	an.*tu*.mā sa.ta.bī.*'ān*	You will sell (dual/M/F)
هما سيبيعان	*hu*.mā sa.ya.bī.*'ān*	They will sell (dual/M)
هما ستبيعان	*hu*.mā sa.ta.bī.*'ān*	They will sell (dual/F)

Here are some other common irregular verbs:

- وصل/يصل (*wa*.ṣa.la/*ya*.ṣil) (*arrived/to arrive*)
- زار/يزور (*zā*.ra/ya.*zūr*) (*visited/to visit*)
- مشى/يمشي (*ma*.shā/*yam*.shī) (*walked/to walk*)
- اشترى/يشتري (ish.*ta*.rā/yash.*ta*.rī) (*bought/to buy*)
- ردّ/يردّ (*rad*.da/ya.*rudd*) (*answered/to answer*)
- جاء/يجيء (*jā*.'a/ya.*jī'*) (*came/to come*)
- أعطى/يعطي (*a'*.ṭā; *yu'*.ṭī) (*gave/to give*)

FUN & GAMES

Match the personal pronouns on the left column with their Arabic equivalents on the right.

you (MS)	هو
we	أنتِ
they (FP)	أنتَ
you (FS)	نحن
he	أنتم
you (MP)	هنّ

The answers are in Appendix C.

» Using common introductions

» Referring to countries and nationalities

» Talking about the weather

Chapter 4

Getting Started with Basic Expressions

In Arabic culture, you can't underestimate the importance of greetings. First impressions in the Middle East are crucial, and knowing both the verbal and nonverbal nuances of greeting people is one of the most important aspects of mastering Arabic.

In this chapter, I show you how to greet people in Arabic, how to respond to basic greetings, and how to interact with native Arabic speakers. You find out when it's appropriate to use formal and informal terms, how to make small talk, and how to introduce yourself. حظاً سعيداً! (*ḥaẓ.ẓan sa.ʿī.dan*) (*Good luck!*)

REMEMBER

You can listen to all the Talkin' the Talk dialogues featured in this chapter. Go to `www.dummies.com/go/arabicfd` and click on the dialogue you want to hear.

Greeting People Appropriately

In Arabic, you have to choose between formal and informal ways of greeting people. The greeting you use depends on whom you're addressing: If you're greeting someone you don't know for the very first time, you must use the more formal greetings. On the other hand, if you're greeting an old family friend or a colleague you know well, feel free to use the more informal forms of greeting. If you're not sure which form to use, you're better off going formal. I cover both types of greetings as well as some other handy pleasantries in this section.

Saying hello

The formal way of greeting someone in Arabic is السلام عليكم (as.sa.*lā*.mu ʻa.*lay*.kum). Even though it translates into English as "hello," it literally means "May peace be upon you." Arabic is a very poetic language, so you're going to have to get used to the fact that a lot of the phrases used in everyday life are very descriptive.

Using السلام عليكم is appropriate when

- You're greeting a potential business partner.
- You're at a formal event, dinner, or gala.
- You're meeting someone for the first time.

REMEMBER

The most common reply is وعليكم السلام (wa.ʻa.*lay*.kum as.sa.*lām*) (*and upon you peace*).

The phrase أهلاً وسهلاً (*ah*.lan wa.*sah*.lan) is a very informal way of greeting a person or group of people. Translated into English, it resembles the more informal "hi" as opposed to "hello." When someone says أهلاً وسهلاً, you should also reply أهلاً وسهلاً. In some cases, when someone greets you in his home, he may use this phrase. Here are other instances where you may run into this common expression.

Using the informal أهلا وسهلاً is appropriate when

- You're greeting an old friend.
- You're greeting a family member.
- You're greeting someone at an informal gathering, such as a family lunch.

Although وسهلاً is one of the friendliest and most informal greetings in Arabic, you can actually greet someone you know very well, such as a close friend or family member, by simply saying أهلاً. Because it's the most informal way of greeting someone in Arabic, make sure that you use أهلاً only with people you're very comfortable with; otherwise, you may appear disrespectful even if you're trying to be friendly! (Nonverbal signs may also convey disrespect; see the later sidebar "Sending the right nonverbal message.")

CULTURAL WISDOM

Kinship, family relations, and tribal connections are extraordinarily important to people from the Middle East. In the early period of Islam when traders and nomads roamed the Arabian Peninsula, they identified themselves as members of one nation — the أهل الإسلام (*ahl* al.is.*lām*) (*kinship of Islam*). They greeted each other by identifying themselves as part of the أهل (*ahl*) (*kin*) by saying أهلاً. This is how the phrase أهلاً وسهلاً originated, although today it's simply a friendly way of greeting people.

Bidding goodbye

Saying goodbye in Arabic is a little more straightforward than greeting someone, because even though there are different ways of saying goodbye, they aren't divided into formal or informal options. Here are the most common ways of saying goodbye in Arabic:

- مع السلامة (*ma.*'a as.sa.*lā*.mah) (*go with peace,* or *goodbye*)
- إلى اللقاء (*i*.lá al.li.*qā'*) (*until next time*)
- إلى الغد (*i*.lá al.*ghad*) (*see you tomorrow*)

Asking how someone is

After you greet someone, the next part of an Arabic greeting is asking how the person is doing.

REMEMBER

The most common way of asking someone how he's doing is كيف الحال؟ (*kay*.fa al.*ḥāl*). When you break down the phrase, you discover that حال means "state of" and كيف means "how." (The prefix ال [**al-**] attached to حال is a definite article, so الحال means "the state of health.") Therefore, the phrase كيف الحال؟ literally means "How is the health?" but for all intents and purposes, you can translate it into English as "How are you?"

كيف الحال is a gender-neutral phrase for asking people how they're doing, but you should also be aware of gender-defined greeting terms, which are derivatives of the phrase:

- When addressing a man, use كيف حالكَ (*kay*.fa *ḥā*.lu.ka).
- When addressing a woman, use كيف حالكِ (*kay*.fa *ḥā*.lu.ki).

REMEMBER

Another variation of كيف الحال is كيف حالك؟ (*kay*.fa *ḥā*.lak) (*How is your health?*). You can use either greeting, but كيف الحال is preferred when you're meeting someone for the first time because it's a bit more personal and informal.

Responding that you're doing well

When someone asks you how you're doing, if you're doing just fine, the typical response is الحمد لله (al.*ḥam*.du lil.*lāh*) (*I'm doing well*), although it literally translates to "Praise to God." Typically, after you say الحمد لله, you follow up by saying شكراً (*shuk*.ran) (*thank you*). As you expose yourself to more and more Arabic phrases and terms, you'll notice that the reference to Allah is widespread. Many everyday phrases still contain religious references. That's why a phrase as mundane as "I'm doing well" takes on religious overtones.

REMEMBER

A greeting wouldn't be complete if both sides didn't address each other. So after you say I'm doing well, you need to ask the other person how he or she is doing:

- If you're speaking with a man, you say وأنتَ كيف الحال؟ (wa.*'an*.ta, *kay*.fa al.*ḥāl*) (*And you, how are you?*).
- If you're speaking with a woman, you say وأنتِ كيف الحال؟ (wa.*'an*.ti, *kay*.fa al.*ḥāl*) (*And you, how are you?*).

Talkin' the Talk

Myriam and Lisa, who are students at the university still getting to know each other, greet each other at the school entrance.

Myriam: السلام عليكم!
as.sa.*lā*.mu 'a.*lay*.kum!
Hello!

Lisa: وعليكم السلام!
wa.'a.*lay*.kum as.sa.*lām!*
Hello!

Myriam: كيف الحال؟
kay.fa al.*ḥāl*?
How are you?

Lisa: الحمد لله، شكراً. وأنت، كيف الحال؟
al.*ḥam*.du lil.*lāh*, *shuk*.ran. wa.'an.ta !!!, *kay*.
fa al.*ḥāl*?
I'm doing well, thank you. And you, how are you?

Myriam: الحمد لله، شكراً.
al.*ḥam*.du lil.*lāh*, *shuk*.ran!
I'm doing well, thank you!

Lisa: إلى الغد!
i.lá al.*ghad!*
I'll see you tomorrow!

Myriam: إلى الغد!
i.lá al.*ghad!*
I'll see you tomorrow!

SENDING THE RIGHT NONVERBAL MESSAGE

Although familiarizing yourself with the language is the first step to interacting with people from the Middle East, you also need to understand some of the nonverbal signs that can be as meaningful as words in communicating with native speakers. For example, when shaking someone's hand, be sure to avoid pressing the person's palm with too much force. In the United States, a firm and strong handshake is encouraged in order to display a healthy dose of confidence. In most Arab countries, however, a forceful handshake is viewed as an openly hostile act. The reasoning is that you use force against people whom you don't consider friends, so a forceful handshake indicates that you don't consider that person a friend. Therefore, the most acceptable way to shake hands in the Arab world is to present a friendly, not-too-firm grip.

Making Introductions

Carrying on a conversation with someone you haven't exchanged names with is awkward, to say the least. But you can easily remedy this awkwardness when you know a few key phrases. This section explains how to ask people for their names and how to share your name using the possessive form, which may be one of the easiest grammar lessons and linguistic concepts you'll encounter in Arabic.

Asking "What's your name?"

After you go through the basic greeting procedure, which I cover in the preceding section, you're ready to ask people their names. This task is relatively easy given that you only need to know two words: اسم (*ism*) (*name*) and ما (*mā*) (*what*). If you're addressing a man, you ask ما اسمكَ؟ (*mā is*.mu.ka) (*What's your name?*). When addressing a woman, you ask ما اسمكِ؟ (*mā is*.mu.ki).

TIP

If you say ما اسمك (*mā is*.muk) without using the suffixes **–a** or **–i** at the end of اسمك, you're actually using a gender-neutral form, which is perfectly acceptable. You can address both men and women by saying ما اسمك؟ (*mā is*.muk) (*What's your name?*).

Responding with the possessive "My name is . . ."

The possessive form is one of Arabic's easiest grammatical lessons: All you do is add the suffix ي (–ī) (pronounced *ee*) to the noun, and — voilà! — you have the possessive form of the noun. For example, to say "my name," you add ي to اسم and get اسمي (*is*.mī) (*my name*). So to say "My name is Amine," all you say is اسمي أمين ('*is*.mī a.*mīn*). It's that simple!

Saying "It's a pleasure to meet you!"

When someone introduces himself or herself, a polite response is تشرفنا (ta.shar.*raf*.nā) (*It's a pleasure to meet you*). تشرفنا is a formal response, whereas أهلًا وسهلًا (*ah*.lan wa.*sah*.lan) (*Welcome!*) is much more informal.

شرف (*sha*.raf) is the Arabic term for "honor," which means that تشرفنا literally translates to "We're honored." In English, it's the equivalent of "It's a pleasure to meet you."

REMEMBER

أهلاً وسهلاً is a phrase with a dual role: When used at the beginning of a dialogue, it means "hi" (see the section "Saying hello" earlier in this chapter for further explanation). When used right after an introduction, you're informally saying "Nice to meet you."

Talkin' the Talk

Amine walks into a coffee shop in downtown Casablanca and greets Alex.

Amine: أهلًا وسهلًا!
ah.lan wa.*sah*.lan!
Hi!

Alex: أهلًا وسهلًا!
ah.lan wa.*sah*.lan!
Hi!

Amine: اسمي أمين. وأنت، ما اسمك؟
is.mī a.*mīn*. wa.'*an*.ta, *mā is*.muk?
My name is Amine. And you, what's your name?

Alex: اسمي أليكس.
is.mī Alex.
My name is Alex.

Amine: تشرفنا!
ta.shar.*raf*.nā!
It's a pleasure to meet you!

Alex: تشرفنا!
ta.shar.*raf*.nā!
It's a pleasure to meet you!

Talking about Countries and Nationalities

With the growing internationalism of the modern world, when you meet someone for the first time, you may want to know what country he or she is from. Fortunately for English speakers, the names of countries in Arabic are very similar to their names in English. Even more good news is the fact that the terms for nationalities are derivatives of the country names.

Asking "Where are you from?"

If you're speaking with a man and want to ask him where he's from, you use the phrase من أين أنتَ؟ (min *ay*.na *an*.ta) (*Where are you from?*). Similarly, if you want to ask a woman "Where are you from?" you say من أين أنتِ؟ (min *ay*.na *an*.ti).

If you want to ask if a man is from a certain place — for example, America — you say هل أنتَ من أمريكا؟ (hal *an*.ta min am.*rī*.kā) (*Are you from America?*) (M). If you're speaking with a woman, you simply replace أنتَ ('*an*.ta) with أنتِ (*an*.ti).

Saying "I am from . . ."

To say "I am from . . .," you use the preposition من (*min*) (*from*) and the personal pronoun أنا ('*a*.nā) (*I/me*). Therefore, "I'm from America" is أنا من أمريكا (*a*.nā min am.*rī*.kā).

To help you both understand responses to the question "Where are you from?" (see the preceding section) and give your own response to such questions, Table 4-1 lists the names of various countries and corresponding nationalities in Arabic.

TABLE 4-1 Country Names and Nationalities in Arabic

Country/Nationalities	Pronunciation	English
المغرب	al.*magh*.rib	Morocco
مغربي	*magh*.ri.bī	Moroccan (M)
مغربية	magh.ri.*biy*.yah	Moroccan (F)
الجزائر	al.ja.*zā*.'ir	Algeria
جزائري	ja.*zā*.'i.rī	Algerian (M)
جزائرية	ja.zā.'i.*riy*.yah	Algerian (F)
تونس	*tū*.nis	Tunisia
تونسي	*tū*.ni.sī	Tunisian (M)
تونسية	tū.ni.*siy*.yah	Tunisian (F)
مصر	miṣr	Egypt
مصري	*miṣ*.rī	Egyptian (M)

Country/Nationalities	Pronunciation	English
مصرية	miṣ.*riy*.yah	Egyptian (F)
العراق	al.'i.*rāq*	Iraq
عراقي	'i.*rā*.qī	Iraqi (M)
عراقية	'i.rā.*qiy*.yah	Iraqi (F)
السعودية	as.sa.'ū.*diy*.yah	Saudi
سعودي	sa.*'ū*.dī	Saudi (M)
سعودية	sa.'ū.*diy*.yah	Saudi (F)
أمريكا	am.*rī*.kā	America/USA
أمريكي	am.*rī*.kī	American (M)
أمريكية	am.rī.*kiy*.yah	American (F)

To tell someone "I am from Morocco," you say أنا من المغرب (*a*.nā min al.*magh*.rib). Alternatively, you may also say أنا مغربي (*a*.nā *magh*.ri.bī) (*I am Moroccan*) (M).

WORDS TO KNOW

السلام عليكم	as.sa.lā.mu 'a.lay.kum	hello
وعليكم السلا	wa.'a.lay.kum as.sa.lām	hello (reply to)
أهلاً وسهلاً	ah.lan wa.sah.lan	hi; or nice to meet you, depending on the context
الحمد لله	al.ḥam.du lil.lāh	I'm doing well (Praise to God)
اسم	ism	name
اسمي	is.mī	my name
أنا	a.nā	personal pronoun "I"
أنتَ	an.ta	personal pronoun "you" (M)

أنتِ	an.ti	personal pronoun "you" (F)
صباح الخير	ṣa.bāḥ al.khayr	good morning
مساء الخير	ma.sā' al.khayr	good evening
تصبح على خير	tuṣ.biḥ 'a.lā khayr	good night
إلى اللقاء	*i*.lá al.li.qā'	until next time

Shooting the Breeze: Talking about the Weather

If you want to chitchat with a friend or stranger, talking about the الطقس (aṭ.*ṭaqs*) (*weather*) is a pretty safe topic. In conversations about the weather, you're likely to use some of the following words:

- الشمس (ash.*shams*) (*sun*)
- المطر (al.*ma*.ṭar) (*rain*)
- رعد (*ra'*d) (*thunder*)
- برق (*barq*) (*lightning*)
- حرارة (*ḥ*a.*rā*.rah) (*temperature*)
- درجة (*da*.ra.jah) (*degree*)
- بارد (*bā*.rid) (*cold*)
- حار (*ḥār*) (*hot*)
- رطوبة (ru.*ṭū*.bah) (*humidity*)
- ريح (*rīḥ*) (*wind*)
- عاصفة (*'ā*.ṣi.fah) (*storm*)
- ثلج (*thalj*) (*snow*)
- قوس قزح (qaws *qu*.zaḥ) (*rainbow*)

REMEMBER

If you want to express the temperature, as in "It's *x* degrees," you must use the following construct: (insert number) درجة الحرارة. So, 35 درجة الحرارة means "It's 35 degrees."

Because the weather is a quasi-universal topic that interests almost everyone, here are some expressions you can use to start talking about the weather:

- هل ستمطر اليوم؟ (*hal* sa.*tum*.ṭir al.*yawm*) (*Is it going to rain today?*)
- يوم حار، أليس كذلك؟ (yawm *ḥār*, a.*lay*.sa ka.*dhā*.lik) (*Hot day, isn't it?*)
- أصبح الجو باردا فجأة. (*aṣ*.ba.ḥa al.*jaww bā*.ri.dan *faj*.'a.tan) (*It's gotten cold all of a sudden.*)
- هل سيبقى الطقس هكذا؟ (hal sa.*yab*.qá al.*jaww hā*.ka.dhā) (*Will the weather remain like this?*)

CULTURAL WISDOM

Temperatures in the majority of the Middle Eastern countries are stated in Celsius and not Fahrenheit. If you hear someone say that 25 درجة الحرارة (da.ra.jah al.ḥa.rā.rah 25) (*It's 25 degrees*), don't worry that you're going to freeze! The person actually means that it's almost 80 degrees Fahrenheit. To convert degrees from Celsius to Fahrenheit, use the following formula:

(Celsius 1.8) + 32 = Degrees Fahrenheit

Talkin' the Talk

Alexandra and Hassan are talking about the weather.

Hassan:	كيف الطقس في نيو يورك؟ *kayf* aṭ.*ṭaqs* fī New York? *How's the weather in New York?*
Alexandra:	الطقس ممتاز الآن! aṭ.*ṭaqs* mum.*tāz* al.*'ān!* *The weather is excellent right now!*
Hassan:	هل سيكون مشمس؟ *hal* sa.ya.*kūn mush*.mis? *Is it going to be sunny?*

Alexandra: سيكون مشمس طوال الأسبوع.
sa.ya.*kūn mush*.mis ṭu.*wāl* al.us.*bū'*.
It's going to be sunny all week long.

Hassan: وبعد ذلك؟
wa.*ba'*.da *dhā*.lik?
And after that?

Alexandra: لا أعرف.
lā a'.rif.
I don't know.

HURRAY, IT'S RAINING!

One of the happiest times of the year for people of the Middle East is when the rain comes. After all, these hot desert countries get very little rainfall. You'll almost never hear anyone complaining about rain in Arabic — there are no equivalent expressions for "rain, rain, go away." Actually, the opposite is true! There's a song that farmers, students, and children sing when the rain starts falling:

> اشتتتتتتت/اولاد الحرت: صب صب صب/الأولاد في قبي *(ah.she.ta.ta.ta.ta.ta / aw.lād al. ḥah.ra.ta; ṣa.bi, ṣa.bi, ṣa.bi / al.aw.lād fī qu.bi)* (*Oh rain, rain, rain, rain, rain / Children of the plowman; Pour, pour, pour / The children are in the hood of my jellaba*).

A jil.*lā*.ba is a long, flowing garment worn by farmers in the Middle East. It has a big hood in which the farmer puts objects. Of course, children can't fit in the hood of the jil.*lā*.ba, but the hood is big enough that it symbolizes protection against the rain. This is a happy song that expresses people's joy when it rains!

FUN & GAMES

Match the common Arabic greetings and basic expressions in the left column with the English translation in the right column.

1. من أين أنتَ؟	**a.** What's your name?
2. الحمد لله	**b.** See you tomorrow.
3. السلام عليكم!	**c.** It's a pleasure to meet you.
4. ما اسمكَ؟	**d.** I'm doing well.
5. وعليكم السلام	**e.** Until next time
6. إلى اللقاء	**f.** Hi!
7. تشرفنا	**g.** Good luck!
8. إلى الغد	**h.** Hello!
9. أهلاً وسهلاً!	**i.** Where are you from?
10. حظا سعيدا!	**j.** And upon you peace.

» Sorting out words for days and months

» Figuring out the right measurements

Chapter 5
Getting Your Numbers, Dates, and Measurements Straight

Being able to communicate effectively in any new language you're studying is essential. Although knowing terms related to the workplace and the home is important, equally important is knowing practical terms, such as numbers and measurements. In this chapter, I identify all the practical terms so that you can communicate clearly and effectively. I first start out by showing you the Arabic number system, which is similar to but slightly different from the number system you're used to in English. I then show you other key terms so that you're able to discuss time of the year (days, weeks, and months). And I finally show you critical terms relating to measurements.

REMEMBER

You can listen to all the Talkin' the Talk dialogues featured in this chapter. Go to `www.dummies.com/go/arabicfd` and click on the dialogue you want to hear.

Talking Numbers

Knowing how to express numbers in Arabic is a basic language lesson. You're bound to encounter Arabic numbers in all sorts of settings, including conversation. For example, when you're talking with someone about the weather, you need to know your numbers in order to reference the temperature or understand a reference the other person may make. In this section, I introduce you to the Arabic أرقام (ar.*qām*) (*numbers*). The singular form of أرقام is رقم (*ra*.qam) (*number*).

REMEMBER

Arabic numbers are part of one of the earliest traditions of number notation. Even though the Western world's number system is sometimes referred to as "Arabic numerals," actual Arabic numbers are written differently than the ones used in the West. One of the most important aspects of Arabic numbers to keep in mind is that you read them from left to right. That's right! Even though you read and write Arabic from right to left, you read and write Arabic numbers from left to right! Table 5-1 lays out the Arabic numbers from 0 to 10.

TABLE 5-1 Arabic Numerals 0–10

Arabic	Pronunciation	English
صفر	ṣifr	0 ٠ Zero
واحد	*wā*.ḥid	1 ١One
اثنان	ith.*nān*	2 ٢ Two
ثلاثة	tha.*lā*.thah	3 ٣ Three
أربعة	*ar*.ba.'ah	4 ٤ Four
خمسة	*kham*.sah	5 ٥ Five
ستة	*sit*.tah	6 ٦ Six
سبعة	*sab*.'ah	7 ٧ Seven
ثمانية	tha.*mā*.ni.yah	8 ٨ Eight
تسعة	*tis*.'ah	9 ٩ Nine
عشرة	'*ah*-sha-rah	10 ١٠ Ten

Numbers are important not only for discussing the weather but also for telling time, asking about prices, and conducting everyday business. Table 5-2 contains the numbers from 11 to 20.

TABLE 5-2

Arabic Numerals 11–20

Arabic	Pronunciation	English
أحد عشر	*a*.ḥad '*a*.shar	11 ١١ eleven
اثنا عشر	*ith*.nā '*a*.shar	12 ١٢ twelve
ثلاثة عشر	tha.*lā*.that '*a*.shar	13 ١٣ thirteen
أربعة عشرة	*ar*.ba.'at '*a*.shar	14 ١٤ fourteen
خمسة عشر	*kham*.sat '*a*.shar	15 ١٥ fifteen
ستة عشرة	*sit*.tat '*a*.shar	16 ١٦ sixteen
سبعة عشر	*sab*.'at '*a*.shar	17 ١٧ seventeen
ثمانية عشر	tha.*mā*.ni.yat '*a*.shar	18 ١٨ eighteen
تسعة عشر	*tis*.'at '*a*.shar	19 ١٩ nineteen
عشرون	'ish.*rūn*	20 ٢٠ twenty

TIP

You obtain the numbers from 11 to 19 by combining a derivative form of the number عشرة (10) — specifically عشر (tenth) — with a derivative form of the singular number. In the case of the numbers from 13 to 19, all you do is add the suffix **-ta** to the regular number and add the derivative form عشر. After you're familiar with this pattern, remembering these numbers is much easier.

Table 5-3 shows the numbers in increments of 10 from 20 to 100.

TIP

In English, you add the suffix **-ty** to get thirty, forty, and so on. In Arabic, the suffix ون (-ūn) plays that role, as in أربعون (40) or خمسون (50).

TABLE 5-3 **Arabic Numerals 20–100**

Arabic	Pronunciation	English
عشرون	'ish.*rūn*	20 ٢٠ twenty
ثلاثون	tha.lā.*thūn*	30 ٣٠ thirty
أربعون	ar.ba.*'ūn*	40 ٤٠ fourty
خمسون	kham.*sūn*	50 ٥٠ fifty
ستون	sit.*tūn*	60 ٦٠ sixty
سبعون	sab.*'ūn*	70 ٧٠ seventy
ثمانون	tha.mā.*nūn*	80 ٨٠ eighty
تسعون	tis.*'ūn*	90 ٩٠ ninety
مائة	*mā*.'ah	100 ١٠٠ one hundred

Referring to Days and Months

When you're engaged in conversation, you may find that you need to refer to certain days of the week or months. Fortunately the days of the أسبوع (us.*bū*') (*week*) are number derivatives — that is, they're derived from Arabic numbers. So recognizing the roots of the words for days of the week is key:

- الأحد (al.*'a*.ḥad) (*Sunday*)
- الاثنين (al.ith.*nayn*) (*Monday*)
- الثلاثاء (ath.thu.lā.*thā'*) (*Tuesday*)
- الأربعاء (al.'ar.ba.*'ā'*) (*Wednesday*)
- الخميس (al.kha.*mīs*) (*Thursday*)
- الجمعة (al.*jum*.'ah) (*Friday*)
- السبت (as.*sabt*) (*Saturday*)

Notice that Sunday is derived from the number 1, Monday from 2, Tuesday from 3, Wednesday from 4, and Thursday from 5. In the Islamic calendar, Sunday is the first day, Monday the second day, and so on.

CULTURAL WISDOM

Friday gets its name from جمع, which means *to gather*; it's the day when Muslims gather around the mosque and pray.

Arabs use two different types of calendars predominantly to note the passage of time.

- The **Gregorian calendar** is basically the same calendar as the one used throughout the Western world.
- The **Islamic calendar,** sometimes also known as the **lunar calendar,** is partly based on the lunar cycle and has radically different names for the months than its Western counterpart.

Tables 5-4 and 5-5 show the أشهر (*ash*.hur) (*months*) in the Gregorian and Islamic calendars, because they're the most widely used calendars.

TABLE 5-4

Gregorian Calendar

Arabic	Pronunciation	English
يناير	ya.*nā*.yir	January
فبراير	fib.*rā*.yir	February
مارس	*mā*.ris	March
أبريل	ab.*rīl*	April
مايو	*mā*.yū	May
يونيو	*yūn*.yū	June
يوليو	*yūl*.yū	July
أغسطس	a.*ghus*.ṭus	August
سبتمبر	sib.*tam*.bir	September
أكتوبر	ak.*tū*.bar	October
نوفمبر	nū.*fam*.bir	November
ديسمبر	dī.*sam*.bir	December

The Arabic names of the Gregorian months are similar to the names in English. However, the names of the Islamic calendar are quite different.

TABLE 5-5 **Islamic Calendar**

Arabic	Pronunciation
المحرّم	al.mu.*ḥar*.ram
صفر	*ṣa*.far
ربيع الأوّل	ra.*bī'* al.'*aw*.wal
ربيع الثاني	ra.*bī'* ath.*thā*.nī
جمادى الأولى	ju.*mā*.dā al.'*ū*.lā
جمادى الثانية	ju.*mā*.dā ath.*thā*.ni.yah
رجب	*ra*.jab
شعبان	sha'.*bān*
رمضان	ra.ma.*ḍān*
شوّال	shaw.*wāl*
ذو القعدة	dhū al.*qi'*.dah
ذو الحجّة	dhū al.*ḥaj*.jah

Because the Islamic calendar is partly based on the lunar cycle, the months don't overlap with the Gregorian calendar, making it difficult to match the months with the Gregorian ones. For example, the month of Ramadan will fall on different Gregorian calendar months each year because the Islamic calendar is based on lunar movements. So don't be surprised if Ramadan is in June one year and then May the following year; it's totally normal since it is based on lunar movements.

Chatting about the months without mentioning the فصول (fu.*ṣūl*) (*seasons*) would be difficult:

- صيف (*ṣayf*) (*summer*)
- خريف (kha.*rīf*) (*fall*)
- شتاء (shi.*tā'*) (*winter*)
- ربيع (ra.*bī'*) (*spring*)

Size Matters: Measuring in Arabic

Measurements are a critical component of any language, and this includes Arabic. If you're going to communicate effectively, you need these tools to be able to get your point across. In this section, I show you some key terms regarding measurements that you'll likely come across:

- حجم (ḥajm) (*size*)
- سنتيمتر (*san*.tī.mitr) (*centimeter*)
- متر (mitr) (*meter*)
- كيلومتر (*kī*.lū.mitr) (*kilometer*)
- وزن (wazn) (*weight*)
- غرام (ghi.*rām*) (*gram*)
- كيلوغرام (*kī*.lū.ghrām) (*kilogram*)
- مليغرام (*mil*.lī.ghrām) (*milligram*)

FUN & GAMES

Name the four seasons:

Illustrations by Elizabeth Kurtzman

A. __________

B. __________

C. __________

D. __________

The answers are in Appendix C.

» Using the imperative verb form

» Relaxing in your home

Chapter 6

At the Office and Around the House

If you're like most people living in the modern world, the two places where you spend the most time probably are your منزل (*man*.zil) (*house*) and your مكتب (*mak*.tab) (*office*). Like many people who are employed by big companies, small businesses, government agencies, or private ventures, you divide your وقت (waqt) (*time*) between العمل (al.'*a*.mal) (*work*) and الحياة الأسرية (al.*ḥa*.yāh al. 'u.sa.*riy*.yah) (*family life*). Achieving التوازن (at.ta.*wā*.zun) (*balance*) between the two is extremely crucial for your happiness, your efficiency at the workplace, and your effectiveness in your home. In this chapter, I cover all the good "work" words you should know and introduce you to all aspects of life at the office and around the house to help you balance life between these two worlds.

REMEMBER

You can listen to all the Talkin' the Talk dialogues featured in this chapter. Go to `www.dummies.com/go/arabicfd` and click on the dialogue you want to hear.

Managing the Office Environment

The office is an essential part of modern life. In most Arabic-speaking and Muslim countries, العمال (al.'um.*māl*) (*workers*) work from الإثنين (al.'ith.*nayn*) (*Monday*) until الجمعة (al.*jum*.'ah) (Friday). Most workers follow a standard الساعة التاسعة إلى الساعة الخامسة (as.*sā*.'ah at.*tā*.si.'ah *i*.lá as.*sā*.'ah al.*khā*.mi.sah) (*9 to 5*) schedule for workdays.

CULTURAL WISDOM

Although most مكاتب (ma.*kā*.tib) (*offices*) around the world give their workers time for غداء (gha.*dā'*) (*lunch*), the duration depends on the employer and the country. For example, in the United States, it's not uncommon for an عامل (*'ā*.mil) (*worker*) to eat lunch while sitting at his مكتب (*mak*.tab) (*desk*). On the other hand, in most Middle Eastern countries, a worker gets two hours and is encouraged to eat his lunch at his home with his أسرة (*us*.rah) (*family*).

Here are some key words and terms to help you navigate the workplace:

- عمل (*'a*.mal) (*work/job*)
- مهنة (*mih*.nah) (*profession*)
- شركة (*sha*.ri.kah) (*company*)
- شركة كبيرة (*sha*.ri.kah ka.*bī*.rah) (*large company*)
- شركة صغيرة (*sha*.ri.kah ṣa.*ghī*.rah) (*small company*)
- مصنع (*maṣ*.na') (*factory*)
- زبون (za.*būn*) (*client*)
- زبائن (za.*bā*.'in) (*clients*)

You can choose from many different kinds of شركات (sha.ri.*kāt*) (*companies*) to work for, including a بنك (*bank*) (*bank*), a شركة محاسبة (*sha*.ri.kat mu.*ḥā*.sa.bah) (*accounting firm*), or a محاماة (mu.ḥā.*māh*) (*law firm*). You also have many choices when it comes to مهن (*mi*.han) (*professions*). Here are some popular professions:

- مصرفي (*maṣ*.ra.fī) (*banker*) (M)
- مصرفية (maṣ.ra.*fiy*.yah) (*banker*) (F)
- رجل أعمال (*ra*.jul a'.*māl*) (*businessman*)
- سيدة أعمال (*say*.yi.dat a'.*māl*) (*businesswoman*)
- محاميc (mu.*ḥā*.mī) (*lawyer*) (M)
- محامية (mu.*ḥā*.mīy.yah) (lawyer) (F)
- شرطي (*shur*.ṭī) (*police officer*)
- رجل إطفاء (*ra*.jul iṭ.*fā'*) (*firefighter*)

Most companies have a lot of workers with different responsibilities, and most workers find themselves in various إدارات (i.dā.*rāt*) (*divisions/groups/departments*) within the company. Here are some of the common departments you may find in a company:

- إدارة المحاسبة (i.*dā*.rat al.mu.*ḥā*.sa.bah) (*accounting department*)

» إدارة التسويق (i.*dā*.rat at.tas.*wīq*) (*marketing department*)
» إدارة القانون (i.*dā*.rat al.qā.*nūn*) (*legal department*)
» إدارة العاملين (i.*dā*.rat al.'ā.mi.*līn*) (*human resources department*)
» ادارة العملاء (i.*dā*.rat al.'u.ma.*lā'*) (*customer service department*)

Interacting with your colleagues

Unless you're in an office that doesn't require you to interact with people face to face, you need to be able to get along with your زملاء (zu.ma.*lā'*) (*colleagues*). This section reveals the terms that can help you get along with everyone at the office so that you can be as productive and efficient as possible.

Before you build good working relationships with your co-workers, you should know the right words for classifying them:

» زميل (za.*mīl*) (*colleague*) (MS)
» زميلة (za.*mī*.lah) (*colleague*) (FS)
» مدير (mu.*dīr*) (*director*) (MS)
» مديرة (mu.*dī*.rah) (*director*) (FS)
» مدراء (mu.da.*rā'*) (*directors*) (MP)
» مديرات (mu.dī.*rāt*) (*directors*) (FP)
» رئيس (ra.*'īs*) (*president*) (MS)
» رئيسة (ra.*'ī*.sah) (*president*) (FS)
» رؤساء (ru.'a.*sā'*) (*presidents*) (MP)
» رئيسات (ra.'ī.*sāt*) (*presidents*) (FP)

Whether you like it or not, your زملاء المكتب (zu.ma.*lā'* al.*mak*.tab) (*office colleagues*) have a big influence over your time at the office; therefore, getting along with your colleagues is crucial. You can address people you work with in a number of different ways, such as based on rank, age, or gender. These categorizations may seem discriminatory in an American sense, but these terms actually carry the utmost respect for the person being referenced:

» Use سيدي (*say*.yi.dī) (*sir*) to address the director or someone with a higher rank than you.
» Use سيدتي (say.*yi*.da.tī) (*madam*) to address the director or president.

- Use صديقي (ṣa.*dī*.qī) (*friend*) to address a male colleague.
- Use صديقتي (ṣa.*dī*.qa.tī) (*friend*) to address a female colleague.
- Use الأخ (al.*'akh*) (*brother*) to address a male colleague.
- Use الأخت (al.*'ukht*) (*sister*) to address a female colleague.

CULTURAL WISDOM

In Arabic culture, it's okay to address co-workers or people close to you as brother or sister even though they may not be related to you. Here are some phrases to help you interact cordially and politely with your colleagues:

- هل تريد مساعدة؟ (*hal* tu.*rīd* mu.*sā*.'a.dah) (*Do you need help?*) (M)
- هل تريدين مساعدة؟ (*hal* tu.rī.*dīn* mu.*sā*.'a.dah) (*Do you need help?*) (F)
- هل يمكن ان اساعدك؟ (*hal yum*.kin an u.*sā*.'*i*.dak) (*May I help you?*) (M)
- هل يمكن ان اساعدك؟ (*hal yum*.kin an u.*sā*.'*i*.dik) (*May I help you?*) (F)
- سأذهب إلى المطعم. هل تريد شيئاً؟ (sa.'*adh*.hab *i*.lá al.*maṭ*.'am. hal tu.rīd *shay*.'an) (*I'm going to the cafeteria. Do you want anything?*) (M)
- سأذهب إلى المطعم. هل تريدين شيئاً؟ (sa.'*adh*.hab *i*.lā al.*maṭ*.'am. hal tu.rī.*dīn* *shay*.'an) (*I'm going to the cafeteria. Do you want anything?*) (F)
- عندنا اجتماع بعد 5 دقائق. ('*in*.da.nā ij.ti.*mā*' *ba*'.da *khams* da.*qā*.'iq) (*We have a meeting in five minutes.*)
- هل وصلك بريدي الإكتروني؟ (*hal wa*.ṣa.lak ba.*rī*.dī al.'i.lik.ti.*rū*.nī) (*Did you get my email?*)
- هل عندك قلم؟ (*hal* '*in*.dak *qa*.lam) (*Do you have a pen?*) (M)
- هل عندك قلم؟ (*hal* '*in*.dik *qa*.lam) (*Do you have a pen?*) (F)

Talkin' the Talk

Omar and Samir are colleagues working on a project at the office.

Omar: هل كتبت التقرير؟
hal ka.*tab*.ta at.taq.*rīr?*
Did you write the report?

Samir: كتبت نصف التقرير ولكن أريد مساعدتك في كتابته.
ka.*tab*.tu *niṣf* at.taq.*rīr* wa.*lā*.kin u.*rīd* mu.sā.'*a*.da.tak *fī* ki.tā.*ba*.ti.hi.
I wrote half of the report, but I need your help to finish writing it.

Omar: طيب، هيا بنا إلى العمل. أين تريد أن نعمل؟
ṭay.tib *hay*.yā *bi*.nā *i*.lá al. *'a*.mal. *ay*.na tu.*rīd* an *na'*.mal?
Okay, let's get to work. Where would you like us to work?

Samir: هيا بنا إلى قاعة الاجتماع.
hay.yā *bi*.nā *i*.lá *qā*.'at al.ij.ti.*mā'*.
Let's go to the conference room.

Omar and Samir head to the conference room to finish the report.

Omar: هل تريد هذه الصورة في بداية التقرير أو نهايته؟
bi.*dā*.yat at.taq.*rīr* aw ni.*hā*.yat.i.hi?
Do you want this illustration in the beginning or end of the report?

Samir: أظنّ في بداية التقرير أحسن.
a.*ẓunn* fī bi.*dā*.yat at.taq.*rīr* *aḥ*.san.
I believe in the beginning of the report is better.

Omar: هل نزيد صفحة أخرى أو هذا كافي؟
hal nu.*rīd* *ṣaf*.ḥah *ukh*.rá aw *hā*.dhā *kā*.fī?
Should we add another page or is this enough?

Samir: هذا كافي.
hā.dhā *kā*.fī.
This is enough.

Omar: متى تريد أن نوزع هذا التقرير؟
ma.tá tu.*rīd* an nu.*waz*.zi' *hā*.dhā at.taq.*rīr?*
When would you like to distribute this report?

Samir: عندنا اجتماع خلال ساعة. يجب أن يكون التقرير جاهز للاجتماع.
'*in*.da.nā ij.ti.*mā'* khi.*lāl* *sā*.'ah. *ya*.jib an ya.*kūn* at.taq.*rīr* *jā*.hiz li.lij.ti.*mā'*.
We have a meeting in one hour. The report must be ready in time for the meeting.

Omar: سيكون جاهز في نصف ساعة. كم نصخة يجب أن نطبع؟
sa.ya.*kūn* *jā*.hiz fī *niṣf* *sā*.'ah. kam *nus*.khah *ya*.jib an *naṭ*.ba'?
It'll be ready in half an hour. How many copies do we need to print?

Samir: عشر نسخ من فضلك.
'ashr *nu*.sakh min *faḍ*-lik.
Ten copies, please.

Omar:	فوراً. هل هناك شيء آخر؟ *faw*.ran. hal hu.*nā*.ka *shay'* *ā*.khar? *Right away. Is there anything else?*
Samir:	لا شكراً. *lā shuk*.ran. *No. Thank you.*

WORDS TO KNOW

تقرير	**taq.rīr**	**report**
تقارير	**ta.qā.rīr**	**reports**
نصف	**niṣf**	**half**
مساعدة	**mu.sā.'a.dah**	**help**
غرفة	**ghur.fah**	**room**
اجتماع	**ij.ti.mā'**	**meeting/conference**
صور	**ṣu.war**	**pictures**
بداية	**bi.dā.yah**	**beginning**
نهاية	**ni.hā.yah**	**ending**
يزيد	**ya.zīd**	**add**
وزع	**waz.za'**	**distribute**
جاهز	**jā.hiz**	**ready (M)**
جاهزة	**jā.hi.zah**	**ready (F)**
طبع	**ṭa.ba.'a**	**print**
نسخ	**nu.sakh**	**copies**
ممثل	**mu.math.thil**	**representative (M)**
ممثلة	**mu.math.thi.lah**	**representative (F)**
ممثلون	**mu.math.thi.lūn**	**representatives (MP)**
ممثلات	**mu.math.thi.lāt**	**representatives (FP)**
إضافي	**i.ḍā.fī**	**additional (M)**
إضافية	**i.ḍā.fiy.yah**	**additional (F)**

Giving orders

GRAMMATICALLY SPEAKING

The *imperative verb form,* also known as the *command form,* is used to give orders or directions. It's an important verb to know in the workplace because that's where you're usually told what to do and where you tell others what to do. The imperative structure is fairly straightforward. This section shares some quick tips to allow you to master the imperative form.

First, because the imperative is a command form, you can use it only with second-person pronouns such as أنتَ (*an*.ta) (*you*) (M) and أنتِ (*an*.ti) (*you*) (F). You can't use the imperative with third-person pronouns such as هو (*hu*.wa) (*he*) because you can't give an order to someone who isn't present. The following is a list of the personal pronouns to use with the imperative:

- أنتَ (*an*.ta) (*you*) (MS)
- أنتِ (*an*.ti) (*you*) (FS)
- أنتم (*an*.tum) (*you*) (MP)
- أنتنّ (an.*tun*.na) (*you*) (FP)
- أنتما (an.*tu*.mā) (*you*) (dual)

Second, the imperative form is nothing but a derived form of the regular verb in the الماضي (al.*mā*.ḍī) (*the past*) and المضارع (al.mu.*ḍā*.ri') (*the present*) tenses. The following is a list of the most common imperative verbs:

- اكتب (*uk*.tub) (*write*)
- اقرأ (*iq*.ra') (*read*)
- انظر (*un*.ẓur) (*look*)
- اعد (*a*.'id) (*repeat*)
- قل (qul) (*say*)
- كل (kul) (*eat*)
- تكلّم (ta.*kal*.lam) (*talk*)
- قف (qif) (*stop*)
- تحرّك (ta.*ḥar*.rak) (*move*)

One of the more important verb command forms is the verb كتب (*ka*.ta.ba) (*to write*). Table 6-1 shows the imperative (command form) of this verb.

TABLE 6-1 Imperative Form of To Write

Pronoun	Imperative	Pronunciation	English
أنتَ (you/MS)	اكتب	*uk*.tub	write (MS)
أنتِ (you/FS)	اكتبي	*uk*.tu.bī	write (FS)
أنتم (you/MP)	اكتبوا	*uk*.tu.bū	write (MP)
أنتنّ (you/FP)	اكتبنّ	uk.*tub*.na	write (FP)
أنتما (dual)	اكتبا	uk.*tu*.bā	write (dual)

Another verb you should be aware of is the verb تكلّم (ta.*kal*.la.ma) (*to talk*). Table 6-2 shows the imperative form of this verb.

TABLE 6-2 Imperative Form of To Talk

Pronoun	Imperative	Pronunciation	English
أنت (you/MS)	تكلّم	ta.*kal*.lam	talk (MS)
أنتِ (you/FS)	تكلّمي	ta.*kal*.la.mī	talk (FS)
أنتم (you/MP)	تكلّموا	ta.*kal*.la.mū	talk (MP)
أنتنّ (you/FP)	تكلّمنّ	ta.kal.*lam*.na	talk (FP)
أنتما (dual)	تكلّما	ta.*kal*.la.mā	talk (dual)

Supplying your office

In order to function properly and efficiently at the office, you need a number of different work-related items. Here are some common supplies you can expect to find at the office:

- كرسي (*kur*.sī) (*chair*)
- مكتب (*mak*.tab) (*desk*)
- الكمبيوتر (al.kum.bi.*yū*.tar) (*computer*)
- هاتف (*hā*.tif) (*telephone*)

- فاكس (fāks) (*fax machine*)
- طابعة (*ṭā*.bi.'ah) (*printer*)

Besides آلات (ā.*lāt*) (*machines*) and heavy furniture, you also need smaller tools to help you get by at the office:

- قلم جاف (*qa*.lam jāf) (*pen*)
- قلم رصاص (*qa*.lam ra.*ṣāṣ*) (*pencil*)
- ممحاة (mim.*ḥāh*) (*eraser*)
- كتاب (ki.*tāb*) (*book*)
- دفتر (*daf*.tar) (*notebook*)
- أوراق (aw.*rāq*) (*papers*)
- مشبك أوراق (*mash*.bak aw.*rāq*) (*paper clip*)
- صمغ (ṣamgh) (*glue*)
- شريط لاصق (sha.*rīṭ lā*.ṣiq) (*tape*)

If you can't find a notebook or glue, ask a colleague if you can borrow the item. Here's how you ask a colleague a question, depending on whether you're speaking to a man or a woman:

- هل عندك دفتر؟ (hal '*in*.dik *daf*.tar) (*Do you have a notebook?*) (F)
- هل عندك صمغ؟ (hal '*in*.dak ṣamgh) (*Do you have glue?*) (M)
- هل عندك شريط لاصق؟ (hal '*in*.dak sha.*rīṭ lā*.ṣiq) (*Do you have tape?*) (M)
- هل عنده قلم؟ (hal '*in*.da.hu *qa*.lam) (*Does he have a pen?*)

GRAMMATICALLY SPEAKING

The construct "to have" in Arabic isn't a verb (see the preceding list of examples); rather, it's a combination of possessive suffix constructions added to the word عند ('*ind*) (*have*), which is the best word in the language to denote possession. However, for all intents and purposes, you may use this construct — عند followed by a possessive suffix — in the same way as you would a regular verb. Check out this prepositional phrase using all personal pronoun suffixes:

Pronoun	Form	Pronunciation	English
أنا	عندي	'*in*.dī	I have
انتَ	عندك	'*in*.dak	You have (MS)
نتِ	عندك	'*in*.dik	You have (FS)

Pronoun	Form	Pronunciation	English
و	عنده	'*in*.da.hu	He has
هي	عندها	'*in*.da.hā	She has
نحن	عندنا	'*in*.da.nā	We have
أنتم	عندكم	'*in*.da.kum	You have (MP)
أنتنّ	عندكنّ	'in.da.*kun*.na	You have (FP)
هم	عندهم	'*in*.da.hum	They have (MP)
هنّ	عندهنّ	'in.da.*hun*.na	They have (FP)
أنتما	عندكما	'in.*da*.ku.mā	You have (dual)
هما	عندهما	'in.*da*.hu.mā	They have (dual)

Talkin' the Talk

Samira can't find her eraser. She asks some of her colleagues if they have one available for her to borrow.

Samira: عفوا طارق. هل عندك ممحاة؟
'*af*.wan *ṭā*.riq, hal '*in*.dak mim.*ḥāh?*
Excuse me, Tarik. Do you have an eraser?

Tarik: لحظة. سأرى في مكتبي.
laḥ.ẓah, sa.'*a*.rá fi *mak*.ta.bī.
One moment. I'll check my desk.

Tarik looks around his desk but can't find the eraser.

Tarik: أنا آسف. ليس عندي ممحاة.
a.nā *ā*.sif. *lay*.sa '*in*.dī mim.*ḥāh*.
I'm sorry. I don't have an eraser.

Samira: من عنده ممحاة؟
man '*in*.da.hu mim.*ḥāh?*
Who has an eraser?

Tarik: أظنّ أنّ فرانك عنده ممحاة.
a.ẕunn *an*.na frank *'in*.da.hu mim.*ḥāh*.
I believe Frank has an eraser.

Samira: شكراً.
shuk.ran.
Thank you.

Samira stops by Frank's desk to ask him for an eraser.

Samira: أهلًا يا فرانك. هل عندك ممحاة؟
ah.lan yā frank. hal *'in*.dak mim.*ḥāh?*
Hi, Frank. Do you have an eraser?

Frank: نعم. ها هي.
na.'am, *hā hi*.ya.
Yes. Here you go.

Samira: شكراً جزيلًا!
shuk.ran ja.*zī*.lan!
Thank you so much!

WORDS TO KNOW

لحظة	lah.ẕah	one moment
أنا آسف	a.nā ā.sif	I am sorry (M)
أنا آسفة	a.nā ā.si.fah	I am sorry (F)

Life at Home

If you're like most people, you spend a lot of time at your منزل (*man*.zil) (*house*). The house is a bit different than the بيت (bayt) (*home*) because a house can be any old house, whereas the home is the space where you feel most comfortable. In many cultures, a house is a family's or individual's most prized possession or asset. Due to the centrality of the home and house in everyday life, knowing how to talk about them in depth can be very useful. In this section, I tell you all the right words and terms to help you talk about your house.

As you know, a house consists of غرف (*ghu*.raf) (*rooms*). The singular form is غرفة (*ghur*.fah) (*room*) in Arabic. This list can help you become familiar with the major types of rooms in a house:

- غرفة الجلوس (*ghur*.fat al.ju.*lūs*) (*sitting room*)
- غرفة المعيشة (*ghur*.fat al.ma.*'ī*.shah) (*living room*)
- غرفة الطعام (*ghur*.fat aṭ.ṭa.*'ām*) (*dining room*)
- غرفة النوم (*ghur*.fat an.*nawm*) (*bedroom*)
- حمّام (ḥam.*mām*) (*bathroom*)
- غرفة الغسل (*ghur*.fat al.*ghasl*) (*washing/laundry room*)
- مطبخ (*maṭ*.bakh) (*kitchen*)

In addition to rooms, a house may also have a مرأب لإيواء السيارات (*mar*.'ab li'ī.*wā'* as.say.yā.*rāt*) (*garage*) where you can park your سيارة (say.*yā*.rah) (*car*) as well as a حديقة (ḥa.*dī*.qah) (*garden*) where you can play or just relax. Some منازل (ma.*nā*.zil) (*houses*) even have a بركة سباحة (*bir*.kat si.*bā*.ḥa) (*swimming pool*).

Each room in the house usually contains different items. For example, you can expect to find a سرير (sa.*rīr*) (*bed*) in a bedroom. Here are some items you can expect to find in the bathroom:

- مرحاض (mir.*ḥāḍ*) (*toilet*)
- دش (dush) (*shower*)
- مغسل (*magh*.sal) (*sink*)
- فرشاة الأسنان (fur.*shāt* al.'as.*nān*) (*toothbrush*)
- شامبو (*sham*.bū) (*shampoo*)
- صابون (ṣā.*būn*) (*soap*)
- مرآة (mir.*'āh*) (*mirror*)

FAMILY LIFE IN A MIDDLE EASTERN HOME

In most Arabic-speaking and Islamic countries, the بيت (bayt) (*home*) plays a very central role in family life. Unlike in Western countries, the أسرة (*us*.rah) (*family*) structure in the home generally consists of more than the parents and children (the typical immediate family); it extends to other members of the family, such as grandparents, uncles, aunts, and cousins. Therefore, a home in most Middle Eastern countries houses not only parents and their children, but also grandparents, grandchildren, cousins, and other family members.

In countries such as Saudi Arabia, منازل (ma.*nā*.zil) (*houses*) are built to accommodate up to 10 or 15 family members and sometimes more. Like houses in the United States, Europe, and other parts of the world, the Middle Eastern home revolves around the غرفة المعيشة (*ghur*.fat al.ma.'*ī*.shah) (*living room*). Physically and architecturally, the living room is the central part of the house; it's usually surrounded by the مطبخ (*maṭ*.bakh) (*kitchen*) and the غرفة الجلوس (*ghur*.fat al.ju.*lūs*) (*sitting room*) and غرفة الطعام (*ghur*.fat aṭ.ṭa.'*ām*) (dining room).

During the عيد ('*īd*) (*holiday*), the home becomes a place where family members come and celebrate the festivities together. The living room retains its centrality during these festivities, although other parts of the home become more significant, such as the dining room.

You can expect to find the following items in the kitchen:

- تنور (tan.*nūr*) (*oven*)
- ثلاجة (thal.*lā*.jah) (*refrigerator*)
- شوك (*shu*.wak) (*forks*)
- ملاعق (ma.*lā*.'iq) (*spoons*)
- سكاكين (sa.kā.*kīn*) (*knives*)
- أكواب (ak.*wāb*) (*cups*)
- أطباق (aṭ.*bāq*) (*dishes*)

WORDS TO KNOW

جهاز التحكم	ji.<u>hāz</u> at.ta.<u>ḥak</u>.kum	TV remote control
تلفزيون	ti.li.fiz.<u>yūn</u>	television
شاشة	<u>shā</u>.shah	screen
راديو	<u>rad</u>.yū	radio
رأى	<u>ra</u>.'á	see
وجد	<u>wa</u>.ja.da	find
فوق	<u>fawq</u>	above/over
تحت	<u>taḥt</u>	under/below
بجانب	bi.<u>jā</u>.nib	next to
متأكد	mu.ta.'<u>ak</u>.kid	sure/certain
ربّما	<u>rub</u>.ba.mā	perhaps/maybe

Talkin' the Talk

Hassan can't find the remote control for the living room television. He asks his mother whether she has seen it.

Hassan: أين جهاز التحكّم؟
ay.na ji.*hāz* at.ta.*ḥak*.kum?
Where is the remote control?

Mother: كان فوق الطاولة.
kān.na *fawq* aṭ.*ṭā*.wi.lah.
It was on the table.

Hassan: أي طاولة؟
ay *ṭā*.wi.lah?
Which table?

Mother: الطاولة التي في غرفة الطعام.
aṭ.*ṭā*.wi.lah al.*la*.tī fi *ghur*.fat aṭ.ṭa.*'ām*.
The table in the dining room.

Hassan looks for the remote control on the dining room table but can't find it.

Hassan: لا, الجهاز ليس فوق الطاولة.
lā al.ji.*hāz lay*.sa *faw*.qa aṭ.*ṭā*.wi.lah.
No, the remote is not on the table.

Mother: هل أنت متأكد؟
hal *an*.ta mu.ta.'*ak*.kid?
Are you sure?

Hassan: نعم. ليس هنا.
na.'am *lay*.sa *hu*.nā
Yes. It's not here.

Mother: ربّما يكون تحت الطاولة.
rub.ba.mā ya.*kūn taḥt* aṭ.*ṭā*.wi.lah.
Perhaps it's under the table.

Hassan: دقيقة سأرى تحت الطاولة.
da.*qī*.qah sa.'*a*.rá *taḥt* aṭ.*ṭā*.wi.lah.
One minute while I look under the table.

Hassan looks under the table for the remote.

Hassan: وجدته!
wa.*jad*.tu.hu!
I found it!

FUN & GAMES

From the following list, choose the words that describe the rooms pictured here:

- حمّام
- مطبخ
- غرفة النوم
- غرفة المعيشة
- غرفة الطعام

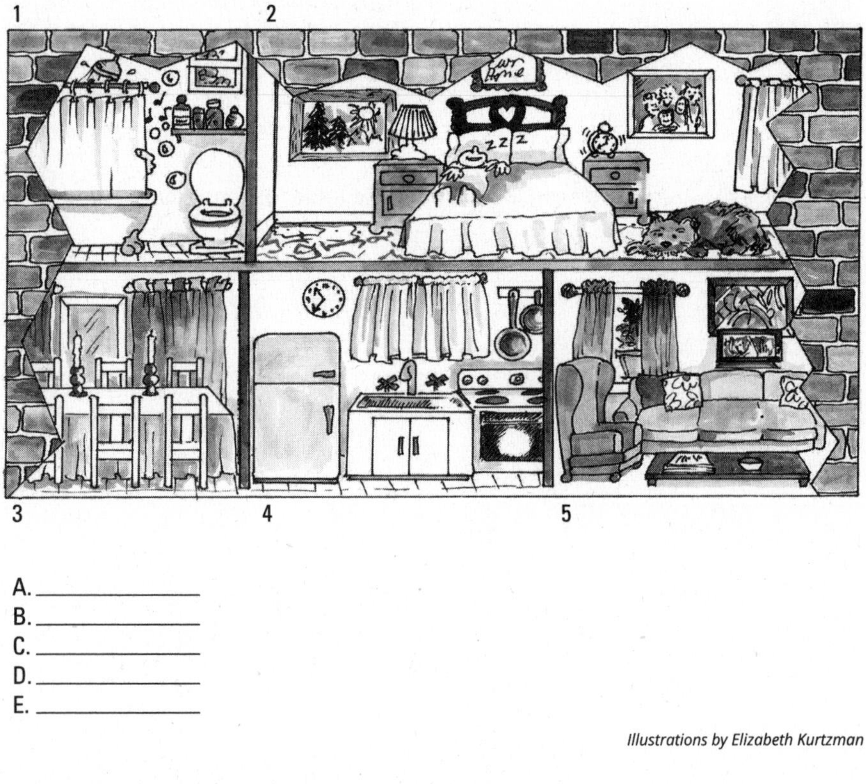

A. ____________

B. ____________

C. ____________

D. ____________

E. ____________

Illustrations by Elizabeth Kurtzman

The answers are in Appendix C.

2 Arabic in Action

IN THIS PART . . .

Try your hand at small talk when getting acquainted with new people.

Discover how to ask for directions when traveling.

Practice using Arabic in a business setting, whether in person or via telecommunications.

Know what to say when trying out a new restaurant or buying food at a market.

Find out some helpful words and phrases to use when going shopping.

Be ready to hit the town with important words for keeping track of time and enjoying museums, religious sites, movie theaters, and more.

Relax and enjoy some downtime playing outside, listening to music, and trying out hobbies.

IN THIS CHAPTER

» Asking simple questions

» Chatting about your family

» Talking about jobs

» Keeping in touch with the phone and email

Chapter 7
Getting to Know You: Making Small Talk

With Arabic speakers, محادثة قصيرة (mu.*ḥā*.da.thah qa.*ṣī*.rah) (*small talk*) plays an important role during interactions. Sometimes you need to engage in small talk when you meet people for the first time. You may know their اسم (ism) (*name*), but you want to find out more about them, such as where they're from and what they do. Small talk allows you to find out more about the person you're interacting with as well as lets you tell a little bit about yourself. Small talk may also take place between people who know each other but prefer to make small talk in order to avoid awkward silence! Whatever the case, the ability to engage in small talk is important.

You need to be aware of a number of rules when you make small talk in Arabic. This chapter explains how to make small talk in Arabic, including how to ask simple questions to find out more about the person or people you're talking to. I discuss how to talk about your أسرة (*us*.rah) (*family*) and your مهنة (*mih*.nah) (*job*).

REMEMBER

You can listen to all the Talkin' the Talk dialogues featured in this chapter. Go to `www.dummies.com/go/arabicfd` and click on the dialogue you want to hear.

Asking Key Questions

One of the best ways to start a conversation is to ask a سؤال (su.*'āl*) (*question*). To get you started, here are some key question words in Arabic:

- من؟ (*man*) (*who*)
- أين؟ (*ay*.na) (*where*)
- متى؟ (*ma*.tá) (*when*)
- ما؟ (mā) (*what*)
- ماذا؟ (*mā*.dhā) (*what*) (used with verbs)
- لماذا؟ (li.*mā*.dhā) (*why*)
- كيف؟ (*kay*.fa) (*how*)
- كم؟ (kam) (*how many* or *how much*)

You may use these question words to ask more elaborate and detailed questions. Here are some examples:

- ما اسمكَ؟ (mā *is*.mu.ka?) (What's your name?) (MS)
- ما اسمكِ؟ (*mā is*.mu.ki?) (*What's your name?*) (FS)
- ما هي مهنتكَ؟ (*mā hi*.ya mih.*na*.tu.ka?) (*What do you do?*; Literally: *What is your job?*) (MS)
- ما هي مهنتكِ؟ (*mā hi*.ya mih.*na*.tu.ki?) (*What do you do?*; Literally: *What is your job?*) (FS)
- ماذا تفعل؟ (*mā*.dhā *taf*.'al?) (*What are you doing?*) (MS)
- ماذا تفعلين؟ (*mā*.dhā taf.'a.*līn?*) (*What are you doing?*) (FS)
- من أين أنتَ؟ (*min ay*.na *an*.ta?) (*Where are you from?*) (MS)
- من أين أنتِ؟ (*min ay*.na *an*.ti?) (*Where are you from?*) (FS)
- ماذا يكتب؟ (*mā*.dhā yak.*tub?*) (*What is he writing?*)
- هل تحب القراءة؟ (*hal* tu.*ḥib* al.qi.*rā*.'ah?) (*Do you like to read?*) (MS)
- هل تحبّين القراءة؟ (*hal* tu.ḥib.*bī*.na al.qi.*rā*.'ah?) (*Do you like to read?*) (FS)
- هل هذا كتابك؟ (*hal hā*.dhā ki.*tā*.bu.ka?) (*Is this your book?*) (MS)
- هل هذا كتابك؟ (*hal hā*.dhā ki.*tā*.bu.ki?) (*Is this your book?*) (FS)
- أين محطة القطار؟ (*ay*.na ma.*ḥaṭ*.ṭat al.qi.*ṭār?*) (*Where is the train station?*)

» متى تذهب إلى المطار؟ (*ma*.tá *tadh*.ha.bu *i*.lá al.ma.*ṭār?*) (*When is she going to the airport?*)

» أين أفضل مطعم؟ (*ay*.na *af*.ḍal *maṭ*.'am?) (*Where is the best restaurant?*)

» لماذا تذهب إلى السوق؟ (li.*mā*.dhā *tadh*.hab *i*.lā as.*sūq?*) (*Why are you going to the market?*) (MS)

TIP

Notice that some of the preceding questions refer to either masculine or feminine subjects. When you ask a question in Arabic, you choose the gender of the subject by modifying the gender suffix of the noun in question. For example, كتاب (ki.*tāb*) means "book," but كتابكَ (ki.*tā*.bu.ka) means "your book" (M), and كتابكِ (ki.*tā*.bu.ki) means "your book" (F). So if you want to ask a man for his book, you use كتابكَ.

Talkin' the Talk

Yassin and Youssef are both incoming freshmen at al-Azhar University in Cairo, Egypt. They strike up a friendly conversation outside the cafeteria.

Yassin: إسمح لي. هل أنتَ طالب في الجامعة؟
is.maḥ lī. hal *an*.ta *ṭā*.lib fī al.*jā*.mi.'ah?
Excuse me. Are you a student at the university?

Youssef: **نعم. أنا في السنة الأولى. وأنتَ؟**
na.'am, *a*.nā fī as.*sa*.nah al.*'ū*.lá. wa.*an*.ta?
Yes. I'm in the freshman class. And you?

Yassin: أنا أيضاً في السنة الأولى!
a.nā *ay*.ḍan fī as.*sa*.nah al.*'ū*.lá!
I'm also in the freshman class!

Youssef: ممتاز! هل تعيش في المدينة الجامعية؟
mum.*tāz!* hal. ta.*'īsh* fī al.ma.*dī*.nah al.jā.mi.*'iy*.yah?
Excellent! Are you living on campus?

Yassin: نعم. أنا في مساكن أحمد.
na.'am *a*.nā fī ma.*sā*.kin *aḥ*.mad.
Yes. I'm in the Ahmed dorms.

Youssef: أنا في مساكن فيصل.
a.nā fī ma.*sā*.kin *fay*.ṣal.
I'm in the Faysal dorms.

Yassin: إلى اللقاء.
i.lá al.li.*qā'*.
See you around.

Youssef: إلى اللقاء.
i.lá al.li.*qā'*.
See you around.

WORDS TO KNOW		
طالب	<u>ṭā</u>.lib	college student (M)
تلميذ	til.<u>mīdh</u>	student (M)
أستاذ	us.<u>tādh</u>	professor (M)
مدرس	mu.<u>dar</u>.ris	teacher (M)
جامعة	<u>jā</u>.mi.'ah	university
كلية	kul.<u>liy</u>.yah	college
سنة	<u>sa</u>.nah	year/class
أول	<u>aw</u>.wal	first (M)
أولى	<u>ū</u>.lá	first (F)
السنة الأولى	as.<u>sa</u>.nah al.'<u>ū</u>.lá	first year/freshman

Talking about Yourself and Your Family

When you meet someone for the first time, you want to get to know a little more about him or her. One of the best ways to get acquainted with the person you're talking to is by finding out more about his or her أسرة (*us*.rah) (*the family*). The family is one of the best topics of conversation because it generates a lot of interest and endless conversation. Table 7-1 lists some important family members who may come up in casual conversation.

TABLE 7-1

All in the Family

Arabic	Pronunciation	Translation
اب	*abb*	*father*
أم	*umm*	*mother*
والدان	*wā.li.dān*	*parents*
ابن	*ibn*	*son*
بنت	*bint*	*daughter*
أبناء	ab.*nā'*	*children*
زوج	*zawj*	*husband*
زوجة	*zaw*.jah	*wife*
أخّ	*akhkh*	*brother*
أخت	*ukht*	*sister*
جدّ	*jadd*	*grandfather*
جدّة	*jad*.dah	*grandmother*
حفيد	ḥa.*fīd*	*grandson*
حفيدة	ḥa.*fī*.dah	*granddaughter*
عمّ	*'amm*	*paternal uncle (father's brother)*
عمّة	*'am*.mah	*paternal aunt (father's sister)*
خال	*khāl*	*maternal uncle (mother's brother)*
خالة	*khā*.lah	*maternal aunt (mother's sister)*
ابن عمّ	*ibn 'amm*	*male cousin from the father's side*
بنت عمّ	*bint 'amm*	*female cousin from the father's side*
ابن خال	*ibn khāl*	*male cousin from the mother's side*

(continued)

TABLE 7-1 ***(continued)***

Arabic	Pronunciation	Translation
بنت خال	*bint khāl*	*female cousin from the mother's side*
أهل الزّوج	*ahl* az.*zawj*	*in-laws* (M; collective)
أهل الزّوجة	*ahl* az.*zaw*.jah	*in-laws* (F; collective)
حمو	*ḥa*.mū	*father-in-law*
حماة	ḥa.*māh*	*mother-in-law*
سلف	*silf*	*brother-in-law*
سلفة	*sil*.fah	*sister-in-law*
زوج الأم	*zawj* al.'*umm*	*stepfather*
زوجة الأب	*zaw*.jat al.'*abb*	*stepmother*

CULTURAL WISDOM

THE ROLE OF FAMILY IN ARAB CULTURE

The أسرة (*us*.rah) (*family*) plays a very important role in Arab life, society, and culture, and the Arab family structure is very different than the Western family unit. The notion of the family is much more comprehensive and reinforced in the Arab world and the Middle East than the United States or other Western countries. The family unit most prevalent in the West is the nuclear family — generally comprised of two parents and their children — but the family in the Arab world is an extended, close-knit family network made up of parents, children, grandparents, aunts, uncles, and cousins.

It's not uncommon to find an Arab household in which children live not only with their parents but also with their aunts and uncles, cousins, and grandparents. In Arab culture, the idea of the immediate family extends to second- and even third-degree cousins! In addition, lineage is important, and the terms for family relatives are specifically designed to differentiate between cousins from the mother's side ابن الخال (*ibn* al.*khāl*) and cousins from the father's side ابن العمّ (*ibn* al.'*amm*). Thus, if you're talking to someone from the Arab world about his or her family, you can be sure that you'll have a lot to talk about!

Talkin' the Talk

Hassan is on a flight to New York from Casablanca, Morocco. He strikes up a conversation with Alexandra, who is sitting next to him.

Hassan: عفواً. هل أنتِ أمريكية؟
'*af*.wan, hal *an*.ti am.rī.*kiy*.yah?
Excuse me. Are you American?

Alexandra: نعم, أنا أمريكية. وأنتَ؟
na.'am *a*.nā am.rī.*kiy*.yah. wa.'*an*.ta?
Yes, I'm American. And you?

Hassan: أنا مغربي. هل أنتِ في زيارة لأسرتك في المغرب؟
a.nā *magh*.ri.bī. hal *an*.ti fī zi.*yā*.rah li.'us.*ra*.tik fī al.*magh*.rib?
I'm Moroccan. Are you visiting family in Morocco?

Alexandra: نعم. خالتي في طنجة. أي جزء من الولايات المتحدة تزور؟
na.'am, *khā*.la.tī fī *ṭan*.jah. ayy juz' *min* al.wa.lā.*yāt* al.mut.*ta*.ḥi.dah ta.*zūr?*
Yes. My aunt lives in Tangiers. What part of the United States are you visiting?

Hassan: أنا ذاهب لزيارة أخي في نيو يورك.
a.nā *dhā*.hib li.zi.*yā*.rit *a*.khī fī New York.
I'm going to visit my brother in New York.

Alexandra: أتمنى لك رحلة سعيدة.
a.ta.*man*.ná *la*.ka *riḥ*.lah sa.'ī.dah.
I wish you a pleasant trip.

Hassan: وأنتِ كذلك.
wa.*an*.ti ka.*dhā*.lik.
Same to you.

WORDS TO KNOW		
زيارة	zi.yā.rah	visit
أزور	a.zūr	I visit
سفر	sa.far	traveling
كذلك	ka.dhā.lik	same/similar
سعيد	sa.'īd	happy

Making Small Talk on the Job

You can generally find out a lot about a person based on his or her مهنة (*mih*.nah) (*job*). A lot of people identify themselves with their occupations, so being able to make small talk about jobs is essential.

GRAMMATICALLY SPEAKING

Professions in Arabic always have a gender distinction. If you want to ask someone about his or her profession, you have two options:

- ما مهنتكَ؟ (*mā* mih.*na*.tu.ka) (*What is your job?*; Literally: *What do you do?*) (M)
- ما مهنتكِ؟ (*mā* mih.*na*.tu.ki) (*What is your job?*; Literally: *What do you do?*) (F)
- أينت تعمل؟ (*ay*.na *ta'*.mal) (*Where do you work?*) (M)
- أين تعملين؟ (*ay*.na ta'.ma.*līn*) (*Where do you work?*) (F)

Table 7-2 contains some important words relating to different occupations.

Table 7-2 gives the masculine forms of professions. You'll be pleased to know that converting the masculine forms of professions into the feminine forms involves simply adding a تاء مربوطة to the end of the masculine profession. For example, to say "translator" in the feminine, you add a تاء مربوطة to مترجم to get مترجمة (mu.*tar*.ji.mah) (*translator*) (F).

TABLE 7-2

Professions

Arabic	Pronunciation	Translation
مصرفي	*maṣ*.ra.fī	*banker* (M)
صحفي	sa.ḥa.*fī*	*journalist* (M)
كاتب	*kā*.tib	*writer* (M)
ممثل	mu.*math*.thil	*actor* (M)
مهندس	mu.*han*.dis	*architect* (M)
طبيب	ṭa.*bīb*	*doctor* (M)
فنان	fan.*nān*	*artist* (M)
مغني	mu.*ghan*.nī	*singer* (M)
مترجم	mu.*tar*.jim	*translator* (M)
ممرض	mu.*mar*.riḍ	*nurse* (M)
محامي	mu.*ḥā*.mī	*lawyer* (M)
طباخ	ṭab.*bākh*	*cook* (M)
تاجر	*tā*.jir	*merchant* (M)
محاسب	mu.*ḥā*.sib	*accountant* (M)
سمسار	sim.*sār*	*real estate broker* (M)
حلاق	ḥal.*lāq*	*barber* (M)
فلاح	fal.*lāḥ*	*farmer* (M)
راقص	*rā*.qiṣ	*dancer* (M)
شرطي	*shur*.ṭī	*police officer* (M)
رجل إطفاء	*ra*.jul iṭ.*fā'*	*fireman*
رجل أعمال	*ra*.jul a'.*māl*	*businessman*

Talkin' the Talk

Hassan and Amanda, two passengers on a plane from Casablanca to New York, are talking about their respective jobs.

Alexandra: ما مهنتكَ؟
mā mih.*na*.tu.ka?
What do you do?

Hassan: أنا مهندس في الدار البيضاء.
a.nā mu.*han*.dis fī ad.*dār* al.bay.*ḍa'*.
I'm an architect in Casablanca.

Alexandra: هذا ممتاز!
hā.dhā mum.*tāz!*
That's excellent!

Hassan: وأنتِ, أين تعملين؟
wa.'*an*.ti *ay*.na ta'.ma.*līn*?
And you, where do you work?

Alexandra: أنا صحفية.
a.nā ṣa.ḥa.*fiy*.yah.
I'm a journalist.

Hassan: في أي جريدة؟
fī ayy ja.*rī*.dah?
In which newspaper?

Alexandra: في النيو يورك تيمز.
fī al New York Times.
At The New York Times.

Staying in Touch by Phone and Email

One of the fun things about meeting new people is staying in touch with them so as to have future encounters that are enjoyable, pleasant, and enriching. Therefore, being able to initiate and provide contact information in order to remain in touch with friends, both old and new, is important. In this section, I give you the basics to help you stay in touch with people. Staying in touch is also an important tool in helping improve your Arabic — the more Arabic speakers you interact with, the faster your Arabic will improve.

- ما هي أفضل طريقة للبقاء على الاتصال؟ (mā *hi*.ya *af*-ḍal ṭa-*rī*-qah lil-ba.*qā'* '*a*.lá al.it.ti.*ṣāl*?) (*What's the best way to stay in touch?*)
- ما هو رقم هاتفك؟ (mā *hu*.wa raqm *hā*.ti.fak) (*What's your telephone number?*)
- هل لديك رقم هاتف جوّال؟ (hal la.*day*.ka *ra*.qam *hā*.tif ja.*wāl*?) (*Do you have a mobile phone number?*)
- ما هو البريد الإلكتروني الخاص بك؟ (mā *hu*.wa al.ba.*rīd* al.'i.lik.*trū*.nī al.khāṣ bik) (*What's your email address?*)

These questions can help you stay in touch with new people whom you meet. Another popular tool that's now helpful for people to stay in touch is فيسبوك (*fīs*.būk) (*Facebook*). A lot of people in the Arab world are increasingly becoming regular Facebook users, which will help you even more when interacting with new friends. Check Chapter 9 for specific information for how to carry on a phone conversation and what to include in an email.

FUN & GAMES

Name four members of the family:

1. ___________

2. ___________

3. ___________

4. ___________

The answers are in Appendix C.

questions

» Clarifying directions

» Exploring ordinal numbers

Chapter 8
Asking Directions and Finding Your Way

Being able to ask for — and understand — اتجاهات (it.ti.jā.*hāt*) (*directions*) is an important skill. In order to interact with others and get assistance, you need to know how to ask questions that can help you get where you want to be. And you also need to understand the directions that are being given to you. In this chapter, I tell you how to get relevant information to help you find what you're looking for.

REMEMBER

You can listen to all the Talkin' the Talk dialogues featured in this chapter. Go to `www.dummies.com/go/arabicfd` and click on the dialogue you want to hear.

Focusing on the "Where"

In order to ask for and give directions, you need to be able to answer and ask "where" questions. In this section, I tell you how to do just that.

Asking "where" questions

The best way to get directions-related information is to ask أين (*ay*.na) (*where*) questions. Luckily, the structure of a where question is relatively straightforward: You use أين followed by the subject. For example:

- أين الفندق؟ (*ay*.na al.*fun*.duq) (*Where is the hotel?*)
- أين الهاتف؟ (*ay*.na al.*hā*.tif) (*Where is the phone?*)
- أين الحمّام؟ (*ay*.na al.ḥam.*mām*) (*Where is the bathroom?*)

REMEMBER

Be sure to define the subject following أين. As I explain in Chapter 3, you define a subject by adding the definite article prefix ال (al) (*the*) to the subject noun. For example, فندق means "hotel," and الفندق means "the hotel." So if you're asking where the hotel is located, you say, أين الفندق (*Where is the hotel?*) and not أين فندق, which translates to *Where is a hotel?*

"Where" questions are useful for more than just asking for directions. You may also apply the where question format to human subjects, such as friends or family. For instance:

- أين مريم؟ (*ay*.na *mar*.yī.am) (*Where is Miriam?*)
- أين الأطفال؟ (*ay*.na al.'aṭ.*fāl*) (*Where are the children?*)
- أين أمي؟ (*ay*.na *um*.mī) (*Where is my mom?*)

REMEMBER

You don't need to use the definite article ال when referring to a noun that's already defined. For instance, in one of the preceding examples, مريم doesn't require the definite article prefix ال because she's a specific person. So make sure that you don't go around adding the prefix ال to every subject after أين because sometimes there's no question about what subject you're referring to.

Answering "where" questions

Answering where questions isn't always as clear-cut as asking a where question. You can answer a where question in a number of different ways, ranging from the simple to the convoluted. In order to answer where questions, you have to understand the structure of the where question response, which usually follows this format: subject, preposition, object.

Take a look at some common where questions and their corresponding replies:

» أين المستشفى؟ (*ay*.na al.mus.*tash*.fá) (*Where is the hospital?*)

المستشفى في المدينة. (al.mus.*tash*.fá fī al.ma.*dī*.nah) (*The hospital is in the city.*)

» أين المطعم؟ (*ay*.na al.*maṭ*.'am) (*Where is the restaurant?*)

المطعم قريب من الفندق. (al.*maṭ*.'am qa.*rīb* min al.*fun*.duq) (*The restaurant is close to the hotel.*)

» أين الكتاب؟ (*ay*.na al.ki.*tāb*) (*Where is the book?*)

» الكتاب تحت الطاولة. (al.ki.*tāb* *taḥt* aṭ.*ṭā*.wi.lah) (*The book is under the table.*)

TIP

Notice that in these examples, you use a preposition to establish a connection between the subject (in this case, what or whom you're looking for) and the object (the location of the desired subject). In order to establish the desired relationship, you need to be familiar with some of these common prepositions:

» على ('*a*.lá) (*on*)
» في (fī) (*in*)
» إلى (*i*.lá) (*to*)
» قريب من (qa.*rīb* min) (*close to*)
» بعيد عن (ba.*'īd* '*an*) (*far from*)
» بجانب (bi.*jā*.nib) (*next to*)
» فوق (*fawq*) (*on top of*)
» تحت (*taḥt*) (*underneath/below*)
» أمام (a.*mām*) (*in front of*)
» وراء (wa.*rā*.'a) (*behind*)
» على يمين ('*a*.lá ya.*mīn*) (*to the right of*)
» على يسار ('*a*.lá ya.*sār*) (*to the left of*)

REMEMBER

You must define the subject in the أين interrogatory sentence (see "Asking 'where' questions" earlier in the chapter for details); similarly, you must also define the subject in the reply to a where question. In addition, you should define the object in the response statement as well, either by using the definite article prefix ال or by including a predefined object.

Getting Direction about Directions

Understanding the format of the where question and reply structures is an important first step in having a firm grasp on how to ask for directions. These sections help you so you can ask and respond to direction questions.

Asking for directions

Of course, you can't just go up to a person and bluntly ask him or her, أين الفندق (*Where is the hotel?*). That wouldn't be very polite. The proper etiquette for approaching someone and asking for directions is to first say السلام عليكم (as.sa.*lā*.mu 'a.*lay*.kum) (*hello*) or أهلًا وسهلًا (*ah*.lan wa.*sah*.lan) (*hi*) and then ask if he or she would permit you to ask a question. For example, you begin the exchange by saying, عفواً. هل يمكن أن أسألك؟ ('*af*.wan hal *yum*.kin an *as*.'a.lak su.'*ā*.lan?) (*Excuse me. May I ask you a question?*).

After the person agrees to take your question, you may proceed to ask for directions. (For more information on greetings and introductions, see Chapter 4.)

Talkin' the Talk

While visiting Casablanca, John is trying to find the museum. He stops Ahmed, a passerby, and asks him for directions.

John: السلام عليكم.
as.sa.*lā*.mu 'a.*lay*.kum.
Hello.

Ahmed: وعليكم السلام.
wa.'a.*lay*.kum as.sa.*lām*.
Hello.

John: عفواً. هل يمكن أن أسألك سؤالًا؟
'*af*.wan *hal yum*.kin an as.'*a*.lak su.'*ā*.lan?
Excuse me. May I ask you a question?

Ahmed: طبعاً.
ṭab.'an.
Of course.

John: أين المتحف؟
ay.na al.*mat*.ḥaf?
Where is the museum?

Ahmed: المتحف بجانب المسجد.
al.*mat*.ḥaf bi.*jā*.nib al.*mas*.jid.
The museum is next to the mosque.

John: شكراً جزيلًا!
shuk.ran ja.*zī*.lan!
Thank you very much!

Ahmed: لا شكر على واجب.
lā shukr '*a*.lá *wā*.jib.
You're welcome.

WORDS TO KNOW		
متحف	ma̲t̲.ḥaf	museum
مسجد	ma̲s̲.jid	mosque
مستشفى	mus.ta̲sh̲.fá	hospital
مطعم	ma̲ṭ̲.'am	restaurant
فندق	fu̲n̲.duq	hotel
سفارة	si.f̲ā̲.rah	embassy
مدرسة	ma̲d̲.ra.sah	school
مكتبة	ma̲k̲.ta.bah	library
مسرح	*mas*.raḥ	theater
سوق	sūq	market
مخبز	ma̲kh̲.baz	bakery
مدينة	ma.d̲ī̲.nah	city

قرية	<u>qar</u>.yah	village
شارع	<u>shā</u>.ri'	street/avenue
حي	ḥayy	neighborhood
بناية	bi.<u>nā</u>.yah	building

Could you repeat that?

Sometimes, when you ask for directions, the person who tries to help you starts talking too fast and you can't quite understand what he is saying. Other times, you may be in a loud area, such as near a downtown traffic jam, and you can't make out what the other person is saying. In either case, you have to ask the person who's giving you directions to speak more slowly or to repeat what he has just said. These phrases can help you cope with these situations:

- عفواً (*'af*.wan) (*Excuse me/Pardon me*)
- لم أفهم (lam *af*.ham) (*I didn't understand*)
- تكلّم ببطء من فضلك (ta.*kal*.lam bi.*buṭ'* min *faḍ*.lik) (*Speak slowly please*)
- اعد من فضلك . (*a*.'id min *faḍ*.lik) (*Repeat please*)
- ماذا قلت؟ (*mā*.dhā qult) (*What did you say?*)

Talkin' the Talk

John is in downtown Casablanca where the traffic is really loud. He stops Maria, a passerby, to ask her for directions but can't make out what she's saying due to the noise. He asks her to repeat what she said.

John: عفواً. هل يمكن أن أسألك سؤالًا؟
'af.wan *hal yum*.kin an as.'*a*.la.ki su.'*ā*.lan?
Excuse me. May I ask you a question?

Maria: نعم.
na.'am.
Yes.

John: أين المدرسة؟
ay.na al.*mad*.ra.sah?
Where is the school?

Maria: المدرسة بعيدة عن هنا.
al.*mad*.ra.sah ba.'ī.dah min *hu*.nā.
The school is far from here.

John: لم أفهم. هل يمكن أن تعيدي من فضلك؟
lam af.ham. *hal yum*.kin an tu.'*ī.dī* min *faḍ*.lik?
I don't understand. Could you repeat please?

Maria: المدرسة ليست قريبة من هنا. يجب أن تأخذ الحافلة إلى وسط المدينة.
al.*mad*.ra.sah *lay*.sat qa.*rī*.bah min *hu*.nā. *ya*.jib an *ta'*.khudh al.*ḥā*.fi.lah *i*.lá *wa*.saṭ al.ma.*dī*.nah.
The school is not close to here. You must take the bus to the center of the city.

John: ما اسم المدرسة؟
mā ism al.*mad*.ra.sah?
What's the name of the school?

Maria: المدرسة الأمريكية.
al.*mad*.ra.sah al.'am.rī.*kiy*.yah.
The American school.

John: فهمت. شكراً جزيلًا.
fa.*himt*. *shuk*.ran ja.*zī*.lan.
I understand! Thank you very much.

Maria: عفواً.
'*af*.wan.
You're welcome.

WORDS TO KNOW

بعيد	ba.'ī̲d̲	far (M)
بعيدة	ba.'ī̲.dah	far (F)
قريب	qa.r̲ī̲b̲	close (M)
قريبة	qa.r̲ī̲.bah	close (F)
هنا	h̲u̲.nā	here

هناك	hu.nāk	there
أفهم	af.ham	understand
حافلة	ḥā.fi.lah	bus
تاكسي	tāk.sī	taxi
قطار	qi.ṭār	train
محطة	ma.ḥa.ṭah	station

Using command forms

When you ask someone for directions, the person directs you to a specific location. Essentially, she tells you where to go, which qualifies as a *command form*. The command form is uniform, which means it applies to all second-person pronouns. However, the command form is gender-defined, which means that you use different commands for men and women. Here are some common command forms:

Masculine Command	Feminine Command
أعد (*a*.'id) (*repeat*)	أعيدي (a.'ī.dī) (*repeat*)
إذهب (idh.hab) (*go*)	إذهبي (idh.*ha*.bī) (*go*)
خذ (khudh) (*take*)	خذي (*khu*.dhī) (*take*)
قف (qif) (*stop*)	قفي (*qi*.fī) (*stop*)

Talkin' the Talk

Susan is trying to get back to her فندق (*fun*.duq) (*hotel*) in Tunis. She stops Rita and asks her how to get there.

Susan: عفواً. هل يمكن أن أسألك سؤالًا؟
'*af*.wan, *hal yum*.kin an as.'*a*.la.ki su.'*ā*.lan?
Excuse me. May I ask you a question?

Rita: طبعاً.
ṭa.ba.'an.
Of course.

Susan: أين فندق الجوهرة؟
ay.na *fun*.duq al.*jaw*.ha.rah?
Where is the Jawhara Hotel?

Rita: أظنّ أنّ هذا الفندق في وسط المدينة.
a.*ẓunn an*.na *hā*.dhā al.*fun*.duq fī *wa*.saṭ al.ma.*dī*.nah.
I believe that this hotel is in the center of the city.

Susan: نعم, كيف أذهب هناك؟
na.'am, *kay*.fa *adh*.hab hu.*nāk*?
Yes. How can I go there?

Rita: إهذبي إلى شارع حسن, ثمّ اتجهي يميناً.
idh.*ha*.bī *i*.lá *shā*.ri' *ḥa*.san, *thum*.ma it.*ta*.ji.hī ya.*mī*.nan.
Go to Avenue Hassan, and then turn right.

Susan: حسناً.
ḥa.sa.nan.
Okay.

Rita: ثمّ إمشي نحو المكتبة وتوقفي. ويقع الفندق أمام المكتبة. تجاه الشمال.
thum.ma *im*.*shī nah*.wa al.*mak*.ta.bah wa.ta.*waq*.qa.fī. wa.*ya*.qa' al.*fun*.duq a.*mām* al.*mak*.ta.bah. ti.*jāh* ash. sha.*māl*.
Then walk toward the library and stop. The hotel is in front of the library. The hotel is facing north.

Susan: شكراً على مساعدتك.
shuk.ran '*a.lá* mu.sā.'*a*.da.tik.
Thank you for your help.

WORDS TO KNOW

أظنّ	a.<u>ẓunn</u>	I believe
ثمّ	<u>thum</u>.ma	then
حسناً	<u>ḥa</u>.sa.nan	okay
مساعدة	mu.sā.'a.dah	help

شمال	sha.mal	north
جنوب	ja.nūb	south
شرق	sharq	east
غرب	gharb	west

Discovering Ordinal Numbers

Ordinal numbers are used to order things in a first-second-third kind of format. Unlike cardinal numbers, which are mostly used for counting, you use ordinals when giving directions. For example, you would tell someone to "turn right on the second street" and not "turn right on two street." Hear the difference?

REMEMBER

Ordinal numbers in Arabic are gender-defined, so you need to be familiar with both the masculine and feminine ordinal forms, which I present in Table 8-1.

TABLE 8-1 Ordinal Numbers

Ordinal (M)	Pronunciation	Ordinal (F)	Pronunciation	English
أول	*aw*.wal	أولى	ū.lá	*first*
ثاني	*thā*.nī	ثانية	*thā*.ni.yah	*second*
ثالث	*thā*.lith	ثالثة	*thā*.li.thah	*third*
رابع	*rā*.bi'	رابعة	*rā*.bi.'ah	*fourth*
خامس	*khā*.mis	خامسة	*khā*.mi.sah	*fifth*
سادس	*sā*.dis	سادسة	*sā*.di.sah	*sixth*
سابع	*sā*.bi'	سابعة	*sā*.bi.'ah	*seventh*
ثامن	*thā*.min	ثامنة	*thā*.mi.nah	*eighth*
تاسع	*tā*.si'	تاسعة	*tā*.si.'ah	*ninth*
عاشر	'*ā*.shir	عاشرة	'*ā*.shi.rah	*tenth*

Ordinal (M)	Pronunciation	Ordinal (F)	Pronunciation	English
حادي عشر	*hā*.dī *'a*.shar	حادية عشر	*hā*.di.yat *'a*.shar	*eleventh*
ثاني عشر	*thā*.nī *'a*.shar	ثانية عشر	*thā*.ni.yat *'a*.shar	*twelfth*
ثالث عشر	*thā*.lith *'a*.shar	ثالثة عشر	*thā*.li.that *'a*.shar	*thirteenth*
رابع عشر	*rā*.bi' *'a*.shar	رابعة عشر	*rā*.bi.'at *'a*.shar	*fourteenth*
خامس عشر	*khā*.mis *'a*.shar	خامسة عشر	*khā*.mi.sat *'a*.shar	*fifteenth*
سادس عشر	*sā*.dis *'a*.shar	سادسة عشر	*sā*.di.sat *'a*.shar	*sixteenth*
سابع عشر	*sā*.bi' *'a*.shar	سابعة عشر	*sā*.bi.'at *'a*.shar	*seventeenth*
ثامن عشر	*thā*.min *'a*.shar	ثامنة عشر	*thā*.mi.nat *'a*.shar	*eighteenth*
تاسع عشر	*tā*.si' *'a*.shar	تاسعة عشر	*tā*.si.'at *'a*.shar	*nineteenth*
عشرون	'ish.*rūn*	عشرون	'ish.*rūn*	*twentieth*
ثلاثون	tha.lā.*thūn*	ثلاثون	tha.lā.*thūn*	*thirtieth*

GRAMMATICALLY SPEAKING

If you want to tell a friend that your house is "the fifth house," you say, **المنزل الخامس** (al.*man*.zil al.*khā*.mis). Note that you use the masculine ordinal form خامس because منزل is a masculine noun subject. To say that you're taking the "eighth bus," you would say, **الحافلة الثامنة** (al.*ḥā*.fi.lah ath.*thā*.mi.nah). The ordinal الثامنة is feminine because الحافلة is a feminine noun subject.

So if you want to tell your friend to "turn left on the second street," you say, **طف إلى اليسار في الشارع الثاني** (*ṭuff* i.lá al.ya.*sār* fī ash.*shā*.ri' ath.*thā*.nī). Because الشارع (ash.*shā*.ri') (*street*) is a masculine subject, the corresponding ordinal ثاني (*second*) should also be masculine.

FUN & GAMES

Match the Arabic statements in Section 1 with their English translations in Section 2.

Section 1: الجملة العربية (al.*jum*.lah al.'a.ra.*biy*.yah) (*Arabic sentence*)

1. طف إلى اليمين.
2. هل يمكن أن تعيد من فضلك؟
3. إذهبي إلى الغرب.
4. الفندق قريب.
5. البناية العاشرة.

Section 2: الجملة الإنجليزية (al.*jum*.lah al.in.jli.*zīy*.yah) (*English sentence*)

A. Please repeat that.

B. The hotel is close.

C. It's the tenth building.

D. Turn right.

E. Go west.

The answers are in Appendix C.

IN THIS CHAPTER

» Beginning a phone conversation

» Making plans over the phone

» Leaving a phone message

» Sending and receiving emails

Chapter 9

Taking Care of Business and Telecommunicating

Personally, I really enjoy talking on the هاتف (*hā*.tif) (*phone*). It's a great way to catch up with friends, make social arrangements, and plan other aspects of your life with ease. With just a phone, you can get in touch with anyone in the world and talk about anything you like — from sports to social events and schoolwork to office gossip!

A few decades ago you may have been limited as to where you could hold a مكالمة هاتفية (mu.*kā*.la.mah hā.ti.*fiy*.yah) (*phone conversation*). Today, with the ubiquity of cellphones and other portable phone units, you can literally take your conversation anywhere! This flexibility makes knowing how to hold a phone conversation in Arabic even more important. In this chapter, I explain how to properly begin and end a phone conversation, how to make plans over the phone, and how to leave a proper phone message in Arabic. With all that information, you can be confident that you're carrying on a proper phone conversation like a native speaker!

REMEMBER

You can listen to all the Talkin' the Talk dialogues featured in this chapter. Go to `www.dummies.com/go/arabicfd` and click on the dialogue you want to hear.

Making a Call: Phone Basics

Before you can chat on the phone with your friends like a native speaker, you need to be familiar with the following basic terminology:

- هاتف عام (*hā*.tif *'ām*) (*public phone*)
- هاتف جوال (*ḥā*.tif jaw.*wāl*) (*cellphone*)
- رقم الهاتف (*raqm* al.*hā*.tif) (*phone number*)
- بطاقة الهاتف (bi.*ṭā*.qat al.*hā*.tif) (*phone card*)
- مكالمة هاتفية (mu.*kā*.la.mah hā.ti.*fiy*.yah) (*phone conversation*)

The following sections explain how to start talking on the phone and how to ask for someone in Arabic.

Beginning a phone conversation

You can begin a phone conversation in a number of ways. The most common, whether you're the caller or the person answering the phone, is to simply say ألو (a.*lū*) (*hello*). Hello is one of the most common phrases in the Arabic language and is used consistently throughout in conversation.

TIP

Stating your name right after the person on the phone says hello is proper etiquette, particularly if you don't know that person. If you're the caller, you may say أنا (*a*.nā) (*I am*) followed by your name. Alternatively, you may say هذا (M)/ هذه (F) (*hā*.dhā/*hā*.dhi.hi) (*this is*) followed by your name. A familiar phrase you can also use after you say hello is السلام عليكم (as.sa.*lā*.mu 'a.*lay*.kum) (*hello*) or أهلاً و سهلاً (*ah*.lan wa.*sah*.lan) (*hi*). Flip to Chapter 3 for more on greetings and making small talk.

Talkin' the Talk

Kamal calls his friend Rita at home.

Kamal: ألو.
a.*lū*.
Hello.

Rita: ألو.
a.*lū*.
Hello.

Kamal: أنا كمال.
a.nā ka.*māl*.
This is Kamal.

Rita: أهلًا و سهلًا كمال!
ah.lan wa.*sah*.lan ka.*māl!*
Hi, Kamal!

Kamal: أهلًا و سهلًا ريتا!
ah.lan wa.*sah*.lan *rī*.tā!
Hi, Rita!

Rita: كيف الحال؟
kayf al.*ḥāl?*
How are you doing?

Kamal: الحمد لله، شكراً.
al.*ḥam*.du lil.*lāh*, *shuk*.ran.
I'm doing well, thank you.

Asking to speak to someone

Sometimes, a person other than the one you want to talk to answers the phone. A common phrase to help you ask for the person you called to speak with is هل (اسم) هنا؟ (*hal [name] hu*.nā), which means "*Is (name) here?*"

Alternatively, you can also use the personal pronouns هو (*hu*.wa) (if the person you're looking for is a man) or هي (*hi*.ya) (in the case of a woman) instead of using the person's name.

Talkin' the Talk

Kamal calls his friend Rita at home. Rita's mom, Souad, answers the phone, and Kamal asks to speak with Rita.

Kamal: ألو.
a.*lū*.
Hello.

Souad: ألو.
a.*lū*.
Hello.

Kamal:	السلام عليكم. أنا صديق ريتا. هل هي هنا؟ as.sa.*lā*.mu 'a.*lay*.kum. *a*.nā ṣa.*dīq* *rī*.tā. hal *hi*.ya *hu*.nā? *Hello. I am a friend of Rita. Is she here?*
Souad:	نعم هي هنا. ما اسمك؟ *na*.'am *hi*.ya *hu*.nā. mā *is*.muk? *Yes, she is here. What's your name?*
Kamal:	أنا كمال. *a*.nā ka.*māl.* *This is Kamal.*
Souad:	انتظر دقيقة من فضلك. *in*.ta.ẓir da.*qī*.qah min *faḍ*.lik. *Wait one minute, please.*
Rita:	ألو كمال. a.*lū* ka.*māl.* *Hello, Kamal.*

WORDS TO KNOW

أنا	a.nā	I
هي	hi.ya	she
هو	hu.wa	he
صديق	ṣa.dīq	friend (M)
صديقة	ṣa.dī.qah	friend (F)
هنا	hu.nā	here
انتظر	in.ta.ẓir	wait
دقيقة	da.qī.qah	minute

Planning while on the Phone

The phone is useful not only for staying in touch with friends and family, but also for making ارتباطات اجتماعية (ir.ti.bā.*ṭāt* ij.ti.mā.'*iy*.yah) (*social arrangements*) as well as ارتباطات العمل (ir.ti.bā.*ṭāt* al.'*a*.mal) (*business arrangements*). This section covers the specific terminology you need for each of these situations.

Making social plans

If you're talking with a friend, you're free to be a bit more informal than if you were calling a business. Some common words to help you make social arrangements with your friends are the following:

- هيا بنا! (*hay*.yā *bi*.nā) (*Let's!*)
- مطعم (*maṭ*.'am) (*restaurant*)
- قاعة سينما (*qā*.'*at si*.ni.mā) (*movie theater*)
- متحف (*mat*.ḥaf) (*museum*)
- وقت فراغ (*waqt* fa.*rāgh*) (*free time*)

Talkin' the Talk

Selma calls her friend Mark on his هاتف جوال (*hā*.tif jaw.*wāl*) (*cellphone*) so that they can make dinner plans.

Selma: ألو.
a.*lū*.
Hello.

Mark: ألو.
a.*lū*.
Hello.

Selma: أهلًا مارك. أنا سلمى.
ah.lan *mārk*. *a*.nā *sal*.má.
Hi, Mark. I am Selma.

Mark: أهلًا سلمى! شكراً لمكالمتك.
ah.lan *sal*.má! *shuk*.ran li.mu.*kā*.la.ma.tik.
Hi, Selma! Thanks for your call.

Selma: عفواً. كيف حالك؟
'*af*.wan. *kayf ḥā*.lak?
You're welcome. How are you?

Mark: الحمد لله. وأنت؟
al.*ḥam*.du lil.*lāh*. wa.'*an*.ti?
I'm doing well. And you?

Selma: الحمد لله. هل عندك وقت فراغ غداً؟
al.*ḥam*.du lil.*lāh*. hal '*in*.dak waqt fa.*rāgh gha*.dan?
I'm doing well. Do you have any free time tomorrow?

Mark: نعم. حوالي الساعة السادسة.
na.'am *ḥa*.*wā*.lī as.*sā*.'ah as.*sā*.di.sah.
Yes, around six o'clock.

Selma: هل تريد أن تذهب معي إلى المطعم الساعة السابعة؟
hal tu.*rīd* an *tadh*.hab *ma*.'ī *i*.lá al.*maṭ*.'am as.*sā*.'ah as.*sā*.bi.'ah?
Would you like to go with me to the restaurant at seven o'clock?

Mark: طبعاً! سيكون ذلك عظيماً.
ṭa.ba.'an! sa.ya.*kūn dhā*.lik 'a.*ẓī*.man.
Of course! I would like that.

Selma: ممتاز! إلى الغد.
mum.*tāz! i*.lá al.*ghad*.
Excellent! See you tomorrow.

Mark: إلى الغد!
i.lá al.*ghad!*
See you tomorrow!

WORDS TO KNOW

مكالمتكَ	mu.kā.la.ma.tu.ka	your call (M)
مكالمتكِ	mu.kā.la.ma.tu.ki	your call (F)
عندكَ	'in.da.ka	you have (M)
عندكِ	'in.da.ki	you have (F)

وقت	waqt	time
وقت فراغ	waqt fa.rāgh	free time
ساعة	sā.'ah	hour
أحب	u.ḥib.bu	I like
ذلك	dhā.li.ka	that
الغد	al.ghad	tomorrow

Making business appointments

Arranging personal get-togethers with friends or family is always fun, but at times you have to conduct business over the phone, whether you're setting up a موعد (*maw.*'id) (*appointment*) with the dentist or arranging a business اجتماع (ij.ti.*mā*') (*meeting*) with a client. Interacting with businesses in Arabic requires specific terminology.

Talkin' the Talk

Susan is calling the Rialto, a company in Casablanca. She reaches the كاتبة (kā.ti.bah) (secretary) and asks to speak with Mr. Ahmed.

Susan: ألو.
a.*lū*.
Hello.

Katiba: ألو. شركة ريالتو. دقيقة من فضلك؟
a.*lū*. *sha*.ri.kat ri.*yāl*.tū. da.*qī*.qah min *faḍ*.lik?
Hello. Rialto Inc. Can you wait one minute, please?

Susan: طبعاً.
ṭa.ba.'an.
Of course.

Katiba: عفواً للتأخر. كيف أساعدك؟
'*af*.wan lit.ta.'*akh*.khur. *kay*.fa u.*sā*.'i.dak?
Sorry to keep you waiting. How may I help you?

Susan: أريد أن أتكلم مع السيد أحمد.
u.*rīd* an a.ta.*kal*.lam *ma*.'a as.*say*.yid *aḥ*.mad.
I would like to speak with Mr. Ahmed.

Katiba: السيد أحمد مشغول. هو في اجتماع.
as.*say*.yid *aḥ*.mad mash.*ghūl*. *hu*.wa fī ij.ti.*mā'*.
Mr. Ahmed is busy. He is in a meeting.

Susan: متى سيكون غير مشغول؟
ma.tá sa.ya.*kūn* ghayr mash.*ghūl*?
When will he be available?

Katiba: أي دقيقة.
ayy da.*qī*.qah.
Any minute now.

Susan: شكراً جزيلًا. سأبقى على الخط.
shuk.ran ja.*zī*.lan. sa.'*ab*.qá '*a*.lá al.*khaṭ*.
Thank you very much. I'll stay on the line.

WORDS TO KNOW

موعد	maw.'id	appointment
اجتماع	ij.ti.mā'	meeting
سيد	say.yid	Mr./Sir
سيدة	say.yi.dah	Mrs./Ms.
رئيس	ra.'īs	president
كاتبة	kā.ti.bah	secretary/assistant
شركة	sha.ri.kah	company
أساعدك	u.sā.'i.dak	I help you
أريد	u.rīd	I would like
مشغول	mash.ghūl	busy

Leaving a Message

Sometimes you just run out of luck and can't get ahold of the person you're trying to reach. You're forced to leave a رسالة (ri.*sā*.lah) (*message*) either on a voice mailbox or with a person. These sections explain how to do so and the important related vocabulary.

Dealing with voice mail

When you leave a voice-mail message, you want to make sure to include the following:

- Your اسم (*ism*) (*name*)
- The وقت المكالمة (*waqt* al.mu.*kā*.la.mah) (*time of the call*)
- Your رقم الهاتف (*raqm* al.*hā*.tif) (*phone number* or *callback number*)
- The أحسن وقت للمكالمة (*aḥ*.san *waqt* lil.mu.*kā*.la.mah) (*best times you're available to talk*)

For example, Salma tries to reach Karim by phone but gets this recording instead:

> أهلًا, أنا كريم. أنا لست هنا ولكن إذا تركت اسمك ورقمك سأكلمك في أسرع وقت
>
> (*ah*.lan, *a*.nā ka.*rīm*. *a*.nā *las*.tu *hu*.nā wa.*lāk*.in *i*.dhā ta.*rak*.ta *is*.muk wa.*raq*.muk sa.'u.kal.*li*.muk fī *'as*.ra' *waqt*)
>
> (*Hi, this is Karim. I'm not in right now, but if you leave your name and number, I'll get back to you as soon as possible.*)

Salma's voice-mail message sounds something like this:

> أهلاً وسهلاً كريم. أنا سلمى. الساعة الواحدة والنصف يوم الخميس. اتصل بي من فضلك عند سماعك هذه الرسالة في أي وقت بعد الساعة الخامسة. رقمي صفر واحد اثنين ثلاثة. شكراً.
>
> (*ah*.lan wa.*sah*.lan ka.*rīm*. *a*.nā *sal*.má. as.*sā*.'ah al.*wā*.ḥi.dah wan.*niṣf yawm* al.*kha*.mīs. it.*ta*.ṣil bī min *faḍ*.lik *'in*.da sa.*mā*.'ik *hā*.dhi.hi ar.ri.*sā*.lah fī ayy waqt ba'd as.*sā*.'ah al.*khā*.mi.sah. *raq*.mī ṣifr *wā*.ḥid *ith*.nayn tha.*lā*.thah. *shuk*.ran.)
>
> (*Hi, Karim. This is Salma. It's 1:30 in the afternoon on Thursday. Please give me a call back when you get this message any time after 5 o'clock. My number is 0123. Thanks!*)

Leaving a message with a person

If you have to leave a message directly with a person, make sure you include your name and ask the person who picks up the phone to pass along word that you called.

Talkin' the Talk

Kamal calls his friend Rita at home. Rita isn't home, and Souad, her mom, answers the phone. Kamal leaves a message for Rita with her mother.

Souad: ألو.
a.*lū*.
Hello.

Kamal: ألو. أنا كمال.
a.lū. *a*.nā ka.*māl*.
Hello. This is Kamal.

Souad: أهلًا كمال.
ah.lan ka.*māl*.
Hi, Kamal.

Kamal: هل ريتا في البيت؟
hal rī.ta *fī* al.*bayt?*
Is Rita home?

Souad: لا. ذهبت إلى الدكان.
lā. *dha*.ha.bat *i*.lá ad.duk.*kān*.
No. She went to the store.

Kamal: متى سترجع؟
ma.tá sa.*tar*.ji'?
When will she be back?

Souad: سترجع بعد ساعة.
sa.*tar*.ji' *ba'*.da *sā*.'ah.
She will be back in an hour.

Kamal: هل يمكن أن تخبريها بمكالمتي؟
hal *yum*.kin an tukh.bi.*rī*.hā bi.mu.*kā*.la.ma.tī?
Is it possible for you to tell her that I called?

Souad: طبعاً!
ṭa.ba.'an!
Of course!

Kamal: شكراً! مع السلامة.
shuk.ran! *ma*.'a as.sa.*lā*.mah.
Thank you! Good-bye.

Souad: مع السلامة.
ma.'a as.sa.*lā*.mah.
Good-bye.

WORDS TO KNOW

بيت	bayt	home
ذهب	dha.ha.ba	he went
ذهبت	dha.ha.bat	she went
دكان	duk.kān	store
متى	ma.tá	when
ترجع	tar.ji'	she come back
بعد	ba'.da	after
هل يمكن	hal yum.kin	is it possible
مكالمتي	mu.kā.la.ma.tī	my call

CULTURAL WISDOM

Most phones in Arabic-speaking countries use the familiar Arabic numerals (see Chapter 5). Thank goodness you won't have to struggle to identify the Arabic numbers on the keypad while dialing a number!

Sending and Getting Emails

Increasingly, the phone is being complemented, and in some cases even replaced, by email messaging. In this section, I show you some key terms to allow you to compose, send, and receive emails.

» إنشاء (*in*.sha') (*compose*)
» البريد الوارد (al.ba.*rīd* al.*wā*.rid) (*inbox*)
» علبة الصادر ('ul.bat aṣ.*ṣā*.dir) (*outbox*)
» مسودة (mis.*wad*.da) (*draft*)
» من (*min*) (*from*)
» إلى (*i*.lá) (*to*)
» موضوع (maw.*ḍū*') (*subject*)

These sections give you some helpful advice for sending emails in Arabic and in English to an Arabic-speaking individual. I also discuss some etiquette to ensure that you don't offend anyone.

Sending an email in Arabic

When you're sending out an email message in Arabic, you always want to start off with the basic term السلام عليكم, the most common greeting that I introduce in Chapter 1. Here are other common expressions to use:

» أشكركم على الرسالة (ash.*ku*.ru.kum *'a*.lá ar.ri.*sā*.lah) (*Thank you for the message*)
» مع أطيب التحيات (*ma*.'ah *aṭ*.yab at.ta.ḥiy.*yāt*) (*With best regards*)

If you're sending an email message to a friend or colleague, I encourage you to use these two expressions to begin and end your message to express that you know the individual.

Sending an email in English

When you're sending an email to a native Arabic-speaking person, feel free to use the same expressions that you would use in composing the email to an English-speaking person. If the individual or individuals you're sending the email understand English, then it's completely valid to use everyday English expressions. If you need to compose an email in Arabic, please see the sections immediately preceding this one.

Following proper etiquette

As a general rule, don't use any language in an Arabic email that you wouldn't use in an English email. Make sure to begin and end the message with the terms I provide earlier in this section, and keep your message to the point. Arabic culture is now getting more and more accustomed to communicating via email, and in a few years, email will be even more prevalent than it is today.

Sometimes you may want to look up terms while you're typing the email. One tool that I find helpful that provides an etiquette-friendly interface is Google Translate. If you're looking for a term or a phrase while typing your email, visit `translate.google.com` and click on English-to-Arabic or Arabic-to-English, depending on what your target language for the email will be.

FUN & GAMES

Here are some questions commonly asked on the phone. Match the questions with the appropriate answers.

أسئلة (*as*.'i.lah) (questions)

1. متى سترجع؟ (*When will she be back?*)
2. هل عندك وقت فراغ؟ (*Do you have free time?*)
3. هل هو هنا؟ (*Is he here?*)
4. كيف الحال؟ (*How are you doing?*)
5. ما اسمك؟ (*What's your name?*)

الأجوبة (al.*aj*.wi.bah) (*answers*)

A. نعم. دقيقة من فضلك.

B. لا. أنا مشغول.

C. اسمي سعاد.

D. الحمد لله، شكراً.

E. سترجع بعد ساعة.

The answers are in Appendix C.

IN THIS CHAPTER

» Finding your way around the kitchen

» Eating at home

» Dining at a restaurant

Chapter 10
This Is Delicious! Eating In and Dining Out

You can explore a new culture with طعام (ṭa.'*ām*) (*food*). You can find out a lot about a people by exploring what they eat, how they eat it, and how they prepare it. Like in many other cultures, food plays a central role in Arabic culture. In this chapter, you can expand your vocabulary with the Arabic words for some popular meals and foods, and you find out how to place an order at a restaurant and how to interact appropriately with your server.

REMEMBER

You can listen to all the Talkin' the Talk dialogues featured in this chapter. Go to `www.dummies.com/go/arabicfd` and click on the dialogue you want to hear.

Consuming Food: All about Mealtime

The three basic وجبات (wa.ja.*bāt*) (*meals*) in Arabic are as follows:

- فطور الصباح (fu.*ṭūr* aṣ.ṣa.*bāḥ*) (*breakfast*)
- غداء (gha.*dā'*) (*lunch*)
- عشاء ('a.*shā'*) (*dinner*)

Sometimes when you're feeling a little جائع (*jā*.'i') (*hungry*) but aren't ready for a full-course meal, you may want a small وجبة خفيفة (*waj*.bah kha.*fī*.fah) (*snack*) instead. These sections take a closer look at these different meals.

Starting the day off with breakfast

I'm sure you've heard it before, but breakfast is the most important meal of the day. When you start your day on a full stomach, you feel better and accomplish more. In the mornings, I like to start my day with a cup of قهوة (*qah*.wah) (*coffee*). I usually like to drink it كحلة (*kaḥ*.lah) (*black*), but sometimes I add a little حليب (ḥa.*līb*) (*milk*) and some سكر (*suk*.kar) (*sugar*) to give it a bit of flavor. Some days, I prefer to drink شاي (shāy) (*tea*) instead of coffee. My favorite accompaniments for my coffee or tea are حلويات (ḥa.la.wiy.*yāt*) (*pastries*).

Here are some other things you can expect in a regular breakfast:

- عسل ('*a*.sal) (*honey*)
- قهوة بالحليب (*qah*.wah bil.ḥa.*līb*) (*coffee with milk*)
- قهوة بالسكر (*qah*.wah bis.*suk*.kar) (*coffee with sugar*)
- قهوة بالحليب والسكر (*qah*.wah bil.ḥa.*līb* was.*suk*.kar) (*coffee with milk and sugar*)
- شاي بالعسل (shāy bil.'*a*.sal) (*tea with honey*)
- خبز محمر (khubz mu.*ḥam*.mar) (*toasted bread*)
- خبز بالزبدة (khubz biz.*zub*.dah) (*bread with butter*)
- خبز بالزبدة والعسل (khubz biz.*zub*.dah wal.'*a*.sal) (*bread with butter and honey*)
- شفنج (shi.*fanj*) (*donuts*)
- حبوب الفطور (ḥu.*būb* al.fu.*ṭūr*) (*breakfast cereal*)
- بيض (bayḍ) (*eggs*)

Having الفطور في المنزل (al.fu.*ṭūr* fī al.*man*.zil) (*breakfast at home*) is a nice, relaxing way to start the day.

Talkin' the Talk

Fatima prepares breakfast for her daughter Nadia at home before sending her off to school.

Fatima: هل تقيدين عصيراً هذا الصباح؟
hal tu.rī.*dīn* 'a.*ṣī*.ran *hā*.dhā aṣ.ṣa.*bāḥ?*
Would you like juice this morning?

Nadia: نعم يا أمي.
na.'am yā *um*.mī.
Yes, Mommy.

Fatima: أي نوع من العصير: عصير برتقال، عصير تفاح، عصير جزر؟
ayy naw' *min* al.'a.*ṣīr*: 'a.*ṣīr* bur.tu.*qāl*, 'a.*ṣīr* tuf.*fāḥ*, 'a.*ṣīr* *ja*.zar?
What kind of juice do you want: orange juice, apple juice, or carrot juice?

Nadia: أريد عصير برتقال.
u.*rīd* 'a.*ṣīr* bur.tu.*qāl*.
I want orange juice.

Fatima: ممتاز! هذا رائع للصحة. وهل تريدين حبوب الفطور ايضاً؟
mum.*tāz! hā*.dhā *rā*.'i' lil.*ṣi*.ḥah. wa.*hal* tu.rī.*dīn* ḥu.*būb* al.fu.*ṭūr ay*.ḍan?
Excellent! It's great for your health. And do you want cereal as well?

Nadia: نعم ومعها حليب كثير.
na.'am wa.*ma*.'a.hā ḥā.*līb* ka.*thīr*.
Yes, and with lots of milk.

Fatima: وها هو الخبز بالزبدة.
wa.*hā hu*.wa al.*khubz* biz.*zub*.dah.
And here's some bread with butter.

Nadia: شكراً. سأذهب إلى المدرسة الآن.
shuk.ran. sa.'*adh*.hab *i*.lá al.*mad*.ra.sah al.'*ān*.
Thank you. I'm going to go to school now.

Fatima: لحظة. نسيت الموزة.
laḥ.ẓah, na.*say*.ti al.*maw*.zah.
One moment. You forgot the banana.

Nadia: طبعاً! شكراً.
ṭa.ba.'an! *shuk*.ran.
Of course! Thank you.

WORDS TO KNOW

عصير	'a.ṣīr	juice
عصير برتقال	'a.ṣīr bur.tu.qāl	orange juice
عصير تفاح	'a.ṣīr tuf.fāḥ	apple juice
عصير جزر	'a.ṣīr ja.zar	carrot juice
برتقالة	bur.tu.qā.lah	an orange
تفاحة	tuf.fā.ḥah	an apple
جزرة	ja.za.rah	a carrot
موزة	maw.zah	a banana
صحة	si.ḥah	health
حليب	ḥa.līb	milk
الآن	al.'ān	now
لحظة	laḥ.ẓah	one moment
نسي	na.si.ya	forgot
ينسى	yan.sá	to forget
نسيتِ	na.say.ti	you forgot (FS)
نسيتَ	na.say.ta	you forgot (MS)

If you're on the go, stopping by a قهوة (*qah*.wah) (*coffee shop*) in the صباح (ṣa.*bāḥ*) (*morning*) is a good alternative to getting your breakfast at home. (***Note:*** The word قهوة denotes both the beverage as well as the coffee shop. Remember this distinction so that you don't get confused unnecessarily!)

Talkin' the Talk

Laura stops by the local coffee shop in the morning to order breakfast from Ahmed.

Laura: صباح الخير يا أحمد.
ṣa.*bāḥ* al.*khayr yā aḥ*.mad.
Good morning, Ahmed.

Ahmed: صباح النور يا لورا. ماذا تحبّين هذا الصباح؟
ṣa.*bāḥ* an.*nūr yā lū*.rā. *mā*.dhā tu.ḥib.*bīn hā*.dhā aṣ.ṣa.*bāḥ?*
Good morning, Laura. What would you like this morning?

Laura: مثل كلّ يوم.
mith.la kull yawm.
Like every day.

Ahmed: فوراً. قهوة بالحليب, نعم؟
faw.ran. *qah*.wah bil.ḥa.*līb*, *na*.ʻam?
Right away. Coffee with milk, right?

Laura: نعم.
na.ʻam.
Yes.

Ahmed: كم ملعقة سكّر؟
kam *mil*.ʻa.qat *suk*.kar?
How many spoons of sugar?

Laura: ملعقتين.
mil.ʻaq.*tayn*.
Two spoons.

Ahmed: هل تحبّين قهوة صغيرة أو متوسطة أو كبيرة؟
hal tu.ḥib.*bīn qah*.wah ṣa.*ghī*.rah aw mu.ta.*was*.si.ṭah aw ka.*bī*.rah?
Would you like a small, medium, or large coffee?

Laura: أحبّ قهوة كبيرة اليوم.
u.*ḥibb* *qah*.wah ka.*bī*.rah al.*yawm*.
I'd like a large coffee today.

Ahmed: وهل تريدين أن تأكلي شيئاً؟
wa.*hal* tu.rī.*dīn* an *ta'*.ku.lī *shay*.'an?
And would you like anything to eat?

Laura: هل عندك شفنج؟
hal *'in*.dak shi.*fanj*?
Do you have donuts?

Ahmed: نعم. كم شفنجة تريدين؟
na.'am, kam shi.*fin*.jah tu.rī.*dīn*?
Yes. How many donuts do you want?

Laura: أريد ثلاث شفنجات من فضلك.
u.*rīd* tha.*lāth* shi.fin.*jāt* min *faḍ*.lak.
I'd like three donuts, please.

WORDS TO KNOW

عادي	'<u>ā</u>.dī	regular
ملعقة	<u>mil</u>.'a.qah	spoon
صغير	ṣa.<u>ghīr</u>	small (M)
صغيرة	ṣa.<u>ghī</u>.rah	small (F)
متوسط	mu.ta.<u>was</u>.siṭ	medium (M)
متوسطة	mu.ta.<u>was</u>.siṭ.ah	medium (F)
كبير	ka.<u>bīr</u>	large (M)
كبيرة	ka.<u>bī</u>.rah	large (F)
الأكل	al.<u>'akl</u>	eating
شفنجة	shi.<u>fin</u>.jah	donut

Having a piece of فاكهة (*fā*.ki.hah) (*fruit*) such as a برتقالة (bur.tu.*qā*.lah) (*an orange*) or تفاحة (tuf.*fā*.ḥah) (*an apple*) is a healthy addition to your meal. Because فواكه (fa.*wā*.kih) (*fruits*) play an important role in any healthy meal, here are some of the more common fruits:

- توت (tūt) (*blackberry*)
- بطيخ (baṭ.*ṭīkh*) (*cantaloupe*)
- ليمون هندي (lay.*mūn hin*.dī) (*grapefruit*)
- عنب (*'i*.nab) (*grapes*)
- ليمون (lay.*mūn*) (*lemon*)
- ليمون مالح (lay.*mūn mā*.liḥ) (*lime*)
- العنبج (al.*'an*.baj) (*mango*)
- خوخ (khawkh) (*peach*)
- إجاص (i.*jāṣ*) (*pear*)

Eating lunch

Eating your breakfast keeps you شبعان (shab.'*ān*) (*satisfied*) for a few hours — time to get some work done and remain productive. Later, though, you're bound to get جائع (*jā*.'i') (*hungry*) again. Perhaps a piece of fruit can keep you going until it's time for lunch.

CULTURAL WISDOM

Lunch is a very important meal. In most Middle Eastern countries, workers don't sit in their cubicles and eat their lunch. Rather, most offices close and employees get two hours or more for lunch.

Unlike breakfast, the food during lunch is quite different. Here are some of the common foods you can expect during lunch:

- لحم (laḥm) (*meat*)
- لحم البقر (laḥm al.*ba*.qar) (*beef*)
- لحم الغنم (laḥm al.*gha*.nam) (*lamb*)
- لحم العجل (laḥm al.*'ijl*) (*veal*)
- سمك (*sa*.mak) (*fish*)
- دجاج (da.*jāj*) (*chicken*)
- أرز (*a*.ruz) (*rice*)

Sometimes, your lunch may consist of a simple ساندويش (sān.da.*wīsh*) (sandwich). Other times, you may prefer a nice, healthy سلطة (*sa*.la.ṭah) (salad). I'm convinced that خضر (khu.*ḍar*) (vegetables) make or break the salad. Here are some vegetables to help you make your salad لذيذة (la.*dhī*.dhah) (delicious):

- خرشوف (khar.*shūf*) (*artichokes*)
- هليون (hil.*yūn*) (*asparagus*)
- أفوكادو (a.fū.*kā*.dū) (*avocado*)
- قرنبيط (qar.na.*bīṭ*) (*broccoli*)
- قنبيط (qun.*bīṭ*) (*cauliflower*)
- ذرة (*dhu*.rah) (*corn*)
- خيار (khi.*yār*) (*cucumber*)
- فول (*fūl*) (*fava beans*)
- خس (*khass*) (*lettuce*)
- فقاع (fu.*qā'*) (*mushrooms*)
- بصل (*ba*.ṣal) (*onions*)
- بازلاء (bā.zil.*lā'*) (*peas*)
- بطاطا (ba.*ṭā*.ṭā) (*potatoes*)
- سبانخ (sa.*bā*.nikh) (*spinach*)
- طماطم (ṭa.*mā*.ṭim) (*tomatoes*)

In order to make a sandwich even more delicious, add some of the following توابل (ta.*wā*.bil) (*condiments*):

- صلصة طماطم (*ṣal*.sat ṭa.*mā*.ṭim) (*ketchup*)
- خردل (*khar*.dal) (*mustard*)
- مايونيز (mā.yū.*nīz*) (*mayonnaise*)
- مخللات (mu.khal.la.*lāt*) (*pickles*)

Talkin' the Talk

Matt is on his lunch break and decides to stop by the local cafeteria to order a sandwich. Nawal takes his order.

Nawal: أهلًا. كيف يمكن أن أساعدك؟
ah.lan. *kay*.fa *yum*.kin an u.sā.'*i*.dak?
Hi. How may I help you?

Matt: أريد ساندويش من فضلك.
u.*rīd* sān.da.*wīsh* min *faḍ*.lik.
I would like a sandwich, please.

Nawal: أي حجب تريد: كبير أو صغير؟
ayy ḥajm tu.*rīd*: ka.*bīr* aw ṣa.*ghīr*?
What size do you want: large or small?

Matt: كبير.
ka.*bīr.*
Large.

Nawal: أي نوع من الخبز تحبّ: خبز أبيض أو خبز أسمر؟
ayy naw' min al.*khubz* tu.*ḥibb*: khubz *ab*.yaḍ aw khubz *as*.mar?
What type of bread would you like: white bread or whole wheat bread?

Matt: خبز أبيض.
khubz *ab*.yaḍ.
White bread.

Nawal: عندنا جميع أنواع اللحوم: لحم الغنم ولحم البقر ولحم العجل. وعندنا دجاج أيضاً. أي نوع لحم تريد في الساندويش؟
'*in*.da.nā ja,*mī*' an.*wā*' al.lu.*ḥūm*: laḥm al.*gha*.nam wa.*laḥm* al.*ba*.qar wa.*laḥm* al.'*ijl*. wa.'*in*.da.nā da.*jāj ay*.ḍan. ayy naw' laḥm tu.*rīḍ* fī as.sān.da.*wīsh*?
We have all sorts of meat: lamb, beef, and veal. And we also have chicken. What kind of meat do you want in the sandwich?

Matt: دجاج من فضلك.
da.*jāj* min *faḍ*.lik.
Chicken, please.

Nawal: وهل تحبّ خضاراً في الساندويش؟
wa.*hal* tu.*ḥibb* khu.*ḍā*.ran fī as.sān.da.*wīsh*?
And would you like any vegetables in your sandwich?

Matt: نعم. هل عندكم طماطم؟
na.'am, hal '*in*.da.kum ṭa.*mā*.ṭim?
Yes. Do you have any tomatoes?

Nawal: نعم. شيء آخر؟
na.'am, shay' *ā*.khar?
Yes. Anything else?

Matt: خس وقرنبيط وبصل.
khass wa.qar.na.*bīṭ* wa.*ba*.ṣal.
Lettuce, broccoli, and onions.

Nawal: آسفة. ليس عندنا قرنبيط.
ā.si.fah, *lay*.sa '*in*.da.nā qar.na.*bīṭ*.
I am sorry. We don't have broccoli.

Matt: طيب. خس وطماطب فقط.
ṭay.yib. khass wa.ṭa.*mā*.ṭim *fa*.qaṭ.
That's okay. Just lettuce and tomatoes.

Nawal: وهل تريد بعض التوابل؟
wa.hal tu.*rīd* baḍ at.ta.*wā*.bil?
And do you want some spices?

Matt: مخللات فقط. شكراً.
mu.khal.la.*lāt* *fa*.qaṭ. *shuk*.ran.
Pickles only. Thank you.

WORDS TO KNOW

أطلب	at.lub	I order
حجم	ḥajm	size
نوع	naw'	type
أبيض خبز	khubz ab.yaḍ	white bread

أسمر خبز	khubz as.mar	whole wheat bread
جميع	ja.mī'	all
فقط	fa.qaṭ	only

GRAMMATICALLY SPEAKING

The most important فعل (*fi'l*) (*verb*) you should know relating to food is the verb أكل (*a*.ka.la), which means "ate" in the past tense. In the present, you conjugate it as يأكل (*ya'*.kul) (*to eat*).

Here is the verb "to eat" conjugated in the past form:

Form	Pronunciation	Translation
أنا أكلتُ	*a*.nā a.*kal*.tu	I ate
أنتَ أكلتَ	*an*.ta a.*kal*.ta	You ate (MS)
أنتِ أكلتِ	*an*.ti a.*kal*.ti	You ate (FS)
هو أكل	*hu*.wa *a*.ka.la	He ate
هي أكلتْ	*hi*.ya *a*.ka.lat	She ate
نحن أكلنا	*naḥ*.nu a.*kal*.nā	We ate
أنتم أكلتم	*an*.tum a.*kal*.tum	You ate (MP)
أنتنّ أكلتنّ	an.*tun*.na a.kal.*tun*.na	You ate (FP)
هم أكلوا	hum *a*.ka.lū	They ate (MP)
هنّ أكلنّ	*hun*.na a.*kal*.na	They ate (FP)
أنتما أكلتما	an.*tu*.mā a.kal.*tu*.mā	You ate (dual/M/F)
هما أكلا	*hu*.mā a.ka.*lā*	They ate (dual/M)
هما أكلتا	*hu*.mā a.ka.la.*tā*	They ate (dual/F)

Because "to eat" is a regular verb, you conjugate it using the form "eating" in the present:

Form	Pronunciation	Translation
أنا آكل	*a*.nā *ā*.kul	I am eating
أنتَ تأكل	*an*.ta *ta'*.kul	You are eating (MS)
أنتِ تأكلين	*an*.ti ta'.ku.*līn*	You are eating (FS)
هو يأكل	*hu*.wa *ya'*.kul	He is eating
هي تأكل	*hi*.ya *ta'*.kul	She is eating
نحن نأكل	*naḥ*.nu *na'*.kul	We are eating
أنتم تأكلون	*an*.tum ta'.ku.*lūn*	You are eating (MP)
أنتنّ تأكلنّ	*an*.tun.na ta'.*kul*.nna	You are eating (FP)
هم يأكلون	hum ya'.ku.*lūn*	They are eating (MP)
هنّ يأكلنّ	*hun*.na ya'.*kul*.nna	They are eating (FP)
أنتما تأكلان	an.*tu*.mā ta'.ku.*lān*	You (two) are eating (dual) (dual/M/F)
يأكلان هما	*hu*.mā ya'.ku.*lān*	They (two) are eating (dual)(dual/M)
تأكلان هما	*hu*.mā ta'.ku.*lān*	They (two) are eating (dual/F)

Supping at dinner

Dinner is an important meal in the course of the day. In most Arab countries, many people usually eat dinner very late, around 9 p.m. or even 10 p.m. Because people eat more at breakfast and lunch, and due to the traditionally late hour of dinner, most people in the Arab world have light meals for dinner.

A typical dinner usually consists of some sort of سمك (*sa*.mak) (*fish*), دجاج (da.*jāj*) (*chicken*), or other kind of لحم (laḥm) (*meat*).

Enjoying a Meal at Home

Grabbing a quick bite on the go is often convenient if you have a busy schedule, but there's nothing like a home-cooked meal. This section covers the key terms to help you prepare and set the table for a وجبة لذيذة في المنزل (*waj*.bah la.*dhī*.dhah fī al.*man*.zil) (*a delicious home-cooked meal*)!

Here are some common items you might find in your مطبخ (maṭ.bakh) (kitchen):

- فرن (furn) (*oven*)
- ثلاجة (thal.*lā*.jah) (*refrigerator*)
- مغسلة (*magh*.sa.lah) (*sink*)
- خزانات (khaz.zā.*nāt*) (*cupboards*)
- ملح (malḥ) (*salt*)
- فلفل (*ful*.ful) (*pepper*)
- زيت الزيتون (zayt az.zay.*tūn*) (*olive oil*)

When you're done الطبخ (aṭ.*ṭabkh*) (*cooking*) داخل (*dā*.khil) (*inside*) the kitchen, you're ready to step into the غرفة الطعام (*ghur*.fat aṭ.ṭa.*'ām*) (*dining room*) and set up the food on top of the مائدة (*mā*.'i.dah) (*dining table*). Here are some items you may find on your dining table:

- صحون (ṣu.*ḥūn*) (*plates*)
- أطباق (aṭ.*bāq*) (*dishes*)
- أكواب (ak.*wāb*) (*glasses/cups*)
- شوك (*shu*.wak) (*forks*)
- ملاعق (ma.*lā*.'iq) (*spoons*)
- سكاكين (sa.kā.*kīn*) (*knives*)
- مناديل (ma.nā.*dīl*) (*napkins*)

Dining Out

Going to a nice مطعم (*maṭ*.'am) (*restaurant*) is one of my favorite things to do. I enjoy interacting with the نادل (*nā*.dil) (*waiter*) and the نادلة (*nā*.di.lah) (*waitress*), and I like taking my time picking and choosing from the قائمة الطعام (*qā*.'i.mat aṭ.ṭa.'*ām*) (*menu*). In this section, you find out how to make your trip to the restaurant as enjoyable as possible, from interacting with the waiter to displaying proper dining etiquette and choosing the best food from the menu.

CULTURAL WISDOM

The dining experience in most restaurants in the Middle East, as well as in Middle Eastern restaurants all over the world, is truly an enchanting and magical experience. The décor is usually very ornate and sumptuous, with oriental patterns and vivid colors adorning the rooms. The waitstaff usually wears traditional جلابة (jal.*lā*.bah), which are long, flowing garments that are pleasing to the eye, and the food is very exotic, spicy, and delicious. When you go to a Middle Eastern restaurant, allow at least a couple of hours for the dining experience — don't be surprised if you end up savoring a five- or even seven-course meal!

Perusing the menu

As in other restaurants, the menu in Middle Eastern restaurants is usually divided into three sections:

- مقبلات (mu.qab.bi.*lāt*) (*appetizers*)
- طبق رئيسي (*ṭa*.baq ra.ʾī.sī) (*main dish/entrees*)
- تحلية (*taḥ*.li.yah) (*dessert*)

Appetizers

In the appetizers section of the menu, you find some طعام خفيف (ṭa.'*ām*.kha.*fīf*) (*light food*) to help build your appetite. Here are some common appetizers:

- باذنجان (bā.dhin.*jān*) (*eggplant*)
- ثوم محمر (thawm mu.*ḥam*.mar) (*roasted garlic*)
- ورق عنب (*wa*.raq *'i*.nab) (*stuffed grape leaves*)
- عدس ('*a*.das) (*lentils*)
- حريرة (ḥa.*rī*.ra) (*Moroccan soup*)
- روبيان (rub.*yān*) (*shrimp*)
- حساء (ḥi.*sā'*) (*soup*)
- كماة (ka.*māh*) (*truffles*)

Entrees

The main dishes or entrees section of a menu consists of dishes featuring chicken, various other لحم (laḥm) (*meat*), and fish. Fish is usually a very popular dish because it's tasty, healthy, and light. Most restaurants have a pretty extensive selection of fish, including:

- شبوط (shab.*būṭ*) (*carp*)
- القد (al.*qud*) (*cod*)
- اسقمري (is.*qam*.rī) (*mackerel*)
- سلمون (*sa*.la.mūn) (*salmon*)
- قرش (qirsh) (*shark*)
- موسى (*mū*.sá) (*sole*)
- العطروط (al.'aṭ.*rūṭ*) (*trout*)
- تون (tūn) (*tuna*)

Desserts

Like a lot of people, my favorite part of a restaurant menu is, of course, the dessert section. The تحلية (*taḥ*.li.yah) (*dessert*) is a great way to wrap up a nice meal. I like dessert because there are a lot of حلويات (ḥa.la.wiy.*yāt*) (*sweets*) to choose from. Here are some popular desserts:

- كعك (ka'k) (*cake*)
- كعك الشكلاطة (ka'k ash.shu.ku.*lā*.ṭah) (*chocolate cake*)
- مثلجات (mu.tha.la.*jāt*) (*ice cream*)
- جبن (jubn) (*cheese*)

Beverages

You may also notice a portion of the menu — or an entirely different menu — introducing different kinds of مشروبات (mash.rū.*bāt*) (*drinks*). The following are some beverages you may come across on the menu:

- ماء (mā') (*water*)
- ماء غازي (mā' *ghā*.zī) (*sparkling water*)
- عصير ليمون ('a.*ṣīr* lay.*mūn*) (*lemonade*)

- نبيذ (khamr) (*wine*)
- بيرة (*bī*.rah) (*beer*)
- نبيذ (na.*bīdh*) (*wine*)
- نبيذ أحمر (na.*bīdh aḥ*.mar) (*red wine*)
- نبيذ ابيض (na.*bīdh ab*.yaḍ) (*white wine*)

Placing your order

After you peruse the menu, place your order with the waiter or waitress. Restaurant staff are usually highly trained individuals who know the ins and outs of the food that the restaurant serves, so don't be afraid of asking lots of أسئلة (*as*.'i.lah) (*questions*) about things on the menu that sound good to you.

Talkin' the Talk

Sam and Atika go to Restaurant Atlas for a romantic dinner for two. They place their drink orders with their waitress.

Waitress: مرحباً بكما في مطعم أطلس. كيف يمكن أن أساعدكما؟
mar.ḥa.ban *bi*.ku.mā *fī maṭ*.'am *aṭ*.las. *kay*.fa *yum*.kin an u.sā.'i.da.*ku*.mā?
Welcome to Restaurant Atlas. How may I help you?

Sam: ما المشروبات التي عندكم؟
mā al.mash.rū.*bāt* al.la.*tī 'in*.da.kum?
What do you have to drink?

Waitress: عندنا ماء وماء غازي وعصير ليمون.
'*in*.da.nā mā' wa.mā' *ghā*.zī wa.'a.*ṣīr* lay.*mūn*.
We have water, sparkling water, and lemonade.

Sam: سنبدأ بالماء من فضلك.
sa.*nab*.da' bil.*mā*' min *faḍ*.lik.
We'll start with water, please.

Waitress: هل تريدان ماءً طبيعياً أو ماءً عادياً؟
hal tu.rī.*dān mā*.'an ṭa.bī.'*iy*.yan aw *mā*.'an 'ā.*diy*.yan?
Do you want mineral (bottled) water or regular (tap) water?

Sam: ماء طبيعي.
mā' ṭa.*bī*.'ī.
Mineral water.

Waitress: فوراً. هل تريدان بعض الخمور ايضاً؟
faw.ran. hal tu.rī.*dān ba'ḍ* al.khu.*mūr ay*.ḍan?
Right away. And would you like any alcoholic drinks as well?

Atika: هل عندكم نبيذ؟
hal '*in*.da.kum na.*bīdh*?
Do you have any wine?

Waitress: نعم. عندنا نبيذ أبيض ونبيذ أحمر.
na.'am '*in*.da.nā na.*bīdh ab*.yaḍ wa.na.*bīdh aḥ*.mar.
Yes. We have white wine and red wine.

Atika: سنأخذ نبيذ أحمر من فضلك.
sa.*na'*.khudh na.*bī*.dh *aḥ*.mar min *faḍ*.lik.
We'll have red wine, please.

Waitress: ممتاز. سأعطيكما وقتاً لتقرآ القائمة.
mum.*tāz*. sa.'u'.*ṭī*.ku.mā *waq*.tan li.taq.*ra*.'ā al.*qā*.'i.mah.
Excellent. I'll give you some time to read through the menu.

Sam: شكراً.
shuk.ran.
Thank you.

After Sam and Atika peruse the menu, they're ready to place their order.

Waitress: هل أنتما مستاعدان لطلب الطعام؟
hal an.tu.*mā* mus.ta.'id.*dān* li.*ṭa*.lab aṭ.ṭa.'*ām*?
Are you ready to place your order?

Atika: نعم. للمقبلات سنبدأ بروبيان وكماة.
na.'am. lil.mu.qab.bi.*lāt* sa.*nab*.da' bi.rub.*yān* wa.ka.*māh*.
Yes. For appetizers, we'd like shrimp and truffles.

Waitress: اختيار ممتاز.
ikh.ti.*yār* mum.*tāz*.
Excellent selection.

Sam: وبعد ذلك سنأخذ سلمون.
wa.*ba'*.da *dhā*.li.ka sa.*na'*.khudh *sa*.la.mūn.
And after that we'd like to have salmon.

Waitress: شيء آخر؟
shay' ā.khar?
Anything else?

Atika: نريد كعك الشكلاطة للتحلية.
nu.*rīd* ka'k ash.shu.ku.*lāṭ*.ah lit.*taḥ*.li.yah.
We'd like the chocolate cake for dessert.

WORDS TO KNOW

ماء طبيعي	mā' ṭa.<u>bī</u>.'ī	bottled/mineral water
ماء عادي	mā' '<u>ā</u>.dī	regular/tap water
مستعد	mus.<u>ta</u>.'id	ready
اختيار	ikh.ti.<u>yār</u>	selection

Finishing your meal and paying the bill

When you finish your meal, you're ready to leave, but before you do, you need to take care of your حساب (ḥi.*sāb*) (*bill*). You may ask your waiter for the bill by saying الحساب من فضلك (al.ḥi.*sāb* min *faḍ*.lik) (*the bill, please*). Another option is to ask the server كم الكامل؟ (kam al.*kā*.mil) (*What's the total?*).

Like in the United States, tipping your server is customary in Arabic-speaking countries and Middle Eastern restaurants. The amount of the بقشيش (baq.*shīsh*) (*tip*) depends on the kind of service you received, but usually 15 percent to 20 percent is average.

FUN & GAMES

You need to go to the grocery store and get the following items. Write the Arabic words for the following five foods.

Illustrations by Elizabeth Kurtzman

1. __________
2. __________
3. __________
4. __________
5. __________

Answers are in Appendix C.

IN THIS CHAPTER

» Browsing inside the store

» Comparing items and costs

» Identifying clothing sizes and colors

Chapter 11
Going Shopping

Whether you're in a foreign country or at the local mall, shopping can be a lot of fun. Not only do you get to buy things to maintain your lifestyle, but you also can discover new items, purchase gifts, and buy things you hadn't even considered.

This chapter exposes you to the important words and terms that help you shop. Discover how to choose the right dress size, how to choose the best item from an electronics store, and even how to shop for nice jewelry. You also find out how to interact with sales staff so that you're sure to find and purchase the item that you want.

REMEMBER

You can listen to all the Talkin' the Talk dialogues featured in this chapter. Go to `www.dummies.com/go/arabicfd` and click on the dialogue you want to hear.

Going to the Store

When you want to buy something, you head to the محل (ma.*ḥal*) (*store*). Depending on your shopping list, you can choose from different types of محلات (ma.ḥal.*lāt*) (*stores*). If you want to buy some خبز (*khubz*) (*bread*), then you want to head to the مخبز (*makh*.baz) (*bakery*). If you're trying to find a particular كتاب (ki.*tāb*) (*book*), then your destination is the مكتبة (*mak*.ta.bah) (*bookstore/library*). To buy ملابس (ma.*lā*.bis) (*clothes*), head to the محل ملابس (ma.*ḥal* ma.*lā*.bis) (*clothing store*).

And if you want to buy a راديو (*rād*.yū) (*radio*) or تلفزيون (ti.li.fiz.*yūn*) (*television*), the محل إلكترونيات (ma.*ḥal* i.lik.trū.niy.*yāt*) (*electronics store*) is your best bet.

Here are some additional specialty stores you may need to visit:

- محل حلويات (ma.*ḥal* ḥa.la.wiy.*yāt*) (*pastry shop*)
- محل سمك (ma.*hal sa*.mak) (*fish store*)
- جواهري (*ja.wā*.hi.rī) (*jeweler*)

Not all stores sell only goods or products. Other types of stores provide services, such as haircuts and manicures. Here are some stores that are more service-oriented:

- وكالة أسفار (wi.*kā*.lat as.*fār*) (*travel agency*)
- حلاق (ḥal.*lāq*) (*barber*)

If you need to shop for a variety of goods, then your destination is the مركز تسوق (*mar*.kaz. ta.*saw*.wuq) (*mall*). At the mall, you can find almost everything and anything you want. Or if you're not sure what to buy, going to the mall is a great idea because you have so many choices that you're bound to find something that you need or want to purchase.

Browsing the merchandise

If you're at the store and aren't quite sure what to purchase, then browsing and checking out the different items is a good idea. You don't have to buy anything, and that's what can be so much fun about window shopping. Feel free to look through a واجهة المحل (*wā*.ji.hat al.ma.*ḥal*) (*store window*) for any items that may attract your attention. While you're browsing, a بائع (*bā*.'i') (*store clerk*) (M) or a بائعة (*bā*.'i.'ah) (*store clerk*) (F) may ask:

- هل يمكن أن أساعدك؟ (*hal yum*.kin an u.sā.'*i*.dak?) (*May I help you?*) (M)
- هل يمكن أن أساعدك؟ (*hal yum*.kin an u.sā.'*i*.dik?) (*May I help you?*) (F)
- هل تريد شيئاً معيناً؟ (*hal* tu.*rīd shay*.'an mu.'*ay*.ya.nan?) (*Are you looking for anything special?*) (M)
- هل تريدين شيئاً معيناً؟ (*hal* tu.rī.*dīn shay*.'an mu.'*ay*.ya.nan?) (*Are you looking for anything special?*) (F)

If you need مساعدة (mu.*sā*.'a.dah) (*help/assistance*), simply respond by saying نعم (*na*.'am) (*yes*). (For more on how to ask for and get help, skip to the section "Asking for a Particular Item," later in this chapter.) Otherwise, if you want to continue browsing, لا شكراً (lā *shuk*.ran) (*no, thank you*) should do the trick.

Getting around the store

If you visit a mall, you probably need some sort of help because department stores can be very big and very confusing. If you want اتجاهات (it.ti.jā.*hāt*) (*directions*), head to the مكتب المعلومات (*mak*.tab al.ma'.lū.*māt*) (*information desk*) to have your أسئلة (*as*.'i.lah) (*questions*) answered. Here are some common questions you may ask:

- هل يمكن أن تساعدني؟ (*hal yum*.kin an tu.sā.'*i*.da.nī?) (*Is it possible for you to help me?*)
- أين الطابق الأول؟ (*ay*.na aṭ.*ṭā*.biq al.'*aw*.wal?) (*Where is the first floor?*)
- أين المصعد؟ (*ay*.na al.*miṣ*.'ad?) (*Where is the elevator?*)
- أين قسم الملابس؟ (*ay*.na qism al.ma.*lā*.bis?) (*Where is the section for clothes?*)
- في أي طابق يوجد الجواهري؟ (fī ayy *ṭa*.biq *yū*.jad al.ja.*wā*.hi.rī?) (*On which floor is the jeweler located?*)
- هل هناك مخبز في مركز التسوق؟ (hal hu.*nā*.ka *makh*.baz fi *mar*.kaz at.ta.*saw*.wuq?) (*Is there a bakery in the mall?*)

Talkin' the Talk

Jessica is at the mall and is trying to figure out where the clothing section is located. She asks the attendant at the information desk for assistance.

Attendant: هل يمكن أن أساعدك؟
hal yum.kin an u.sā.'*i*.dik?
May I help you?

Jessica: نعم. أنا أبحث عن محل للملابس.
na.'am. *a*.nā *ab*.ḥath 'an ma.*ḥal* lil.ma.*lā*.bis.
Yes. I'm searching for the clothing section.

Attendant: هل تبحثين عن محل لملابس النساء أو الرجال؟
hal tab.ḥa.*thīn* 'an ma.*ḥal* li.ma.*lā*.bis an.ni.*sā*' aw ar.ri.*jāl*?
Are you searching for the women's or men's clothing section?

Jessica:	أبحث عن محل لملابس النساء والرجال معاً. *ab*.ḥath ‘an ma.*ḥal* li.ma.*lā*.bis an.ni.*sā*’ war.ri.*jāl ma*.‘an. *I'm looking for both the men's and women's clothing sections.*
Attendant:	محل ملابس النساء في الطابق الخامس. ma.*ḥal* ma.*lā*.bis an.ni.*sā*’ fī aṭ.*ṭā*.biq al.*khā*.mis. *The women's clothing section is located on the fifth floor.*
Jessica:	هل هناك مصعد إلى الطابق الخامس؟ hal hu.*nā*.ka *miṣ*.‘ad *i*.lá aṭ.*ṭā*.biq al.*khā*.mis? *Is there an elevator to the fifth floor?*
Attendant:	نعم، على يمينك. *na*.‘am, ‘*a*.lá ya.*mī*.nik. *Yes, to your right.*
Jessica:	شكراً. *shuk*.ran. *Thank you.*
Attendant:	محل ملابس الرجال في الطابق السابع. ma.*ḥal* ma.*lā*.bis ar.ri.*jāl fī* aṭ.*ṭā*.biq as.*sā*.bi‘. *The men's clothing section is on the seventh floor.*
Jessica:	هل هناك جواهري في مركز التسوق؟ hal hu.*nā*.ka ja.*wā*.hi.rī fī *mar*.kaz at.ta.*saw*.wuq? *Is there a jeweler inside the mall?*
Attendant:	لا ليس داخل مركز التسوق. ولكن هناك جواهري في وسط المدينة. lā, *lay*.sa *dā*.khil *mar*.kaz at.ta.*saw*.wuq. wa.*lā*.kin hu.*nā*.ka ja.*wā*.hi.rī fī *wa*.saṭ al.ma.*dī*.nah. *No, there isn't a jeweler inside the mall. But there is a jeweler located in the city center.*
Jessica:	شكراً جزيلًا. *shuk*.ran ja.*zī*.lan. *Thank you very much.*

WORDS TO KNOW

يبحث	yab.ḥath	searching
مكان	ma.kān	location
نساء	ni.sā’	women
رجال	ri.jāl	men
بنات	ba.nāt	girls
أولاد	aw.lād	boys
طابق	ṭā.biq	floor
مصعد	miṣ.‘ad	elevator
يمين	ya.mīn	right
يسار	ya.sār	left
يمينك	ya.mī.nik	your right (F)
يمينك	ya.mī.nak	your right (M)
يسارك	ya.sā.rik	your left (F)
يسارك	ya.sā.rak	your left (M)
داخل	dā.khil	inside
خارج	khā.rij	outside

Getting to know the verb "to search"

GRAMMATICALLY SPEAKING

Shopping usually involves searching for particular items. In order to help with your بحث (baḥth) (*search*), you should be familiar with the verbs بحث (*ba.ḥa.tha*) (*searched*) and يبحث (*yab.ḥath*) (*searching*). Luckily, search is a regular verb, meaning that it has three consonants and is conjugated in the ماضي (*mā.ḍī*) (*past*) tense and مضارع (mu.*ḍā*.ri‘) (*present*) tense using the same patterns of prefixes and suffixes as most other regular verbs.

Here's the verb "to search" in the past tense:

Form	Pronunciation	English
أنا بحثتُ	*a*.nā ba.*ḥath*.tu	I searched
أنتَ بحثتَ	*an*.ta ba.*ḥath*.ta	You searched (MS)
أنتِ بحثتِ	*an*.ti ba.*ḥath*.ti	You searched (FS)
هو بحثَ	*hu*.wa *ba*.ḥa.tha	He searched
هي بحثتْ	*hi*.ya *ba*.ḥa.that	She searched
نحن بحثنا	*naḥ*.nu ba.*ḥath*.nā	We searched
أنتم بحثتم	*an*.tum ba.*ḥath*.tum	You searched (MP)
أنتنّ بحثتنّ	an.*tun*.na ba.ḥath.*tun*.na	You searched (FP)
هم بحثوا	hum *ba*.ḥa.thū	They searched (MP)
هنّ بحثنّ	*hun*.na ba.*ḥath*.na	They searched (FP)
أنتما بحثتما	an.*tu*.mā ba.ḥath.*tu*.mā	You searched (dual/M/F)
هما بحثا	*hu*.mā *ba*.ḥa.thā	They searched (dual/MP)
هما بحثتا	*hu*.mā ba.ḥa.*tha*.tā	They searched (dual/FP)

Here is the present tense:

Form	Pronunciation	English
أنا أبحث	*a*.nā *ab*.ḥath	I am searching
أنت تبحث	*an*.ta *tab*.ḥath	You are searching (MS)
أنت تبحثين	*an*.ti tab.ḥa.*thīn*	You are searching (FS)
هو يبحث	*hu*.wa *yab*.ḥath	He is searching
هي تبحث	*hi*.ya *tab*.ḥath	She is searching
نحن نبحث	*naḥ*.nu *nab*.ḥath	We are searching
أنتم تبحون	*an*.tum tab.ḥa.*thūn*	You are searching (MP)
أنتنّ تبحثنّ	an.*tun*.na tab.*ḥath*.na	You are searching (FP)

Form	Pronunciation	English
هم يبحثون	hum yab.ḥa.*thūn*	They are searching (MP)
هنّ يبحثنّ	*hun*.na yab.*ḥath*.na	They are searching (FP)
أنتما تبحثان	an.*tu*.mā tab.ḥa.*thān*	You are searching (dual/M/F)
هما يبحثان	*hu*.mā yab.ḥa.*thān*	They are searching (dual/M)
هما تبحثان	*hu*.mā tab.ḥa.*thān*	They are searching (dual/F)

Asking for a Particular Item

Oftentimes, you head to the store not to window shop or browse, but because you have a specific item in mind that you want to purchase. When you want to direct a clerk to a particular item, you're likely to need a demonstrative word, such as "that one" or "this" or "those over there." *Demonstratives* are the little words used to specify particular items. Arabic has a number of different demonstratives, depending on the number of items (singular or plural) and gender (in case of human nouns), as well as state (present or absent). Table 11-1 presents the common demonstratives in Arabic.

TABLE 11-1 **Arabic Demonstratives**

Arabic	Pronunciation	English
هذا	*hā*.dhā	this (MS)
هذه	*hā*.dhi.hi	this (FS)
ذلك	*dhā*.li.ka	that (MS)
تلك	*til*.ka	that (FS)
هؤلاء	hā.'u.*lā*.'i	these (gender neutral)
اولائك	u.*lā*.'i.ka	those (gender neutral)

Notice that the singular demonstratives (هذا, هذه, ذلك, تلك) are all gender-defined, meaning that you use a specific demonstrative corresponding to whether the object being referred to is masculine or feminine. On the other hand, the plural demonstratives, هؤلاء and أولئك, are gender-neutral, meaning that the gender of the object being pointed to doesn't matter.

REMEMBER

In a sentence, you always place the demonstrative word *before* the object being pointed to, which is often a noun. In addition, you must define the noun using the definite prefix pronoun **al-**. Here are some examples to illustrate the use of the definite prefix pronoun:

- هذا الولد (*hā*.dhā al.*wa*.lad) (*this boy*)
- هذه البنت (*hā*.dhi.hi al.*bint*) (*this girl*)
- ذلك الرجل (*dhā*.li.ka ar.*ra*.jul) (*that man*)
- تلك امرأة (*til*.ka al.mar.'ah) (*that woman*)
- هؤلاء البنات (ḥa.'u.*lā*.'i al.ba.*nāt*) (*these girls*)
- أولئك النساء (u.*lā*.'i.ka an.ni.*sā'*) (*those women*)

REMEMBER

It's important to not only follow the specific order of the demonstrative phrase (demonstrative word followed by the noun), but also to make sure you define the noun. If the noun isn't defined with the definite article prefix **al-**, the meaning of the demonstrative phrase changes dramatically. Arabic has no verb "to be" in the present tense, but because every language requires "is/are" sentences to function appropriately, you create "is/are" sentences in Arabic by manipulating these little definite articles. If you include a demonstrative followed by an undefined noun, you create a demonstrative "is/are" sentence. Using the examples from the earlier list, look at what happens to the demonstrative phrase when the definite article isn't included:

- هذا ولد. (*hā*.dhā *wa*.lad.) (*This is a boy.*)
- هذه بنت. (*hā*.dhi.hi *bint.*) (*This is a girl.*)
- ذلك رجل. (*dhā*.li.ka *ra*.jul.) (*That is a man.*)
- تلك مرأة. (*til*.ka *mar.*'ah.) (*That is a woman.*)
- هؤلاء بنات. (*ḥā*.'u.lā.'i ba.*nāt.*) (*These are girls.*)
- أولئك نساء. (u.*lā*.'i.ka ni.*sā'.*) (*Those are women.*)

As you can see by comparing these two lists, one small prefix can radically alter the meaning of a sentence.

Talkin' the Talk

Omar is looking to buy a black leather jacket, so he asks the salesperson for this particular item.

Omar: هل عندكم معاطف؟
hal 'in.da.kum ma.*'ā*.ṭif?
Do you have jackets?

Salesperson: نعم. عندنا أنواع كثيرة.
na.'am. *'in*.da.nā an.*wā'* ka.*thī*.rah.
Yes. We have many different kinds of jackets.

Omar: أريد معطفاً من الجلد.
u.*rīd mi'*.ṭa.fan *min* al.*jild*.
I want a leather jacket.

Salesperson: حسناً. إتبعني من فضلك.
ḥa.sa.nan, it.*ba'*.nī min *faḍ*.lik.
Okay. Follow me, please.

Omar follows the salesperson to the jacket section.

Salesperson: هذه كل المعاطف التي عندنا.
hā.dhi.hi *kul* al.ma.*'ā*.ṭif al.*la*.tī *'in*.da.nā.
Those are all the jackets we have.

Omar: أحب هذه المعاطف.
u.*ḥib hā*.dhi.hi al.ma.*'ā*.ṭif.
I love these jackets.

Salesperson: إنها جميلة جداً.
in.na.hā ja.*mī*.lah *jid*.dan.
They are very beautiful.

Omar: أريد أن أجرب هذا.
u.*rīd* an u.*jar*.rib *hā*.dhā.
I would like to try on this one.

Salesperson: فوراً. هل تريد لوناً معيناً؟
faw.ran. *hal* tu.*rīd law*.nan mu.*'ay*.ya.nan?
Right away. Are you looking for any particular color?

Omar: أريد ذلك اللون.
u.*rīd dhā*.li.ka al.*lawn*.
I want that color.

WORDS TO KNOW		
مطعف	mi'.ṭaf	jacket
نوع	naw'	type/kind
جلد	jild	leather
يتبع	yat.ba'	following
إتبع	it.ba'	follow (imperative)
إتبعني	it.ba'.nī	follow me
موافق	mu.wā.fiq	agree
جميل	ja.mīl	beautiful (M)
جميلة	ja.mī.lah	beautiful (F)
أجرب	u.jar.rib	to try (I/me)
لون	lawn	color
معين	mu.'ay.yan	particular (M)
معينة	mu.'ay.ya.nah	particular (F)
فوراً	faw.ran	right away

Comparing Merchandise

Have you ever been shopping and found yourself debating between two or more comparable items? Perhaps you have a general idea of what you want to buy — a television, for instance — but you aren't sure what year, make, or model you want. In these instances, being able to compare merchandise is important. In this section, you discover how to evaluate comparable (and incomparable) items based on a variety of important criteria, such as price, quality, and durability.

In order to be able to compare different items, you need to have an understanding of degrees of adjectives and superlatives. In English, degrees of adjectives have straightforward applicability. For example, in order to say that something is bigger than another thing, you simply add the suffix **-er** to the adjective; hence, "big" becomes "bigger." Furthermore, when you're comparing two or more items, you use comparatives, meaning you use both the degree of adjectives followed by the preposition "than." For instance, "the truck is bigger *than* the car." To say that something is the biggest, you only need to add the suffix **-est** to the adjective; so "big" becomes "biggest," as in "it's the biggest car." This form is called a *superlative.*

Fortunately, the structures of degrees of adjectives, comparatives, and superlatives in Arabic are fairly similar to those in English.

Comparing two or more items

Adjectives are the linguistic backbone that allow for comparisons between different items, products, or goods. Table 11-2 lists some of the most common adjectives followed by their comparative forms.

TABLE 11-2 Arabic Adjectives and Their Comparative Forms

Adjective	Pronunciation	English	Comparative	Pronunciation	English
كبير	ka.*bīr*	big	أكبر	*ak*.bar	bigger
صغير	ṣa.*ghīr*	small	أصغر	*aṣ*.ghar	smaller
حسن	*ḥa*.san	good	أحسن	*aḥ*.san	better
سيء	*say*.yi'	bad	أسوأ	*as*.wa'	worse
رخيص	ra.*khīṣ*	cheap	أرخص	*ar*.khaṣ	cheaper
غالي	*ghā*.lī	expensive	أغلى	*agh*.lá	more expensive
سريع	sa.*rī'*	fast	أسرع	*as*.ra'	faster
بطيء	ba.*ṭī'*	slow	أبطأ	*ab*.ṭa'	slower
ثقيل	tha.*qīl*	heavy	أثقل	*ath*.qal	heavier
خفيف	kha.*fīf*	light	أخفّ	a.*khaff*	lighter
جميل	ja.*mīl*	pretty	أجمل	*aj*.mal	prettier
قبيح	qa.*bīḥ*	ugly	أقبح	*aq*.baḥ	uglier
بعيد	ba.*'īd*	far	أبعد	*ab*.'ad	farther
قريب	qa.*rīb*	near	أقرب	*aq*.rab	nearer
جديد	ja.*dīd*	new	أجدد	*aj*.dad	newer
قديم	qa.*dīm*	old	أقدم	*aq*.dam	older

Place these adjectives in their appropriate context in the phrase or sentence — using these adjectives independently changes their meanings. Similar to the English language structure, the comparative form of adjectives always follows this pattern:

noun + adjective comparative form + preposition من (*min*) (*than*) + second adjective

REMEMBER

It's essential that you include the preposition من right after every comparative adjective. In addition, all nouns being compared need to be defined by attaching to them the definite article prefix ال.

Here are some common examples of comparative sentences using the adjective forms:

- البنت أكبر من الولد. (al.*bint ak*.bar min al.*wa*.lad.) (*The girl is bigger than the boy.*)
- التلفزيون أغلى من المذياع. (at.ti.li.fiz.*yūn agh*.lá min al.midh.*yā'*.) (*The television is more expensive than the radio.*)
- السيارة أسرع من الشاحنة . (as.say.*yā*.rah *as*.ra' min ash.*shā*.ḥi.nah.) (*The car is faster than the truck.*)

When forming these types of sentences, you may add demonstratives to be even more specific. Here are examples of comparative sentences used in conjunction with demonstratives:

- هذه البنت أكبر من ذلك الولد . (*hā*.dhi.hi al.*bint ak*.bar min *dhā*.li.ka al.*wa*.lad.) (*This girl is bigger than that boy.*)
- هذه السيارات أسرع من تلك الحافلات. (*hā*.dhi.hi as.say.yā.*rāt as*.ra' min *til*.ka al.ḥā.fi.*lāt*.) (*These cars are faster than those buses.*)
- تلك امرأة أجمل من ذلك الرجل. (*til*.ka al.*mar*.'ah *aj*.mal min *dhā*.li.ka ar.*ra*.jul.) (*That woman is prettier than that man.*)
- هذا الولد أكبر من هؤلاء البنات. (*hā*.dhā al.*wa*.lad *ak*.bar min hā.'u.*lā*.'i al.ba.*nāt*) (*This boy is bigger than those girls.*)

GRAMMATICALLY SPEAKING

Notice in the examples that the adjective comparative form remains constant whether the nouns being compared are a combination of singular/singular, singular/plural, or plural/plural. In other words, the adjective comparatives are gender-neutral: They remain the same regardless of both gender and number.

Picking out the best item

A *superlative* describes something that is of the highest order, degree, or quality. Some common superlatives in English are "best," "brightest," "fastest," "cleanest," "cheapest," and so on. Superlatives in Arabic are actually very straightforward and shouldn't be hard for you to understand if you have a good grasp of comparatives (see the preceding section).

Basically, a superlative in Arabic is nothing more than the comparative form of the adjective! The only difference is that comparatives include the preposition من (*than*) and superlatives don't include any preposition. For example, to tell someone, "This is the biggest house," you say هذا أكبر منزل (*hā*.dhā *ak*.bar *man*.zil).

REMEMBER

The biggest differences between superlatives and comparatives are

- The superlative adjective always comes before the noun, unless the adjective is definite.
- When expressing a superlative, the noun is always indefinite.

Here are some common examples of superlative sentences:

- هذه أجمل بنت. (*hā*.dhi.hi *aj*.mal bint) (*This is the prettiest girl.*)
- ذلك أبعد دكان. (*dhā*.li.ka *ab*.'ad duk.*kān*) (*That is the farthest store.*)

If you switch the order of the words to demonstrative + noun + superlative, be sure to define the noun. That's the only other way you can construct a superlative sentence. For example:

- هذه البنت الأجمل. (*hā*.dhi.hi al.*bint* al.*aj*.mal) (*This girl is the prettiest.*)
- ذلك الدكان الأبعد. (*dhā*.li.ka ad.duk.*kān* al.*ab*.'ad) (*That store is the farthest.*)

Talkin' the Talk

Adam stops by an electronics store to buy a camera. The salesman helps him pick the best one.

Salesman: صباح الخير ومرحباً بك في محل الإلكترونيات.
ṣa.*bāḥ* al.*khayr*, wa.*mar*.ḥa.ban *bi*.ka fi ma.*ḥal* al.'i.lik.trū.niy.*yāt*.
Good morning and welcome to the electronics store.

Adam: شكراً. أنا أبحث عن آلة تصوير.
shuk.ran, *a*.nā *ab*.ḥath 'an *ā*.lat taṣ.*wīr*.
Thank you. I am looking for a camera.

Salesman: هل تبحث عن نموذج معين؟
hal *tab*.ḥath 'an na.*mū*.dhaj mu.'*ay*.yan?
Are you looking for a particular model?

Adam: أنا أبحث عن أحسن آلة تصوير.
a.na *ab*.ḥath 'an *aḥ*.san *ā*.lat taṣ.*wīr*.
I'm looking for the best camera.

Salesman: حسناً. لدينا هذا النموذج بألوان مختلفة.
ḥa.sa.nan. la.*day*.nā *hā*.dhā an.na.*mū*.dhaj bi.'al.wān mukh.*ta*.li.fah.
Okay. We have this model with different colors.

Adam: هل عندك نموذج آخر؟
hal '*in*.dak na.*mū*.dhaj *ā*.khar?
Do you have another model?

Salesman: نعم, هذا نموذج آخر يحبه الزبائن.
na.'am, *hā*.dhā na.*mū*.dhaj *ā*.khar yu.*ḥib*.bu.hu az.za.*bā*.'in.
Yes, this model is popular with customers.

Adam: ما هو أفضل نموذج؟
mā hu.wa *af*.ḍal na.*mu*.dhaj?
Which is the best model?

Salesman: النموذج الثاني أحسن من النموذج الأول.
an.na.*mū*.dhaj ath.*thā*.nī *aḥ*.san min an.na.*mū*.dhaj al.'*aw*.wal.
The second model is better than the first model.

Adam: أريد أن أشتري النموذج الثاني من فضلك.
u.*rīd* an *ash*.ta.rī an.na.*mū*.dhaj ath.*thā*.nī min *faḍ*.lik.
I'd like to buy the second model, please.

Salesman: اختيار ممتاز!
ikh.ti.*yār* mum.*tāz!*
Excellent selection!

WORDS TO KNOW

آلة تصوير	ā.lat taṣ.wīr	camera
معين	mu.'ay.yan	particular (M)
معينة	mu.'ay.ya.nah	particular (F)
مختلف	mukh.ta.lif	different (M)
مختلفة	mukh.ta.li.fah	different (F)
زبائن	za.bā.'in	customers
اختيار	ikh.ti.yār	selection (M)

More than a Few Words about Buying and Selling

GRAMMATICALLY SPEAKING

Perhaps the two most important verbs relating to shopping are يشتري (yash.ta.*rī*) (*to buy*) and يبيع (ya.*bī*ʻ) (*to sell*). Unlike other verbs in Arabic, these two critical verbs are irregular, which means they don't follow a particular pattern. Because these verbs are widely used and have their own patterns, you should be familiar with how to conjugate them.

Use the form باع (*bā*.ʻa) (*sold*) to conjugate "to sell" in the past tense:

Form	Pronunciation	English
أنا بعتُ	*a*.nā *bi'*.tu	I sold
أنتَ بعتَ	*an*.ta *bi'*.ta	You sold (MS)
أنتِ بعتِ	*an*.ti *bi'*.ti	You sold (FS)
هو باع	*hu*.wa *bā*.'a	He sold
هي باعتْ	*hi*.ya *bā*.'at	She sold
نحن بعنا	*naḥ*.nu *bi'*.nā	We sold

Form	Pronunciation	English
أنتم بعتم	*an*.tum *bi'*.tum	You sold (MP)
أنتنّ بعتنّ	an.*tun*.na bi'.*tun*.na	You sold (FP)
هم باعوا	*hum bā*.'ū	They sold (MP)
هنّ بعنّ	*hun*.na *bi'*.na	They sold (FP)
أنتما بعتما	an.*tu*.mā bi'.*tu*.mā	You sold (dual/M/F)
هما باعا	*hu*.mā *bā*.'ā	They sold (dual/M)
هما باعتا	*hu*.mā bā.'*a*.tā	They sold (dual/F)

The form يبيع (ya.*bī*') (*selling*) is used to conjugate it in the present tense:

Form	Pronunciation	English
أنا أبيع	*a*.na a.*bī'*	I am selling
أنتَ تبيع	*an*.ta ta.*bī'*	You are selling (MS)
أنتِ تبيعين	*an*.ti ta.bī.'*īn*	You are selling (FS)
هو يبيع	*hu*.wa ya.*bī'*	He is selling
هي تبيع	*hi*.ya ta.*bī'*	She is selling
نحن نبيع	*naḥ*.nu na.*bī'*	We are selling
أنتم تبيعون	*an*.tum ta.bī.'*ūn*	You are selling (MP)
أنتنّ تبيعنّ	an.*tun*.na ta.*bi'*.na	You are selling (FP)
هم يبيعون	*hum* ya.bī.'*ūn*	They are selling (MP)
هنّ يبيعنّ	*hun*.na ya.*bi'*.na	They are selling (FP)
أنتما تبيعان	an.*tu*.mā ta.bī.'*ān*	You are selling (dual/M/F)
هما يبيعان	*hu*.mā ya.bī.'*ān*	They are selling (dual/M)
هما تبيعان	*hu*.mā ta.bī.'*ān*	They are selling (dual/F)

The verb form for "to buy" in the past tense is اشترى (ish.*ta*.rá) (*bought*). This verb is also irregular:

Form	Pronunciation	English
أنا استريتُ	*a*.nā ish.ta.*ray*.tu	I bought
أنتَ اشتريتَ	*an*.ta ish.ta.*ray*.ta	You bought (MS)
أنتِ اشتريتِ	*an*.ti ish.ta.*ray*.ti	You bought (FS)
هو اشترى	*hu*.wa ish.*ta*.rá	He bought
هي اشترتْ	*hi*.ya ish.*ta*.rat	She bought
نحن اشترينا	*naḥ*.nu ish.ta.*ray*.nā	We bought
أنتم اشرتيتم	*an*.tum ish.ta.*ray*.tum	You bought (MP)
أنتنّ اشتريتنّ	an.*tun*.na ish.ta.ray.*tun*.na	You bought (FP)
هم اشتروا	*hum* ish.*ta*.rū	They bought (MP)
هنّ اشترينّ	*hun*.na ish.ta.*ray*.na	They bought (FP)
أنتما اشتريتما	an.*tu*.mā ish.ta.ray.*tu*.mā	You bought (dual/M/F)
هما اشتريا	*hu*.mā ish.*ta*.ra.yā	They bought (dual/M)
هما اشتريتا	*hu*.mā ish.ta.ra.ya.*tā*	They bought (dual/F)

In the present-tense form, the verb "buying" is conjugated using the form يشتري (*yash*.ta.rī):

Form	Pronunciation	English
أنا أشتري	*a*.nā *ash*.ta.rī	I am buying
أنتَ تشتري	*an*.ta *tash*.ta.rī	You are buying (MS)
أنتِ تشترين	*an*.ti tash.ta.*rīn*	You are buying (FS)
هو يشتري	*hu*.wa *yash*.ta.rī	He is buying
هي تشتري	*hi*.ya *tash*.ta.rī	She is buying

Form	Pronunciation	English
نحن نشتري	*naḥ*.nu *nash*.ta.rī	We are buying
أنتم تشترون	*an*.tum tash.ta.*rūn*	You are buying (MP)
أنتنّ تشترينّ	*an*.tun.na tash.ta.*rī*.na	You are buying (FP)
هم يشترون	*hum* yash.ta.*rūn*	They are buying (MP)
هنّ يشترينّ	*hun*.na yash.ta.*rī*.na	They are buying (FP)
أنتما تشتريان	an.*tu*.mā tash.ta.ri.*yān*	You are buying (dual/M/F)
هما يشتريان	*hu*.mā yash.ta.ri.*yān*	They are buying (dual/M)
هما تشتريان	*hu*.mā tash.ta.ri.*yān*	They are buying (dual/F)

Shopping for Clothes

For many people, one of the most essential items to shop for is ملابس (ma.*lā*.bis) (*clothes*). Whether you're in a foreign country or shopping at the local mall, chances are that clothes make it on your shopping list. Table 11-3 lists some basic articles of clothing and accessories you should know.

TABLE 11-3 **Clothing and Accessories**

Arabic	Pronunciation	English
سروال	sir.*wāl*	pants (S)
سراويل	sa.rā.*wīl*	pants (P)
قميص	qa.*mīṣ*	shirt
قمصان	qum.*ṣān*	shirts
بلوزة	*blū*.zah	blouse
معطف	*mi'*.ṭaf	coat
معاطف	ma.*'ā*.ṭif	coats

Arabic	Pronunciation	English
فستان	fus.*tān*	dress
فساتين	fa.sā.*tīn*	dresses
جلابة	jal.*lā*.bah	Regional Arab robe/dress
جلابات	jal.lā.*bāt*	Regional Arab robes/dresses
حزام	ḥi.*zām*	belt
أحزمة	*aḥ*.zi.mah	belts
ربطة عنق	*rab*.ṭat *'u*.nuq	necktie
قبعة	*qub*.ba.'ah	hat
قبعات	qub.ba.*'āt*	hats
جورب	*jaw*.rab	sock
جوارب	ja.*wā*.rib	socks
حذاء	ḥi.*ḍhā'*	shoe
أحذية	*aḥ*.dhi.yah	shoes
خاتم	*khā*.tim	ring
ساعة	*sā*.'ah	watch
تنورة	tan.*nū*.rah	skirt

An important consideration when you're out shopping for clothing is مقاس (ma.*qās*) (*size*). The four standard clothes sizes are

- صغير (ṣa.*ghīr*) (*small*) (American size [Men's]: 34–36; American size [Women's]: 6–8)
- وسط (*wa*.saṭ) (*medium*) (American size [Men's]: 38–40; American size [Women's]: 10–12)
- كبير (ka.*bīr*) (*large*) (American size [Men's]: 42–44; American size [Women's]: 14–16)
- كبير جداً (ka.*bīr jid*.dan) (*extra large*) (American size [Men's]: 46 and above; American size [Women's]: 18–20)

Another important consideration in clothes shopping is the لون (*lawn*) (*color*). Because ألوان (al.*wān*) (*colors*) are adjectives that describe nouns, a color always must agree with the noun in terms of gender. If you're describing a feminine noun, use the feminine form. When describing masculine nouns, use the masculine forms. How do you know whether a noun is feminine or masculine? In about 80 percent of the cases, feminine nouns end with a تاء مربوطة or the "ah" sound. For the rest, simply look up the word in the قاموس (qā.*mūs*) (*dictionary*) to determine its gender. The masculine and feminine forms of some common colors appear in Table 11-4.

TABLE 11-4 **Basic Colors in Arabic**

Color (M)	Pronunciation	Color (F)	Pronunciation	English
أبيض	*ab*.yaḍ	بيضاء	bay.*ḍā'*	white
أسود	*as*.wad	سوداء	saw.*dā'*	black
أحمر	*aḥ*.mar	حمراء	ḥam.*rā'*	red
أخضر	*akh*.ḍar	خضراء	khaḍ.*rā'*	green
أزرق	*az*.raq	زرقاء	zar.qā'	blue
أصفر	*aṣ*.far	صفراء	ṣaf.*rā'*	yellow

FUN & GAMES

Write the Arabic names for the items in the illustrations.

Illustrations by Elizabeth Kurtzman

A. ______________________________

B. ______________________________

C. ______________________________

D. ______________________________

E. ______________________________

F. ______________________________

G. ______________________________

H. ______________________________

The answers are in Appendix C.

» Experiencing the culture of a museum

» Taking in a movie

» Touring religious sites

Chapter 12
Hitting the Town

Part of the fun of mastering a new language is putting your growing language skills to good use; one of the best ways to do that is by exploring a مدينة (ma.*dī*.nah) (*city*). Whether you're visiting a city in your home country or traveling in a Middle Eastern city, this chapter introduces you to key words, phrases, and concepts to help you navigate any city — from entertainment spots to cultural venues — like a native Arabic speaker!

REMEMBER

You can listen to all the Talkin' the Talk dialogues featured in this chapter. Go to `www.dummies.com/go/arabicfd` and click on the dialogue you want to hear.

Telling Time in Arabic

When you're exploring a city, you're guaranteed to have a difficult time catching buses to get around or buying tickets for specific events if you can't ask or tell the time. And telling وقت (waqt) (*time*) in Arabic is an entirely different proposition than telling time in English. In fact, you have to accept a fundamental difference right off the bat: Arabic doesn't use an a.m./p.m. convention to denote the time of day, nor does it use the 24-hour military clock (according to which, for example, 10 p.m. is written as 22:00). So how do you know which part of the day it is if you can't use the 24-hour system *or* the a.m./p.m. convention? It's actually very simple: You specify the time of day! So you say, for example, "It's ten o'clock *in the morning*," or "It's ten o'clock *at night*." Easy enough, don't you think? (For more on this issue, see the section "Specifying the time of day" later in this chapter.)

If you want to ask someone for the time, you ask the following question: كم الساعة؟ (kam as.*sā*.'ah) (*What time is it?*). If someone asks you this question, the appropriate response is الساعة (as.*sā*.'ah) (*the time is*) followed by the ordinal of the hour. So you would say, for instance, "It's the second hour" as opposed to saying "It's two o'clock." Because الساعة is a feminine noun, you use the feminine form of the ordinal numbers, which are listed in Table 12-1. (See Chapter 5 for more on numbers.)

TABLE 12-1

Arabic Ordinals for Telling Time

Arabic	Pronunciation	Translation
الواحدة	al.*wā*.ḥi.dah	first (F)
الثانية	ath.*thā*.nī.yah	second (F)
الثالثة	ath.*thā*.li.thah	third (F)
الرابعة	ar.*rā*.bi.'ah	fourth (F)
الخامسة	al.*khā*.mi.sah	fifth (F)
السادسة	as.*sā*.di.sah	sixth (F)
السابعة	as.*sā*.bi.'ah	seventh (F)
الثامنة	ath.*thā*.mi.nah	eighth (F)
التاسعة	at.*tā*.si.'ah	ninth (F)
العاشرة	al.'*ā*.shi.rah	tenth (F)
الحادية عشرة	al.*ḥā*.di.yat '*ash*.rah	eleventh (F)
الثانية عشرة	ath.*thā*.ni.yat '*ash*.rah	twelfth (F)

REMEMBER

You need to use the definite prefix article **al-** with the ordinals because you're referring to a specific hour and not just any hour.

The following are some additional key words related to telling time in Arabic:

- ساعة (*sā*.'ah) (*hour*)
- دقيقة (da.*qī*.qah) (*minute*)
- ثانية (*thā*.nī.yah) (*second*)
- بعد (*ba'*.da) (*after*)
- قبل (*qab*.la) (*before*)
- اليوم (al.*yawm*) (*today*)
- الغد (al.*ghad*) (*tomorrow*)
- البارحة (al.*bā*.ri.ḥah) (*yesterday*)
- بعد غد (*ba'*.da ghad) (*the day after tomorrow*)
- أول أمس (*aw*.wal ams) (*the day before yesterday*)

Specifying the time of day

Because Arabic uses neither the a.m./p.m. system nor the 24-hour military clock, when giving the time, you need to specify the time of day by actually saying what part of the day it is.

Here are the different times of day you're likely to use:

- الصباح (aṣ.ṣa.*bāḥ*) (*morning*, or *sunrise to 11:59 a.m.*)
- الظهر (aẓ.*ẓuhr*) (*noon*, or *12 p.m.*)
- بعد الظهر (*ba'*.da aẓ.*ẓuhr*) (*afternoon*, or *12:01 p.m. to 4 p.m.*)
- العصر (al.*'aṣr*) (*late afternoon*, or *4:01 p.m. to sunset*)
- المساء (al.ma.*sā'*) (*evening*, or *sunset to two hours after sunset*)
- الليل (al.*layl*) (*night*, or *sunset to two hours to sunrise*)

For example, if the time is 2 p.m., then you attach بعد الظهر (*ba'*.da aẓ.*ẓuhr*) (*after noon*) to the proper ordinal. If sunset is at 6 p.m. and you want to say the time's 7 p.m., then you use المساء (al.ma.*sā'*) (*evening*) and the ordinal because المساء applies to the two-hour period right after sunset; if sunset is at 6 p.m. and you want to say the time's 9 p.m., then you use الليل (al.*layl*) (*night*) and the ordinal because 9 p.m. falls outside the scope of the evening convention (see the preceding list).

The convention used to specify the part of the day is fairly straightforward:

الساعة (as.*sā*.'ah) (*the time*) + ordinal number + في (fī) (*in*) + part of the day

So when someone asks you كم الساعة (kam as.*sā*.'ah) (*what's the time*), your literal reply in Arabic is "It's the ninth hour in the morning," for instance. The following are some examples to better illustrate responses to this question:

- الساعة الواحدة بعد الظهر. (as.*sā*.'ah al.*wā*.ḥi.dah *ba'*.da aẓ.*ẓuhr*) (*It's one o'clock in the afternoon.*)
- الساعة الخامسة عصراً. (as.*sā*.'ah al.*khā*.mi.sah *'aṣ*.ran) (*It's five o'clock in the late afternoon.*)
- الساعة الحادية عشرة صباحاً. (as.*sā*.'ah al.*ḥā*.di.yat *'ash*.rah ṣa.*bā*.ḥan) (*It's eleven o'clock in the morning.*)
- الساعة التاسعة ليلاً. (as.*sā*.'ah at.*tā*.si.'ah *lay*.lan) (*It's nine o'clock in [at] night.*)
- الساعة السابعة مساءً. (as.*sā*.'ah as.*sā*.bi.'ah ma.*sā*.'an) (*It's seven o'clock in the evening.*)

Specifying minutes

When telling time in Arabic, you can specify minutes in two different ways:

- Noting the fractions of the hour, such as a half, a quarter, and a third
- Actually spelling out the minutes

Because these methods have different conventions, this section examines each method separately.

Using fractions of the hour

When using the fraction method of telling minutes, use the following structure:

الساعة (as.*sā*.'ah) (*the time*) + ordinal number + و (wa) (*and*) + fraction

So what you're in fact saying is "It's the second hour and a half," for example. In English transliteration, that's the equivalent of "It's half past two."

The main fractions you use are

- النصف (an.*niṣf*) (*half*)
- الثلث (ath.*thulth*) (*third*)
- الربع (ar.*rub'*) (*quarter*)

The following examples show you how to use the fraction method to specify minutes when telling time:

- الساعة الثانية والربع. (as.*sā*.'ah ath.*thā*.ni.yah war.*rub'*) (*It's a quarter past two.*)
- الساعة التاسعة والنصف. (as.*sā*.'ah at.*tā*.si.'ah wan.*niṣf*) (*It's half past nine.*)
- الساعة الواحدة والثلث. (as.*sā*.'ah al.*wā*.ḥi.dah wath.*thulth*) (*It's twenty past one.*)
- الساعة الخامسة والربع. (as.*sā*.'ah al.*khā*.mi.sah war.*rub'*) (*It's quarter past five.*)
- الساعة الحادية عشرة والنصف. (as.*sā*.'ah al.*ḥā*.di.yat *'ash*.rah wan.*niṣf*) (*It's half past eleven.*)

Using this system, you can cover ten past the hour, quarter past the hour, twenty past the hour, and half past the hour, which are the major fractions. But what if you want to say, "It's a quarter to . . ." or "It's twenty till . . ."? In those cases, you need to use the preposition إلا (*i*.lā), which means "to" or "till." If you think of the preposition *wa* as adding to the hour, then think of *i*.lā as subtracting from the hour.

REMEMBER

Because إلا subtracts from the hour, you must add one hour to whatever hour you're referring to. For example, if you want to say "It's 5:45," then you must say "It's quarter to six" and not "It's a quarter to five," which would be 4:45. Here are some examples that use إلا:

- الساعة السادسة إلا ربع. (as.*sā*.'ah as.*sā*.di.sah *il*.lā rub'.) (*It's a quarter to six,* or *5:45.*)
- الساعة الواحدة إلا ثلث. (as.*sā*.'ah al.*wā*.ḥi.dah *il*.lā thulth.) (*It's twenty to one,* or *12:40.*)

If you want to express minutes as a fraction and specify which time of day (a.m. or p.m.), you simply add في (fī) (in) and the time of day. For example

الساعة الواحدة والنصف بعد الظهر. (as.*sā*.'ah al.*wā*.ḥi.dah wan.*niṣf ba'*.da aẓ.*ẓuhr*.) (*It's 1:30 in the afternoon.*)

Here are other examples:

- الساعة الثانية عشرة وربع ليلًا. (as.*sā*.'ah ath.*thā*.ni.yat *'ash*.rah war.*rub'* *lay*.lan.) (*It's 12:15 at night,* or *12:15 a.m.*)
- الساعة السابعة والنصف مساءً. (as.*sā*.'ah as.*sā*.bi.'ah wan.*niṣf* ma.*sā*.'an.) (*It's 7:30 in the evening.*)
- الساعة الثامنة والربع صباحاً. (as.*sā*.'ah ath.*thā*.mi.nah war.*rub'* ṣa.*bā*.ḥan.) (*It's 8:15 in the morning.*)
- الساعة الخامسة إلا ربع عصراً. (as.*sā*.'ah al.*khā*.mi.sah *il*.lā rub' *'aṣ*.ran.) (*It's quarter to five in the late afternoon,* or *4:45 p.m.*)

Talkin' the Talk

Salim and Wafaa are trying to figure out at what time to go to the movies.

Salim: كم الساعة؟
kam as.*sā*.'ah?
What time is it?

Wafaa: الساعة الخامسة والنصف.
as.*sā*.'ah al.*khā*.mi.sah wan.*niṣf*.
It's 5:30.

Salim: متى سيبدأ الفيلم؟
ma.tá sa.*yab*.da' al.*film*?
When will the movie begin?

Wafaa: أظنّ أنّه سيبدأ في الساعة السادسة والنصف.
a.*ẓunn* an.*na*.hu sa.*yab*.da' fī as.*sā*.'ah as.*sā*.di.sah wan.*niṣf*.
I believe that it will start at 6:30.

Salim: حسناً. هيا بنا إلى السينما في الساعة السادسة.
ḥa.sa.nan. *hay*.yā *bi*.nā *i*.lá as.*sī*.ni.mā as.*sā*.'ah as.*sā*.di.sah.
Okay. Let's go to the theater at six o'clock then.

Wafaa: أنا موافقة.
a.nā mu.*wā*.fi.qah.
I agree.

WORDS TO KNOW		
متى	ma.tá	when
بداية	bi.dā.yah	beginning
يبدأ	yab.da'	to begin
فيلم	fīlm	movie
مسرح	mas.raḥ	theater
ا بنا	*hay*.yā bi.nā	let's
موافق	mu.wā.fiq	(I) agree

Spelling out minutes

When expressing time, you can specify the minutes by actually spelling them out. (Check out Chapter 5 for full coverage of cardinal numbers.) Use the following format:

> الساعة (as.*sā*.'ah) (*the time*) + ordinal/hours + و (wa) (*and*) + cardinal/minutes + دقيقة (da.*qī*.qah) (*minutes*)

So الساعة الخامسة وخمس دقائق (as.*sā*.'ah al.*khā*.mi.sah wa.*khams* da.*qā*.'iq.) means "It's 5:05." Here are some other examples:

- الساعة الواحدة وعشرون دقيقة. (as.*sā*.'ah al.*wā*.ḥi.dah wa.'ish.*rūn* da.*qī*.qah.) (*It's 1:20.*)
- الساعة الرابعة وثلاثون دقيقة. (as.*sā*.'ah ar.*rā*.bi.'ah wa.tha.lā.*thūn* da.*qī*.qah *'aṣ*.ran.) (*It's 4:30 in the afternoon.*)
- الساعة الثامنة وأربعون دقيقة صباحاً. (as.*sā*.'ah ath.*thā*.mi.nah wa.'ar.ba.*'ūn* da.*qī*.qah ṣa.*bā*.ḥan.) (*It's 8:45 in the morning.*)

Talkin' the Talk

Ted is trying to figure out which bus to take.

Ted: متى ستنطلق الحافلة؟
ma.tá sa.tan.*ṭa*.liq al.*ḥā*.fi.lah?
When does the bus leave?

Cashier: ستنطلق الحافلة في الساعة الخامسة وعشرين دقيقة عصراً.
sa.tan.*ṭa*.li.qu al.*ḥā*.fi.lah fī as.*sā*.'ah al.*khā*.mi.sah wa.'ish.*rīn* da.*qī*.qah *'aṣ*.ran.
The bus leaves at 5:30 in the (late) afternoon.

Ted: هل هناك حافلة قبل ذلك؟
hal hu.*nā*.ka *ḥā*.fi.lah *qab*.la *dhā*.lik?
Is there a bus before that?

Cashier: دقيقة من فضلك.
da.*qī*.qah min *faḍ*.lik.
One minute, please.

Ted: طبعاً.
ṭa.ba.'an.
Of course.

Cashier: هناك حافلة في الساعة الخامسة.
hu.*nā*.ka *ḥā*.fi.lah fī as.*sā*.'ah al.*khā*.mi.sah.
There is a bus at five o'clock.

Ted: ممتاز! بطاقة واحدة لحافلة الساعة الخامسة من فضلك.
mum.*tāz!* bi.*ṭā*.qah *wā*.ḥi.dah li.*ḥā*.fi.la as.*sā*.'ah al.*khā*.mi.sah min *faḍ*.lik.
Excellent! One ticket for the 5:00 bus, please.

WORDS TO KNOW		
انطلاق	in.ṭi.lāq	departure
تنطلق	tan.ṭa.liq	to leave
حافلة	ḥā.fi.lah	bus
محطة	ma.ḥaṭ.ṭah	station
قبل	qab.la	before/earlier
بطاقة	bi.ṭā.qah	ticket
سائح	sā.'iḥ	tourist (M)
سائحة	sā.'i.ḥa	tourist (F)
سفر	sa.far	traveling
رحلة	riḥ.lah	voyage/trip

Visiting Museums

I love museums because I can learn so much about virtually any topic, from irrigation systems during the Roman Empire to the brush techniques of the Impressionist artists. The متحف (*mat.*ḥaf) (*museum*) plays a central role in the Arab city; Arab people have a deep sense of history and their role in it, and one way to preserve some of that history, in the form of great Arab and Islamic works of art and achievements, is in the museum.

TIP

Here are some Middle Eastern museums worth visiting, in both the United States and the Middle East:

- The Dahesh Museum in New York, New York
- The Arab-American Museum in Dearborn, Michigan
- Baghdad Museum in Baghdad, Iraq

A زيارة (zi.*yā*.rah) (*visit*) to a museum can be a wonderful experience as long as you follow a number of قواعد (qa.*wā*.'id) (*rules*). These rules ensure that your experience and the experiences of others at the museum are جميلة (ja.*mī*.lah) (*pleasant*).

ARABIC SCHOLARS AND WESTERN CIVILIZATION

Many of the works of the ancient Greek masters, such as Aristotle and Plato, were preserved by Islamic scholars when Europe was plunged into the Dark Ages (from about the fifth through the tenth centuries). Islamic scholars throughout the Muslim world in Cordoba, Spain, and elsewhere translated gargantuan amounts of texts from Greek and Latin into Arabic. They extensively studied these texts and added a significant amount to the pool of knowledge. Thanks to the work of these Islamic scholars, much of the knowledge that serves as the basis of Western thought and civilization was preserved. In fact, while Europe was in the Dark Ages, Islam went through a revival and renaissance period not experienced anywhere else in the world.

The word ممنوع (mam.*nū*') means "prohibited," and the word ضروري (ḍa.*rū*.rī) means "required"; whenever you see the word ممنوع on a sign, it's usually accompanied by a picture of the item that's prohibited with a red line across it. Make sure to pay attention so that you don't get into trouble with the museum management!

When visiting a museum, you may see signs that say the following:

- ممنوع التصوير. (mam.*nū*' at.taṣ.*wīr*.) (*Taking pictures is prohibited.*)
- ممنوع الدخول. (mam.*nū*' ad.du.*khūl*.) (*Do Not Enter.*)
- ممنوع التدخين. (mam.*nū*' at.tad.*khīn*.) (*Smoking is prohibited.*)
- ممنوع الأكل. (mam.*nū*' al.'*akl*.) (*Food is prohibited.*)

Talkin' the Talk

Larry and Samir are trying to decide at what time to go to the museum.

Larry: هيا بنا إلى المتحف اليوم.
hay.yā *bi*.nā *i*.lá al.*mat*.ḥaf al.*yawm*.
Let's go to the museum today.

Samir: هذه فكرة ممتازة!
hā.dhi.hi *fik*.rah mum.*tā*.zah!
That's an excellent idea!

Larry: متى يفتح المتحف؟
ma.tá *yaf*.taḥ al.*mat*.ḥaf?
When does the museum open?

Samir: المتحف يفتح في الساعة الثامنة صباحاً.
al.*mat*.ḥaf *yaf*.taḥ fī as.*sā*.'ah ath.*thā*.mi.nah ṣa.*bāḥ*.an.
The museum opens at eight o'clock in the morning.

Larry: وكم الساعة الآن؟
wa.*kam* as.*sā*.'ah al.*'ān*?
And what time is it now?

Samir: الساعة الآن الثامنة الربع.
as.*sā*.'ah al.*'ān* ath.*thā*.mi.nah war.*rub*'.
It's 8:15 right now.

Larry: عظيم! هيا بنا الآن!
'a.*ẓīm*! *hay*.yā bi.nā al.*'ān*!
Great! Let's go right now!

Samir: هيا بنا!
hay.yā *bi*.nā!
Let's go!

WORDS TO KNOW

يوم	yawm	day
اليوم	al.yawm	today
فتح	fa.ta.ḥa	to open
يفتح	yaf.taḥ	opens
الآن	al.'ān	now

GRAMMATICALLY SPEAKING

Although most verbs in Arabic have three consonants — such as كتب (*ka*.ta.ba) (*to write*), جلس (*ja*.la.sa) (*to sit*), or درس (*da*.ra.sa) (*to study*) — زار (*zā*.ra), the verb form for "to visit," contains only two consonants. This difference makes زار an irregular verb.

If you want to visit a lot of different places around the مدينة (ma.*dī*.nah) (*city*), being able to conjugate the irregular verb زار in both the past and present tenses is particularly helpful. Because "to visit" is irregular, there's no specific form — like the one available for regular verbs in Chapter 2 — where a pattern is apparent.

For the past tense form of visited, use زار:

Form	Pronunciation	English
أنا زرتُ	*a*.nā *zur*.tu	I visited
أنتَ زرتَ	*an*.ta *zur*.ta	You visited (MS)
أنتِ زرتِ	*an*.ti *zur*.ti	You visited (FS)
هو زارَ	*hu*.wa *zā*.ra	He visited
هي زارتْ	*hi*.ya *zā*.rat	She visited
نحن زرنا	*naḥ*.nu *zur*.nā	We visited
أنتم زرتم	*an*.tum *zur*.tum	You visited (MP)
أنتنّ زرتنّ	an.*tun*.na zur.*tun*.na	You visited (FP)
هم زاروا	hum *zā*.rū	They visited (MP)
هنّ زرنّ	*hun*.na *zur*.na	They visited (FP)
أنتما زرتما	an.*tu*.mā zur.*tu*.mā	You visited (dual/M/F)
هما زارا	*hu*.mā *zā*.rā	They visited (dual/M)
هما زارتا	*hu*.mā zā.*ra*.tā	They visited (dual/F)

For the present-tense form, use يزور (ya.*zūr*) (*visiting*) as the basis of the verb:

Form	Pronunciation	English
أنا أزور	*a*.nā a.*zūr*	I am visiting
أنتَ تزور	*an*.ta ta.*zūr*	You are visiting (MS)
أنتِ تزورين	*an*.ti ta.zū.*rīn*	You are visiting (FS)
هو يزور	*hu*.wa ya.*zūr*	He is visiting

Form	Pronunciation	English
هي تزور	*hi*.ya ta.*zūr*	She is visiting
نحن نزور	*naḥ*.nu na.*zūr*	We are visiting
أنتم تزورون	*an*.tum ta.zū.*rūn*	You are visiting (MP)
أنتنّ تزرنّ	an.*tun*.na ta.*zur*.na	You are visiting (FP)
هي يزورون	hum ya.zū.*rūn*	They are visiting (MP)
هنّ يزرنّ	*hun*.na ya.*zur*.na	They are visiting (FP)
أنتما تزوران	an.*tu*.mā ta.zū.*rān*	You are visiting (dual/M/F)
هما يزوران	*hu*.mā ya.zū.*rān*	They are visiting (dual/MP)
هما تزوران	*hu*.mā ta.zū.*rān*	They are visiting (dual/FP)

Talkin' the Talk

Lara is telling her friend Mary about her and her family's visit to the museum.

Lara: زرنا متحف مراكش البارحة.
zur.nā *mat*.ḥaf mur.*rā*.kush al.*bā*.ri.ḥah.
We visited the Museum of Marrakesh yesterday.

Mary: كيف كانتْ زيارتكم؟
kay.fa *kā*.nat zi.yā.*ra*.tu.kum?
How was your visit?

Lara: كانت ممتعة جداً.
kā.nat *mum*.ti.'ah *jid*.dan.
It was very entertaining.

Mary: ماذا رأيتم؟
mā.dhā ra.'*ay*.tum?
What did you see?

Lara: رأينا بعض اللوحات الزيتية.
ra.'*ay*.nā baḍ al.law.*ḥāt* az.zay.*tiy*.yah.
We saw some oil paintings.

Mary: وماذا أيضاً؟
wa.*mā*.dhā *ay*.ḍan?
What else?

Lara: ورأينا رسومات على الزليج. كانت جميلًا جداً.
wa.ra.'*ay*.nā ru.sū.*māt* '*a*.lá az.za.*līj*. *kā*.nat ja.*mī*.lan *jid*.dan
And we saw mosaics. They were really beautiful.

Mary: هذا جميل.
hā.dhā ja.*mīl*.
Sounds beautiful.

Lara: وأخذنا جولة مع مرشد المتحف لمدة نصف ساعة.
wa.'a.*khadh*.nā *jaw*.lah *ma*.'a *mur*.shid al.*mat*.ḥaf li.*mud*.
dat niṣf *sā*.'ah.
And we went on a guided tour around the museum that lasted a half-hour.

Mary: أنا أريد أن أذهب! أين المتحف؟
a.nā u.*rīd* an *adh*.hab! *ay*.na al.*mat*.ḥaf?
I want to go! Where is the museum located?

Lara: المتحف في وسط المدينة ويفتح على الساعة الثامنة في الصباح.
al.*mat*.ḥaf fī *wa*.saṭ al.ma.*dī*.nah wa.*yaf*.taḥ '*a*.lá as.*sā*.'ah
ath.*thā*.mi.nah fī aṣ.ṣa.*bāḥ*.
The museum is in the downtown area, and it opens at 8:00 in the morning.

Mary: وبكم بطاقة الدخول؟
wa.bi.*kam* bi.*ṭā*.qat ad.du.*khūl*?
And how much is the entry ticket?

Lara: بعشرة دراهم.
bi.'*ash*.rat da.*rā*.him.
Ten dirhams.

Mary: شكراً.
shuk.ran.
Thank you.

Lara: عفواً. زيارة سعيدة!
'*af*.wan. zi.*yā*.rah sa.'*ī*.dah!
You're welcome. Have a fun visit!

WORDS TO KNOW

زيارتكم	zi.yā.ra.ta.kum	your visit (MP)
متعة	mut.'ah	entertainment
ممتع	mum.ti'	entertaining
جداً	jid.dan	very
رأى	ra.'á	saw
بعض	ba'ḍ	some
فنّ	fann	art
لوحة	law.ḥah	painting
رسم	rasm	drawing
زليج	za.līj	mosaic
جميل	ja.mīl	pretty/beautiful
جولة	jaw.lah	tour
حول	ḥawl	around
وسط	wa.saṭ	center/downtown
مدخل	mad.khal	entrance
مخرج	makh.raj	exit

Going to the Movies

Going to see a فيلم (*film*) (*movie*) in a قاعة سينما (*qa.*'at *si.*ni.mā) (*movie theater*) is a very popular pastime for people in the Middle East. American action movies are a particularly favorite genre — don't be surprised if you walk into a movie theater in a Middle Eastern city and see Tom Cruise on the big screen! Most of the movies shown in these movie theaters are actually the original versions with ترجمة

(*tar*.ja.mah) (*subtitles*) at the bottom of the screen. Here are some other popular movie genres:

- مغامرة (mu.*ghā*.ma.rah) (*action/adventure*)
- كوميديا (kū.*mīd*.yā) (*comedy*)
- دراما (*drā*.mā) (*drama*)
- رعاة البقر (ru.*'āt* al.*ba*.qar) (*western*)
- وثائقي (wa.*thā*.'i.qī) (*documentary*)
- الرسوم المتحركة (ar.ru.*sūm* al.mu.ta.*ḥar*.ri.kah) (*cartoon*)

The verb most commonly associated with going to the movies is ذهب (*dha*.ha.ba) (*to go*). Using the conjugations that follow, you can say ذهبت إلى قاعة السينما (dha.*hab*.tu *i*.lá *qā*.'at as.*si*.ni.mā) (*I went to the movie theater*), or يذهب إلى قاعة السينما (*yadh*.hab *i*.lá *qā*.'at as.*si*.ni.mā) (*He is going to the movies*) and much more.

Here's the verb "to go" in the past tense:

Form	Pronunciation	English
أنا ذهبتُ	*a*.nā dha.*hab*.tu	I went
أنتَ ذهبتَ	*an*.ta dha.*hab*.ta	You went (MS)
أنتِ ذهبتِ	*an*.ti dha.*hab*.ti	You went (FS)
هو ذهبَ	*hu*.wa *dha*.ha.ba	He went
هي ذهبتْ	*hi*.ya *dha*.ha.bat	She went
نحن ذهبنا	*naḥ*.nu dha.*hab*.nā	We went
أنتم ذهبتم	*an*.tum dha.*hab*.tum	You went (MP)
أنتنّ ذهبتنّ	an.*tun*.na dha.hab.*tun*.na	You went (FP)
هم ذهبوا	*hum dha*.ha.bū	They went (MP)
هنّ ذهبنّ	*hun*.na dha.*hab*.na	They went (FP)
أنتما ذهبتما	an.*tu*.mā dha.hab.*tu*.mā	You went (dual/M/F)
هما ذهبا	*hu*.mā *dha*.ha.bā	They went (dual/M)
هما ذهبتا	*hu*.mā dha.ha.ba.*tā*	They went (dual/F)

Use the form يذهب (*yadh*.hab) (*going*) to conjugate "to go" in the present tense.

Form	Pronunciation	English
أنا أذهب	*a*.nā *adh*.hab	I am going
أنتَ تذهب	*an*.ta *tadh*.hab	You are going (MS)
أنتِ تذهبين	*an*.ti tadh.ha.*bīn*	You are going (FS)
هو يذهب	*hu*.wa *yadh*.hab	He is going
هي تذهب	*hi*.ya *tadh*.hab	She is going
نحن نذهب	*naḥ*.nu *nadh*.hab	We are going
أنتم تذهبون	*an*.tum tadh.ha.*būn*	You are going (MP)
أنتنّ تذهبنّ	an.*tun*.na tadh.*hab*.na	You are going (FP)
هم يذهبون	hum yadh.ha.*būn*	They are going (MP)
هنّ يذهبنّ	*hun*.na yadh.*hab*.na	They are going (FP)
أنتما تذهبان	an.*tu*.mā tadh.ha.*bān*	You are going (dual/M/F)
هما يذهبان	*hu*.mā yadh.ha.*bān*	They are going (dual/M)
هما تذهبان	*hu*.mā tadh.ha.*bān*	They are going (dual/F)

Talkin' the Talk

Adam and Asmaa are debating whether to go to the movies.

Asmaa: هل تريد أن نذهب إلى المتحف اليوم؟
hal tu.*rīd* an *tadh*.hab *i*.lá al.*mat*.ḥaf al.*yawm?*
Do you want to go to the museum today?

Adam: لا. أنا أريد أن أذهب إلى قاعة السينما.
lā. *a*.nā u.*rīd* an *adh*.hab *i*.lá *qā*.'at as.*si*.ni.mā.
No. I would like to go to the movie theater.

Asmaa: ولكن قاعة السينما بعيدة من هنا.
wa.*lā*.kin *qā*.'at as.*si*.ni.mā ba.'*ī*.dah min *hu*.nā.
But the movie theater is far from here.

Adam: يمكن أن نذهب إلى قاعة السينما بالحافلة.
yum.kin an *nadh*.hab *i*.lá *qā*.'at as.*si*.ni.mā bil.*ḥā*.fi.lah.
We can go to the movies by bus.

Asmaa: متى سيبدأ الفيلم؟
ma.tá sa.*yab*.da' al.*film*?
When does the movie begin?

Adam: بعد ساعة ونصف.
ba.'da *sā*.'ah wa.*niṣf*.
In an hour and a half.

Asmaa: أي فيلم تعرضه قاعة السينما اليوم؟
ayy film ta'.*riḍ*.u.hu *qā*.'at as.*si*.ni.mā al.*yawm*?
Which movie is the theater showing today?

Adam: آخر فيلم لأنجلينا جولي.
ā.khir fīlm li.'an.ji.*lī*.na ju.*lī*.
The latest Angelina Jolie movie.

Asmaa: نعم؟ لماذا لم تقُل هذا من قبل؟
na.'am? li.*mā*.dhā lam *ta*.qul *hā*.dhā min qabl?
Really? Why didn't you say so earlier?

Adam: لماذا؟
li.*mā*.dhā?
How come?

Asmaa: أنا أحبّ هذه الممثلة كثيراً!
a.nā u.*ḥibb hā*.dhi.hi al.mu.*math*.thi.lah ka.*thī*.ran!
I like this actress a lot!

Adam: ممتاز. هيا بنا!
mum.*tāz*. *hay*.yā *bi*.nā!
Great. Let's go!

Asmaa: هيا بنا!
hay.yā *bi*.nā!
Let's go!

WORDS TO KNOW

يريد	yu.rīd	to want
بعيد	ba.ʽīd	far
قريب	qa.rīb	close
آخر	ā.khīr	last/latest
كثيرا	ka.thī.ran	a lot
قليلا	qa.lī.lan	a little
ممثل	mu.math.thil	actor
ممثلة	mu.math.thi.lah	actress
مخرج	mukh.rij	director
مشاهد	mu.shā.hid	viewer (MS)
مشاهدة	mu.shā.hi.dah	viewer (FS)

Touring Religious Sites

If you ever get a chance to go to the Middle East, I suggest you visit some of the beautiful religious sites that are spread across the land. If you're in a Middle Eastern or Arab city, be sure to check out a مسجد (*mas*.jid) (*mosque*). The largest مساجد (ma.*sā*.jid) (*mosques*) in the Muslim world are located in Mecca and Medina, Saudi Arabia, and in Casablanca, Morocco.

A few rules to keep in mind

When visiting a mosque, you must follow certain قواعد (qa.*wā*.ʻid) (*rules*):

» **If you're Muslim,** you're allowed to walk into any mosque you like; but before entering, you must remove your shoes and say the شهادة (sha.*hā*.dah) (*religious prayer*): لا إله إلا الله محمد رسول الله (lā i.*lā*.ha *il*.lā al.*lāh* mu.*ḥam*.ma.dan ra.*sū*.lu al.*lāh*) (*There is no god but God and Muhammad is his Prophet.*).

» **If you're non-Muslim,** entry into a mosque is generally forbidden, especially during prayer time, whether you're in the Middle East, the United States, or anywhere else around the world. However, certain mosques, such as the ***mas. jid Hassan II*** (مسجد الحسن الثاني) in Casablanca, have designated wings that are open to both Muslims and non-Muslims. These wings are set aside more as exhibition rooms than as religious or prayer rooms, so you're allowed to enter them, but you still must remove your حذاء (ḥi.*dhā'*) (*shoes*).

CULTURAL WISDOM

The word **mas.jid** comes from the verb سجد (*sa*.ja.da), which means "to prostrate" or "to kneel." Another word for "mosque" is جامع (*jā*.mi'), which comes from the word جماعة (ja.*mā*.'ah) (*a gathering*). So the Arabic words for "mosque" are related to what one actually does in the mosque, which is to gather in a religious setting and pray.

The Hajj

One of the most popular events during the year for Muslims is the حج (*ḥajj*), which is the pilgrimage to Mecca in Saudi Arabia. The Hajj, which generally lasts for five days, takes place once a year, and is actually one of the five pillars of Islam. Technically, attending the Hajj is mandatory for Muslims, but because the pilgrimage can be expensive, it's widely accepted that one can be a Muslim without actually having to attend the Hajj.

During the Hajj, حجاج (ḥuj.*jāj*) (*pilgrims*) must follow a number of rules. As soon as the pilgrims arrive in Mecca, they must shed all their worldly clothing and possessions and change into sandals and a simple إحرام (iḥ.*rām*), which basically consists of a white cloth wrapped around the body. Other than these two items, they aren't allowed to wear any watches, jewelry, or any other types of clothes. The logic behind wearing only the إحرام is that every pilgrim is equal before God, and because no difference exists between a king and a beggar during the Hajj, everyone must wear the same thing.

After they don the إحرام, the pilgrims begin a ritual known as the طواف (ṭa.*wāf*) (*to turn*), in which they walk around the كعبة (*ka'*.bah), a cubelike structure located in the middle of the المسجد الحرام (al.*mas*.jid al.ḥa.*rām*) (*The Sacred Mosque of Mecca*). According to the Quran and other religious texts, the Prophet Abraham built the كعبة for the purpose of worship. The pilgrims must circle the كعبة seven times in a counterclockwise manner. After completing the turns, the pilgrims walk to the hills of Safa and Marwah before walking to Medina, the city where the Prophet Muhammad is buried. From Medina they walk to the hill of Arafat, then to the tent city of Mina before returning to the holy site for a final pilgrimage.

Because the Hajj is one of the five pillars of Islam, a few million people make the journey to Saudi Arabia to participate in this pilgrimage every year, making it by far the largest religious pilgrimage in the world. In fact, it's not uncommon to have at least 5 million pilgrims in the city of Mecca during the Hajj. Once a Muslim has performed the Hajj, he or she receives a special status in society, complete with a title: A man who has completed the Hajj is called الحاج (al.*ḥāj*), and a woman who has done the Hajj is called al-Hajja الحاجة (al.*ḥāj*.jah).

WARNING

Saudi Arabian law prohibits non-Muslims from entering Mecca. If you're non-Muslim, you may be able to visit Saudi Arabia during this period, but you won't be permitted to visit the كعبة and some of the other religious sites related to the Hajj.

FUN & GAMES

Match the hours on the clocks with their Arabic equivalents.

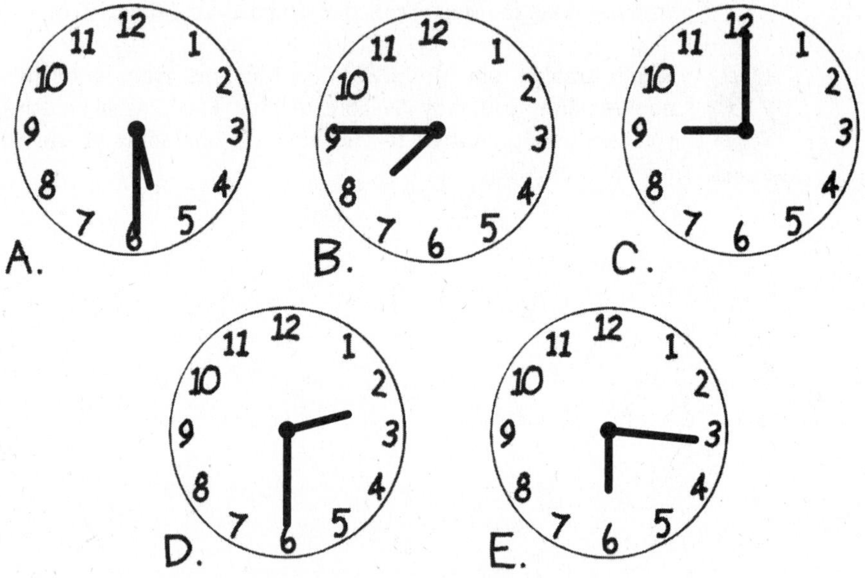

الساعة السادسة والربع صباحاً (as.*sā*.‘ah as.*sā*.di.sah war.*rub‘* ṣa.*bā*.ḥan)

الساعة التاسعة صباحاً (as.*sā*.‘ah at.*tā*.si.‘ah ṣa.*bā*.ḥan)

الساعة الثامنة إلا ربع (as.*sā*.‘ah ath.*thā*.mi.nah *il*.lā rub‘)

الساعة الخامسة والنصف (as.*sā*.‘āh al.*khā*.mi.sah wan.*niṣf*)

الساعة الثانية والنصف بعد الظهر (as.*sā*.‘ah ath.*thā*.ni.yah wan.*niṣf* ba‘.da aẓ.*ẓuhr*)

A. ______________________________

B. ______________________________

C. ______________________________

D. ______________________________

E. ______________________________

The answers are in Appendix C.

» Playing sports

» Exploring the beach

» Playing musical instruments

» Chatting about hobbies

Chapter 13
Enjoying Yourself: Recreation, Music, and the Outdoors

Language teachers may not want you to hear this, but if you want to practice a new language, move outside the classroom. Doing things you enjoy, such as playing sports, creating music, or playing card games, is one of the best ways to immerse yourself in your chosen language. In this chapter, I introduce new words and phrases to help you have fun in Arabic.

REMEMBER

You can listen to all the Talkin' the Talk dialogues featured in this chapter. Go to `www.dummies.com/go/arabicfd` and click on the dialogue you want to hear.

Starting Out with the Doing Verb

One of the most frequently used verbs in the Arabic language is فعل (*fa.*'a.la) (*did*). In the ماضي (*mā.*ḍī) (*past tense*), use the فعل form; for the مضارع (mu.*ḍā*.ri') (*present tense*), use يفعل (*yaf.*'a.lu) (*to do/doing*). Use فعل to describe activities or رياضة (ri.*yā.*ḍah) (*sport*) you're taking part in.

Here's فعل conjugated in the past tense:

Form	Pronunciation	English
أنا فعلتُ	*a*.nā fa.'*al*.tu	I did
أنتَ فعلتَ	*an*.ta fa.'*al*.ta	You did (MS)
أنتِ فعلتِ	*an*.ti fa.'*al*.ti	You did (FS)
هو فعل	*hu*.wa *fa*.'a.la	He did
هي فعلتْ	*hi*.ya *fa*.'a.lat	She did
نحن فعلنا	*naḥ*.nu fa.'*al*.nā	We did
أنتم فعلتم	*an*.tum fa.'*al*.tum	You did (MP)
أنتنّ فعلتنّ	an.*tun*.na fa.'al.*tun*.na	You did (FP)
هم فعلوا	*hum fa*.'al.lū	They did (MP)
هنّ فعلنّ	*hun*.na fa.'*al*.nā	They did (FP)
أنتما فعلتما	an.*tu*.mā fa.'al.*tu*.mā	You did (dual/ M/F)
هما فعلا	*hu*.mā *fa*.'a.lā	They did (dual/M)
هما فعلتا	*hu*.ma fa.'a.*la*.tā	They did (dual/F)

Here are a few examples of فعل in action:

- » الولد ذهب إلى المكتبة وعمل واجبه. (al.*wa*.lad *dha*.ha.ba. *i*.lá al.*mak*.ta.bah wa.'*a*.mi.la. wā.*ji*.ba.hu.) (*The boy went to the library and did his homework.*)
- » انجزت العمل على الطاولة. (an.*jaz*.tu al.'*a*.mal '*a*.lá aṭ.*ṭā*.wi.lah.) (*I did the work on the table.*)
- » أنجزت التمرينات في المنزل. (an.*jaz*.tu at.ta.mrī.*nāt* fī al.*man*.zil.) (*I did the exercises at home.*)

Then use the form يفعل to conjugate "to do" in the present tense:

Form	Pronunciation	English
أنا أفعل	*a*.nā *af*.'al	I am doing
أنتَ تفعل	*an*.ta *taf*.'al	You are doing (MS)
أنتِ تفعلين	*an*.ti taf.'a.*līn*	You are doing (FS)
هو يفعل	huwa *yaf*.'al	He is doing
هي تفعل	*hi*.ya *taf*.'al	She is doing
نحن نفعل	*naḥ*.nu *naf*.'al	We are doing
أنتم تفعلون	*an*.tum taf.'a.*lūn*	You are doing (MP)
أنتنّ تفعلنّ	an.*tun*.na taf.'*al*.na	You are doing (FP)
هم يفعلون	*hum* yaf.'a.*lūn*	They are doing (MP)
هنّ يفعلنّ	*hun*.na yaf.'*al*.na	They are doing (FP)
أنتما تفعلان	an.*tu*.mā taf.'a.*lān*	You are doing (dual/M/F)
هما يفعلان	*hu*.mā yaf.'a.*lān*	They are doing (dual/M)
هما تفعلان	*hu*.mā taf.'a.*lān*	They are doing (dual/FP)

Here are some examples:

» نحن نعمّر الأوراق. (*naḥ*.nu nu.'*am*.mir al.aw.*rāq*.) (*We are doing the paperwork right now.*)

» تقوم بالتجربة في الحديقة. (ta.*qūm* bit.*taj*.ri.bah fī. al.ḥa.*dī*.qah.) (*She is doing the experiments in the garden.*)

» هل تقومون بواجبات الغد؟ (hal ta.qū.*mūn* bi.wā.ji.*bāt* al.*ghad?*) (*Are you doing the work for tomorrow?*)

Sporting an Athletic Side

I don't know about you, but I love playing رياضة (ri.*yā*.ḍah), whether it's an individual sport, such as الغولف (al.*gūlf*) (*golf*) or a team sport like كرة القدم (*ku*.rat al.*qa*.dam) (*soccer*).

Soccer is one of the most popular sports among Arabic-speaking people; in the Middle East, it comes as close as any sport to being the "national" sport. One reason why soccer is so popular is because it's a رياضة مشاهدة (ri.*yā*.ḍat mu.*shā*.ha.dah) (*spectator sport*). In a typical مباراة (mu.bā.*rāh*) (*game*), one فريق (fa.*rīq*) (*team*) with 11 players plays with another team in a ملعب (*mal*.'ab) (*stadium*). Fans closely follow the نتيجة (na.*tī*.jah) (*score*), hoping that their team manages a فوز (*fawz*) (*win*). Not surprisingly, excited fans react to every خطأ (*kha*.ṭa') (*foul*), often disagreeing with the حكم (*ḥa*.kam) (*referee*).

If you find yourself enjoying soccer or a number of other team sports with a friend who speaks Arabic, the following terms may come in handy:

- ملابس رياضية (ma.*lā*.bis ri.yā.*ḍiy*.yah) (*uniforms*)
- خسر (*kha*.si.ra) (*lose*)
- كرة(*ku*.rah) (*ball*)
- لاعب (*lā*.'ib) (*player*) (MS)
- لاعبة (*lā*.'i.bah) (*player*) (FS)

Soccer is only one of the many sports popular with Arabic speakers and peoples of the Middle East. Here are some other favorite sports:

- سباحة (si.*bā*.ḥah) (*swimming*)
- فروسية (fu.rū.*siy*.yah) (*horseback riding*)
- الكرة الطائرة (al.*ku*.rah aṭ.ṭā.'*i*.rah) (*volleyball*)
- كرة السلة (*ku*.rat as.*sal*.lah) (*basketball*)
- التنس (at.*ti*.nis) (*tennis*)
- ركوب الدراجات (ru.*kūb* ad.dar.rā.*jāt*) (*cycling*)
- التزحلق (at.ta.*zaḥ*.luq) (*skiing*)

- التزلج (at.ta.*zal*.luj) (*ice skating*)
- جمباز (jum.*bāz*) (*gymnastics*)
- سباق السيارات (si.*bāq* as.say.yā.*rāt*) (*car racing*)

One of the most common verbs used with sports and other recreational activities is لعب (*la*.'i.ba) (*play*). Because you commonly use this verb, knowing how to conjugate it in both past and present tense is a good idea.

Here's the verb "to play" in the past tense:

Form	Pronunciation	English
أنا لعبتُ	*a*.nā la.'*ib*.tu	I played
أنتَ لعبتَ	*an*.ta la.'*ib*.ta	You played (MS)
أنتِ لعبتِ	*an*.ti la.'*ib*.ti	You played (FS)
هو لعب	*hu*.wa *la*.'i.ba	He played
هي لعبث	*hi*.ya la.'*i*.bat	She played
نحن لعبنا	*naḥ*.nu la.'*ib*.nā	We played
أنتم لعبتم	*an*.tum la.'*ib*.tum	You played (MP)
أنتنّ لعبتنّ	an.*tun*.na la.'ib.*tun*.na	You played (FP)
هم لعبوا	*hum la*.'i.bū	They played (MP)
هنّ لعبنّ	*hun*.na la.'*ib*.na	They played (FP)
أنتما لعبتما	an.*tu*.mā la.'ib.*tu*.mā	You played (dual/M/F)
هما لعبا	*hu*.mā *la*.'i.bā	They played (dual/M)
هما لعبتا	*hu*.mā la.'i.*ba*.tā	They played (dual/F)

Use the form يلعب (*yal.*ʻa.bu) to conjugate "to play" in the present tense:

Form	Pronunciation	English
أنا ألعب	*a*.nā *al*.'ab	I am playing
أنتَ تلعب	*an*.ta *tal*.'ab	You are playing (MS)
أنتِ تلعبين	*an*.ti tal.'a.*bīn*	You are playing (FS)
هو يلعب	*hu*.wa *yal*.'ab	He is playing
هي تلعب	*hi*.ya *tal*.'ab	She is playing
نحن نلعب	*naḥ*.nu *nal*.'ab	We are playing
أنتم تلعبون	*an*.tum tal.'a.*būn*	You are playing (MP)
أنتنّ تلعبنّ	an.*tun*.na tal.'*ab*.na	You are playing (FP)
هم يلعبون	*hum* yal.'a.*būn*	They are playing (MP)
هنّ يلعبنّ	*hun*.na yal.'*ab*.na	They are playing (FP)
أنتما تلعبان	an.*tu*.mā tal.'a.*bān*	You are playing (dual/M/F)
هما يلعبان	*hu*.mā yal.'a.*bān*	They are playing (dual/M)
هما تلعبان	*hu*.mā tal.'a.*bān*	They are playing (dual/F)

GRAMMATICALLY SPEAKING

The sentence structure for creating verbs is such that you use the verb لعب (*la*.ʻi.ba) or يلعب (*yal*.ʻab) followed by the sport or activity you're playing. For example, you may say أنا ألعب كرة السلة (a.nā *al*.ʻab *ku*.rat as.*sal*.lah) (*I am playing basketball*) or هي لعبتْ التنس (*hi*.ya *la*.ʻi.bat at.*ti*.nis) (*She played tennis*). As you can see from these examples, all you do is start with the personal pronoun and verb conjugation, attach the sport you're referring to, and there you go!

Another important phrase commonly used relating to sports and other fun activities is هيا بنا (*hay*.yā *bi*.nā) (*Let's*). You'll often hear friends telling each other "Let's" followed by the activity or location of the activity, such as هيا بنا إلى ملعب كرة القدم (*hay*.yā *bi*.nā i.lá *mal*.ʻab *ku*.rat al.*qa*.dam.) (*Let's go to the soccer field.*).

Talkin' the Talk

Karim and Kamal are scheduling a soccer game.

Karim: هيا نلعب كرة القدم غداً.
hay.yā *nal*.'ab *ku*.rat al.*qa*.dam *gha*.dan.
Let's go play soccer tomorrow.

Kamal: هذه فكرة ممتازة.
hā.dhi.hi *fik*.rah mum.*tā*.zah.
That's an excellent idea.

Karim: في أي ساعة؟
fī *ayy sā*.'ah?
At what time?

Kamal: هل توافقك الساعة الخامسة؟
hal tu.*wā*.fi.qu.ka as.*sā*.'ah al.*khā*.mi.sah?
Does 5:00 work for you?

Karim: نعم. الساعة الخامسة موافقة. أين سنلعب؟
na.'am. as.*sā*.'ah al.*khā*.mi.sah mu.*wā*.fi.qah. *ay*.na sa.*nal*.'ab?
Yes. 5:00 works for me. Where are we going to play?

Kamal: في ملعب المدرسة.
fī *mal*.'ab al.*mad*.ra.sah.
In the school stadium.

Karim: ممتاز! هل عندك كرة؟
mum.*tāz*! *hal 'in*.dak *ku*.rah?
Excellent! Do you have a ball?

Kamal: نعم عندي كرة. ولكن ليس عندي ملابس رياضية.
na.'am *'in*.dī *ku*.rah. wa.*lā*.kin *lay*.sa *'in*.dī ma.*lā*.bis ri.yā.*ḍiy*.yah.
Yes, I have a ball. But I don't have any uniforms.

Karim: لا نحتاج للملابس الرياضية.
lā naḥ.*tāj* lil.ma.*lā*.bis ar.ri.yā.*ḍiy*.yah.
We don't need uniforms.

Kamal: ممتاز. إلى الغد.
mum.*tāz*. *i*.lá al.*ghad*.
Excellent. See you tomorrow.

Karim: إلى الغد.
i.lá al.*ghad*.
See you tomorrow.

WORDS TO KNOW

فكرة	fik.rah	idea
غداً	gha.dan	tomorrow
ساعة	sā.'ah	hour
مدرسة	mad.ra.sah	school
كرة	ku.rah	ball
ملعب	mal.'ab	stadium

Going to the Beach

One of my favorite places is the شاطئ (*shā*.ṭi') (*beach*); whether you go to the beach with your أصدقاء (aṣ.di.*qā*') (*friends*) or your أسرة (*us*.rah) (*family*), it's a really great place to have a fun time! You can do some سباحة (si.*bā*.ḥah) (*swimming*) in the محيط (mu.*ḥīṭ*) (*ocean*) or play around in the رمل (raml) (*sand*).

Talkin' the Talk

Rita is trying to convince her mother to take her to the beach.

Rita: هيا بنا إلى الشاطئ!
hay.yā *bi*.nā *i*.lá ash.*shā*.ṭi'!
Let's go to the beach!

Mother: متى؟
ma.tá?
When?

Rita: هيا بنا الآن!
hay.yā *bi*.nā al.'*ān!*
Let's go now!

Mother: هل عندكِ ملابس سباحة؟
hal 'in.dik ma.*lā*.bis si.*bā*.ḥa?
Do you have your bathing suit?

Rita: نعم!
na.'am!
Yes!

Mother: وهل عندكِ دهان ضد الشمس؟
wa.*hal 'in*.dik da.*hān* ḍid ash.*shams?*
And do you have sunscreen?

Rita: نعم!
na.'am!
Yes!

Mother: ممتاز. هيا بنا.
mum.*tāz. hay*.yā *bi*.nā.
Excellent. Then let's go.

WORDS TO KNOW		
ملابس سباحة	ma.lā.bis si.bā.ḥa	bathing suit
دهان ضد الشمس	da.hān ḍid ash.shams	sunscreen
شمس	shams	sun
سحاب	sa.ḥāb	clouds
شاطئ	shā.ṭi'	beach
محيط	mu.ḥīṭ	ocean
مظلة	mi.ẓal.lah	umbrella
رمل	raml	sand
موجة	maw.jah	wave

Playing Musical Instruments

I happen to agree with the saying that موسيقى (mū.*sī*.qá) (*music*) is a universal language. No matter where you come from or what languages you speak, music has more power to break down barriers and bring people closer together than perhaps any other activity. Popular آلات موسيقية (ā.*lāt* mū.sī.*qiy*.yah) (*musical instruments*) include the following:

- بيانو (bi.*yā*.nū) (*piano*)
- قيثارة (qī.*thā*.rah) (*guitar*)
- كمنجة (ka.*man*.jah) (*violin*)
- طبل (ṭabl) (*drums*)
- ناي (nāy) (*flute*)
- بوق (būq) (*trumpet*)
- ساكسفون (sāks.*fūn*) (*saxophone*)

In order to say that someone plays a particular instrument, use the present tense form of the verb. For example, يعزف على القيثارة (*ya'*.zif '*a*.lá al.qī.*thā*.rah) means

"He plays the guitar" or "He is playing the guitar" because the present tense describes both an ongoing and a habitual action.

CULTURAL WISDOM

Middle Eastern music is one of the most popular types of music in the world. It's characterized by a special kind of string instrument called the عود (*'ūd*) that has six double strings and a round, hollow body. The عود is generally accompanied by a number of percussion instruments, such as the regular drum and the special طبلة (*ṭab.*lah) that keeps the beat and adds extra flavor to the serenading of the عود.

A particularly popular kind of Northern African music is راي (*rāy*), which originated in the early 1990s in Algeria, Morocco, and Tunisia. راي uses a lot of traditional Arabic instruments, such as the عود and the طبلة but adds modern rock 'n' roll and jazz instruments, such as the electric guitar, the saxophone, and the trumpet. One of the most popular singers of راي music is شاب خالد (Sheb Khaled).

Talking about Hobbies

You may enjoy a number of types of hobbies. Do you consider قراءة (qi.*rā*.'ah) (*reading*) a هواية (hu.*wā*.yah) (*hobby*)? Perhaps you're creative and like رسم (rasm) (*drawing*) or فخار (fakh.*khār*) (*pottery*). Almost everyone has a hobby, and because a hobby, by definition, is an activity that a person is really passionate about, you can be sure that he or she will enjoy talking about it! Here are some activities that may be considered hobbies:

- ركوب الدراجات (ru.*kūb* ad.dar.rā.*jāt*) (*bicycling*)
- ورق اللعب (wa.raq al.*la*.'ib) (*cards*)
- الشطرنج (ash.sha.ṭa.*ranj*) (*chess*)
- الرقص (ar.*raqṣ*) (*dancing*)
- الطائرات الورقية (aṭ.ṭā.'i.*rāt* al.wa.ra.*qiy*.yah) (*kite flying*)
- القراءة (al.qi.*rā*.'ah) (*reading*)
- الحياكة (al.ḥi.*yā*.kah) (*sewing*)
- الشعر (ash.*shi'r*) (*poetry*)
- غناء (ghi.*nā'*) (*singing*)

When you want to discuss hobbies and personal activities, use the verb لعب (*la*.'i.ba), which means "to play" (for conjugations, check out "Sporting an

Athletic Side" earlier in this chapter). For example, you say لعبتُ كرة القدم (la.'*ib*.tu *ku*.rat al.*qa*.dam) (*I played soccer*). Here are some other example sentences that pair activities with لعب:

- لعبت الشطرنج . (*la*.'i.bat ash.sha.ṭa.*ranj*.) (*She played chess.*)
- لعبنا كرة السلة. (la.'*ib*.nā *ku*.rat as.*sal*.lah.) (*We played basketball.*)
- لعبا ورق. (*la*.'i.bā *wa*.raq al.*la*.'ib.) (*They played cards.*) (dual/MP/FP)

However, there are times when you're going to use the verb عمل ('*a*.mi.la). Generally speaking, you use this verb to discuss activities that are more work-related than hobbies. For instance, you say عملتُ الواجب ('a.*mil*.tu al.*wā*.jib) (*I did the homework*). As a rule, use the verb لعب when you're discussing hobbies, such as sports.

Talkin' the Talk

Yassin and Youssef, two freshmen students at Al-azhar University, find that they have a hobby in common.

Yassin: ما هي هوايتك؟
mā hi.ya hu.wā.*ya*.tak?
What is your hobby?

Youssef: أحبّ كرة القدم.
u.*ḥibb ku*.rat al.*qa*.dam.
I like soccer.

Yassin: أنا أيضا أحبّ كرة القدم!
a.nā *ay*.ḍan u.*ḥibb ku*.rat al.*qa*.dam!
I also like soccer!

Youssef: يجب أن نلعب معاً!
ya.jib ann *nal*.'ab *ma*.'an!
We must play together sometime!

Yassin: طبعاً!
ṭa.ba.'an!
Definitely!

FUN & GAMES

Draw lines connecting the Arabic activities on the left with their English equivalents on the right.

شطرنج	basketball
رسم	guitar
شعر	swimming
تنس	drawing
سباحة	chess
كرة السلة	tennis
قيثارة	poetry

The answers are in Appendix C.

3 Arabic on the Go

IN THIS PART . . .

Plan a trip, including getting a visa and making hotel reservations.

Decipher foreign currency and practice counting money and making change.

Know the ins and outs of traveling by plane, breezing through customs, and shuttling your way around town.

Figure out the right questions to ask when looking for a place to stay.

Be ready to deal with emergency situations.

» Packing your bags

» Dealing with travel documents

» Consulting a travel agent

Chapter 14 Planning a Trip

I don't know about you, but I simply love traveling. I enjoy visiting exotic locations around the world, meeting new people from different backgrounds, and discovering new cultures. This chapter tells you everything you need to know about planning, organizing, and going on a رحلة (*riḥ*.lah) (*trip*) — in Arabic, of course.

REMEMBER

You can listen to all the Talkin' the Talk dialogues featured in this chapter. Go to `www.dummies.com/go/arabicfd` and click on the dialogue you want to hear.

Choosing Your Destination

When you decide to take a trip, أين (*ay*.na) (*where*) to go is probably the biggest decision you face. For أفكار (af.*kār*) (*ideas*) on a possible travel وجهة (*wij*.hah) (*destination*), you may want to consult a وكيل أسفار (wa.*kīl* as.*fār*) (*travel agent*). Table 14-1 lists the Arabic names of some popular travel destinations you can choose from.

TABLE 14-1 **Names of Countries**

Arabic	Pronunciation	English
المغرب	al.*magh*.rib	Morocco
الجزائر	al.ja.*zā*.'ir	Algeria
تونس	*tū*.nis	Tunisia
ليبيا	*līb*.yā	Libya
مصر	miṣr	Egypt
إسرائيل	is.rā.'*īl*	Israel
فلسطين	fa.las.*ṭīn*	Palestine
لبنان	lub.*nān*	Lebanon
الأردن	al.'*ur*.dun	Jordan
سوريا	*sūr*.yā	Syria
السعودية	as.sa.'ū.*diy*.yah	Saudi Arabia
العراق	al.'i.*rāq*	Iraq
الكويت	al.ku.*wayt*	Kuwait
البحرين	al.baḥ*rayn*	Bahrain
قطر	*qa*.ṭar	Qatar
الإمارات	al.'i.mā.*rāt*	United Arab Emirates
اليمن	al.*ya*.man	Yemen
عمان	'u.*mān*	Oman
السودان	as.sū.*dān*	Sudan
الصومال	aṣ.ṣū.*māl*	Somalia
إيران	ī.*rān*	Iran
امريكا	am.*rī*.kā	United States of America
كندا	*ka*.na.dā	Canada

Arabic	Pronunciation	English
المكسيك	al.mik.*sīk*	Mexico
إنجلترا	in.gil.*ti*.rā	England
فرنسا	fa.*ran*.sā	France
إسبانيا	is.*bān*.yā	Spain
إيطاليا	ī.*ṭāl*.yā	Italy
ألمانيا	al.*mān*.yā	Germany
البرازيل	al.ba.rā.*zīl*	Brazil
الأرجنتين	al.ar.jan.*tīn*	Argentina
اليابان	al.yā.*bān*	Japan
الصين	aṣ.*ṣīn*	China
كوريا	*kūr*.ya	Korea
الهند	al.*hind*	India
باكستان	bā.kis.*tān*	Pakistan
أفغانستان	af.ghā.nis.*tān*	Afghanistan

أسئلة **(*as.*'i.lah) (*questions*) you should ask when choosing your destination include**

- كيف الطقس في هذا البلد؟ (*kay*.fa aṭ.*ṭaqs* fī *hā*.dhā al.*ba*.lad?) (*How is the weather in this country?*)
- كيف الطقس في هذا الوقت من السنة؟ (*kay*.fa aṭ.*ṭaqs* fī *hā*.dhā al.*waqt* min as.*sa*.nah?) (*How is the weather during this time of year?*)
- هل هناك الكثير من السياح؟ (*hal* hu.*nā*.ka al.ka.*thīr* min as.suy.*yāḥ*?) (*Are there a lot of tourists there?*)
- هل هذا المكان يناسب الأسرة والأطفال؟ (*hal hā*.dhā al.ma.*kān* yu.*nā*.sib al.'*us*.rah wal.'aṭ.*fāl*?) (*Is this place suitable for the family and for children?*)
- هل هناك ترفيه للأطفال؟ (*hal* hu.*nā*.ka tar.*fih* lil.'aṭ.*fāl*?) (*Is there entertainment for the children?*)

» هل المدينة نظيفة؟ (*hal* al.ma.*dī*.nah na.*ẓī*.fah?) (*Is the city clean?*)

» هل القرية قريبة من المدينة؟ (*hal* al.*qar*.yah qa.*rī*.bah min al.ma.*dī*.nah?) (*Is the village close to the city?*)

» متى تشرق الشمس؟ (*ma*.tá *tush*.riq ash.*shams?*) (*When does the sun rise?*)

» متى وقت الغروب؟ (*ma*.tá *waqt* al.ghu.*rūb?*) (*What time is sunset?*)

» هل الشاطئ قريب من الفندق؟ (*hal* ash.*shā*.ṭi' qa.*rīb* min al.*fun*.duq?) (*Is the beach close to the hotel?*)

» هل هناك متحف في المدينة؟ (*hal* hu.*nā*.ka *mat.*ḥaf fī al ma.*dī*.nah?) (*Is there a museum in the city?*)

Talkin' the Talk

Stephanie calls her travel agent, Murad, to get his recommendations on where she should go on vacation this year.

Stephanie: أهلًا مراد. هذه ستيفاني.
ah.lan mu.*rād*. *hā*.dhi.hi Stephanie.
Hi, Murad. This is Stephanie.

Murad: أهلًا ستيفاني! كيف يمكن أن أساعدك؟
ah.lan Stephanie! *kay*.fa *yum*.kin an u.sā.'*i*.da.ki?
Hi, Stephanie! How may I help you?

Stephanie: أنا أريد أن أذهب مع أسرتي في رحلة في نهاية السنة.
a.nā u.*rīd* an *adh*.hab *ma*.'a *us*.ra.tī fī *rih*.lah fī ni.*hā*.yit as.*sa*.nah.
I want to go on a trip with my family at the end of the year.

Murad: هذه فكرة ممتازة.
hā.dhi.hi *fik*.rah mum.*tā*.zah.
This is an excellent idea.

Stephanie: هل عندك أي نصائح؟
hal '*in*.dak ayy na.*ṣā*.'iḥ?
Do you have any recommendations?

Murad: هل تريدين أن تذهبي إلى مكان دافئ؟
hal tu.rī.*dīn* an *tadh*.ha.bī *i*.lá ma.*kān* *dā*.fi'?
Do you want to go someplace warm?

Stephanie: نعم, من الأفضل.
na.'am, min al.'*af*.ḍal.
Yes, that is better.

Murad: هل ذهبتِ إلى المغرب من قبل؟
hal dha.*hab*.ti *i*.lá al.*magh*.rib min qabl?
Have you gone to Morocco before?

Stephanie: لا. لم أذهب إلى المغرب من قب ولكن أحبّ أن أزوره.
lā. lam *adh*.hab *i*.lá al.*magh*.rib min qabl wa.*lā*.kin u.*ḥibb* an a.*zū*.ra.hu.
No. I have never visited Morocco before, but I would love to visit it.

Murad: ممتاز! هذا البلد دافئ في كل وقت في السنة.
mum.*tāz! hā*.dhā al.*ba*.lad *dā*.fi' fī *kul*.li waqt fī as.*sa*.naḥ.
Excellent! This country is warm during the whole year.

Stephanie: هذا رائع!
hā.dhā *rā*.'i'!
That's great!

Murad: هناك مدن كثيرة يمكين أن تزوريها.
hu.*nā*.ka *mu*.dun ka.*thī*.rah *yum*.kin an ta.zū.*rī*.hā.
There are a lot of cities you can visit.

Stephanie: ما هي؟
mā hi.ya?
Which ones?

Murad: مراكش والدار البيضاء مدينتان جميلتان.
mur.*rā*.kush wad.*dār* al.bay.*ḍā'* ma.dī.na.*tān* ja.mī.la.*tān*.
Marrakech and Casablanca are two beautiful cities.

Stephanie: ما الفرق بينهما؟
mā al.*farq* bay.*na*.hu.mā?
What's the difference between the two?

Murad: هناك شاطئ في الدار البيضاء لأنها قريبة من المحيط الأطلسي.
hu.*nā*.ka *shā*.ṭi' fī ad.*dār* al.bay.*ḍā'* li.'*an*.na.hā qa.*rī*.bah min al.mu.*ḥīṭ* al.'*aṭ*.la.sī.
There is a beach in Casablanca because it is near the Atlantic Ocean.

Stephanie: جميل.
ja.*mīl*.
Beautiful.

Murad: ومراكش ليس فيها شاطئ ولكنها قريبة من جبال الأطلس.
wa.mur.*rā*.kush *lay*.sa *fī*.hā *shā*.ṭi' wa.lā.*kin*.na.hā qa.*rī*.bah min ji.*bāl* al.'*aṭ*.las.
There is no beach in Marrakech, but it is near the Atlas Mountains.

Stephanie: وهل يمكن أن أتزلج في جبال الاطلس؟
wa.*hal yum*.kin an at.ta.*zal*.laj fī ji.*bāl* al.'*aṭ*.las?
And is it possible to ski in the Atlas Mountains?

Murad: نعم. جبال الأطلس أكبر جبال في شمال افريقيا وفي الشرق الأوسط. هناك الكثير من الثلج فيها.
na.'am. ji.*bāl* al.'*aṭ*.las *ak*.bar ji.*bāl* fī sha.*māl* af.*rīq*.yah wa.fī ash.*sharq* al.'*aw*.saṭ. hu.*nā*.ka al.ka.*thīr* min ath.*thalj* *fī*.hā.
Yes. The Atlas Mountains are the biggest mountain range in North Africa and in the Middle East. There is plenty of snow there.

Stephanie: هذا اختيار صعب جداً.
hā.dhā ikh.tī.*yār* ṣa'b *jid*.dan.
This is a very difficult choice.

Murad: هل ستذهبين مع أسرتك؟
hal sa.tadh.ha.*bīn* ma.'a *us*.ra.tik?
Are you going to go with your family?

Stephanie: نعم مع زوجي وابني.
na.'am. *ma*.'a *zaw*.jī *wab*.nī.
Yes. With my husband and son.

Murad: كم عمر ابنك؟
kam 'umr *ib*.nik?
How old is your son?

Stephanie: عشر سنوات.
'ashr sa.na.*wāt*.
Ten years old.

Murad: أظنّ أنّ مراكش تناسب رحلة للأسرة. ابنك سيحبّها.
a.*ẓunn an*.na mur.*rā*.kush tu.*nā*.sib *riḥ*.lat al.*'us*.rah. *ib*.nik sa.yu.*ḥib*.bu.hā.
I believe that Marrakech is suitable for a family trip. Your son will like it.

Stephanie: حسناً سنذهب إلى مراكش. ولكن أريد أن أذهب إلى الدار. البيضاء. هل هذا ممكن؟
ḥa.sa.nan sa.*nadh*.hab *i*.lá mur.*rā*.kush. wa.*lā*.kin u.*rīd* an *adh*.hab *i*.lá ad.*dār* al.bay.*ḍā'*. *hal hā*.dhā *mum*.kin?
Okay, we'll go to Marrakech. But I'd like to go to Casablanca as well. Is this possible?

Murad: نعم. هذا أحسن إذا زرتم مراكش والدار البيضاء.
na.'am. *hā*.dhā *aḥ*.san i.*dhā zur*.tum mur.*rā*.kush wad.*dār* al.bay.*ḍā'*.
Yes. It's better if you visit both Marrakech and Casablanca.

WORDS TO KNOW

زوج	zawj	husband
زوجة	zaw.jah	wife
فكرة	fik.rah	idea
نصيحة	na.ṣī.ḥah	recommendation/advice
دافئ	dā.fi'	warm
بارد	bā.rid	cold
مكان	ma.kān	place
أفضل	af.ḍal	preferable
زيارة	zi.yā.rah	visit
منذ	mun.dhu	since
مدينة	ma.dī.nah	city
مدن	mu.dun	cities

شاطئ	shā.ṭi'	beach
محيط	mu.ḥīṭ	ocean
سباحة	si.bā.ḥah	swimming
جبل	ja.bal	mountain
جبال	ji.bāl	mountains
ثلج	thalj	snow
تزلج	ta.zal.luj	skiing
شمال	sha.māl	north
جنوب	ja.nūb	south
غرب	gharb	west
شرق	sharq	east

Picking the Right Time for Your Trip

A major part of travel planning is timing. When you have an idea of what you want to do or where you want to go, you need to consider the most appropriate time to take the trip. An obvious example is deciding to go skiing and making sure your mountain destination will have snow when you're there. However, things can get trickier if you're traveling to a Middle Eastern or Islamic country. During some months of the year, such as the holy month of Ramadan, traveling to these countries probably isn't a good idea because the time is sacred to Muslims.

TIP

Look at the تقويم (taq.*wīm*) (*calendar*) and choose the شهر (shahr) (*month*) most suitable not only to your travel plans but also to the دولة (*daw*.lah) (*country*) you're visiting. Flip to Chapter 5 to see the months listed according to the Gregorian and Islamic calendar.

CULTURAL WISDOM

For travel purposes, the Gregorian calendar convention is most widely used, so use it if you're making a reservation.

REMEMBER

After you narrow down the month in which you want to take your trip, you must specify the dates by using numbers. Arabic numbers fall into two categories: cardinals and ordinals. *Cardinals* are regular counting numbers, like "one," "two," or "three"; *ordinals* are the adjective forms of numbers, like "first," "second," and "third." Arabic ordinals differ from cardinals in that every ordinal number has both a masculine and feminine form. Because ordinals are treated as adjectives, they must be in gender agreement with their corresponding nouns.

When you specify a date, you say "December fifth" or "January eighth." Because month is a masculine noun (the terms for months are masculine), you must use masculine ordinals to identify specific dates. For example, you say الخامس من ديسمبر (al.*khā*.mis min dī.*sam*.bir) (*the fifth of December*) or الثامن من يناير (ath.*thā*.min min ya.*nā*.yir) (*January eighth*). In addition, because the ordinal acts as a modifying adjective, you must include the definite prefix ال **(al)**. For more on cardinals and ordinals, flip to Chapters 5 and 8.

Talkin' the Talk

George and his wife Selma are trying to figure out when to visit their favorite country, Morocco.

George: متى تريدين أن نذهب إلى المغرب هذه السنة؟
ma.tá tu.rī.*dīn* an *nadh*.hab *i*.lá al.*magh*.rib *hā*.dhi.hi as.*sa*.nah?
When would you like us to go to Morocco this year?

Selma: في نهاية السنة كالعادة.
fī ni.*hā*.yat as.*sa*.nah kal.*'ā*.dah.
At the end of the year, as usual.

George: ديسمبر؟ هل يمكن أن تذهبي في الخامس من ديسمبر؟
dī.*sam*.bir? *hal yum*.kin an *tadh*.ha.bī fī al.*khā*.mis min dī.*sam*.bir?
December? Can you go on December fifth?

Selma: انتظر دقيقة. سأرى تقويمي.
in.ta.ẓir da.*qī*.qah. sa.*'a*.rá taq.*wī*.mī.
Hold on one minute. I'll check my calendar.

Selma checks her calendar.

Selma: للأسف لا يمكنني أن أذهب في الخامس من ديسمبر. عندي اجتماع مهن في ذلك اليوم.
lil.*'a*.saf *lā* yum.*kin*.nu.nī an *adh*.hab fī al.*khā*.mis min dī.*sam*.bir. *'in*.dī ij.ti.*mā'* mu.*him* fī *dhā*.li.ka al.*yawm*.
Unfortunately I'm not able to leave on December fifth. I have an important meeting that day.

George: هل يمكنك أن تذهبي في الثامن من ديسمبر؟
hal yum.*kin*.u.ki an *tadh*.ha.bī fī ath.*thā*.min min dī.*sam*.bir?
Can you go on December eighth?

Selma: نعم! الثامن من ديسمبر ممتاز!
na.'am. ath.*thā*.min min dī.*sam*.bir mum.*tāz!*
Yes. December eighth is perfect!

George: ممتاز! وهل نرجع في العشرين من ديسمبر؟
mum.*tāz*! wa.hal *nar*.ji' fī al.'ish.*rīn* min dī.*sam*.bir?
Excellent! And should we come back on December twentieth?

Selma: نعم هذا ممكن. ولكن أنا أريد أن أبقى وقتاً أكثر. هل يمكن أن نبقى إلى الرابع والعشرين من ديسمبر؟
na.'am *hā*.dhā *mum*.kin. wa.*lā*.kin *a*.nā u.*rīd* an *ab*.qá *waq*.tan *ak*.thar. *hal yum*.kin an *nab*.qá *i*.lá ar.*rā*.bi' wal.'ish.*rīn* min dī.*sam*.bir?
Yes that's possible. But I'd like to stay a bit longer. Can we stay until December twenty-fourth?

George: حسناً. نبقى إلى الرابع والعشرين.
ḥa.sa.nan. *nab*.qá *il*.lá ar.*rā*.bi' wal.'ish.*rīn*.
Okay. Let's stay until the twenty-fourth.

Selma: شكراً! ستكون رحلة ممتعة!
shuk.ran! sa.ta.*kūn* *riḥ*.lah *mum*.ti.'ah!
Thank you! It's going to be an entertaining trip!

WORDS TO KNOW

ذهب	dha.ha.ba	he went
نذهب	nadh.hab	we go
شهر	shahr	month
أشهر	ash.hur	months
نهاية	ni.hā.yah	end
بداية	bi.dā.yah	beginning
وسط	wa.saṭ	middle

وقت	waqt	time
ترك	ta.ra.ka	to leave
رجع	ra.ji.'a	to return/come back
عمل	'a.mi.la	work
دقيقة	da.qī.qah	minute
تقويم	taq.wīm	calendar
اجتماع	ij.ti.mā'	meeting
مهم	mu.him	important (M)
مهمة	mu.him.mah	important (F)

Tackling Packing

Packing the right items for your trip is a crucial step toward enjoying your travel experience. First, you must gather the أمتعة (*am*.ti.'ah) (*luggage*) you need. Here are some possibilities:

- شنطة (*shan*.ṭah) (*suitcase*)
- شنط (*shu*.naṭ) (*suitcases*)
- محفظة (*maḥ*.fa.ẓah) (*briefcase*)
- محافظ (ma.*ḥā*.fiẓ) (*briefcases*)
- كيس (kīs) (*bag*)
- أكياس (ak.*yās*) (*bags*)
- كيس الحمّام (*kīs* al.ḥam.*mām*) (*toiletry bag*)
- أكياس الحمّام (ak.*yās* al.ḥam.*mām*) (*toiletry bags*)

With your luggage selected, you can now choose what to put in it. Here are some essential items you should carry with you regardless of your destination:

- ملابس (ma.*lā*.bis) (*clothes*)
- قمصان (qa.*mīṣ*) (*shirt*)

- قميص (qum.*ṣān*) (*shirts*)
- سروال (sir.*wāl*) (*pants*)
- سروال قصير (sir.*wāl* qa.*ṣīr*) (*shorts*)
- معطف (*mi'*.ṭaf) (*coat*)
- جاكيت (*jā*.kīt) (*jacket*)
- أحذية (*aḥ*.dhi.yah) (*shoes*)
- صندل (*ṣan*.dal) (*sandals*)
- أحزمة (*aḥ*.zi.mah) (*belts*)
- جوارب (ja.*wā*.rib) (*socks*)
- نظارات (naẓ.ẓā.*rāt*) (*glasses*)
- نظارات الشمس (naẓ.ẓā.*rāt* ash.*shams*) (*sunglasses*)
- قبعة (*qub*.ba.'ah) (*hat*)

In addition to clothing and accessories, you also need grooming items. Here are some toiletries you may pack for your trip:

- فرشات الأسنان (fur.*shāt* al.'as.*nān*) (*toothbrush*)
- معجون الأسنان (ma'.*jūn* al.'as.*nān*) (*toothpaste*)
- مشط (mishṭ) (*comb*)
- غسول الشعر (gha.*sūl* ash.*sha'r*) (*shampoo*)
- صابون (ṣā.*būn*) (*soap*)
- مزيل العرق (mu.*zīl* al.*'a*.raq) (*deodorant*)
- فوطة (*fū*.ṭah) (*towel*)
- ماكنة الحلاقة (mā.*ki*.nat al.ḥi.*lā*.qah) (*shaving razor*)
- معجون الحلاقة (ma'.*jūn* al.ḥi.*lā*.qah) (*shaving cream*)

Preparing Your Travel Documents

The logistics of travel can get pretty complicated, especially when you're traveling internationally. In recent years, travel restrictions have grown more stringent due to growing security concerns. In this section, you can find all the key terms you need to know in order to gather the appropriate وثائق السفر (wa.*thā*.'iq as.*sa*.far) (*travel documents*) to make your trip go as smoothly as possible.

Before you leave on a trip, you need to have at least one شخصية (bi.*ṭā*.qah shakh.*ṣiy*.yah) (*personal identification card*); to be safe, you should probably have two or more. In case you need further confirmation of your identity, carrying three forms of identification is ideal. Here are some بطاقات شخصية (bi.ṭā.*qāt* shakh.*ṣiy*.yah) (*personal identification cards*) you could carry with you:

- رخصة القيادة (*rukh*.ṣat al.qi.*yā*.dah) (*driver's license*)
- بطاقة من الحكومة (bi.*ṭā*.qah min al.ḥu.*kū*.mah) (*government-issued ID*)
- بطاقة من الجيش (bi.*ṭā*.qah min al.*jaysh*) (*military-issued ID*)
- جواز السفر (jaw.*wāz* as.*sa*.far) (*passport*)
- تصريح عمل (taṣ.*rīḥ* '*a*.mal) (*work permit*)

GRAMMATICALLY SPEAKING

The word بطاقة (bi.*ṭā*.qah) literally means "card." However, its meaning may change, depending on the context of the phrase in which you use it. For instance, in the previous list of terms, the word, بطاقة means "license" as well as "permit."

In addition to personal identification documents, if you're traveling overseas, many countries require that you also have a تأشيرة (ta'.*shī*.rah) (*visa*) stamped on your passport. Every دولة (*daw*.lah) (*country*) has different procedures and requirements for obtaining تأشيرات (ta'.*shī*.rāt) (*visas*), so it's your responsibility to find out whether the country you're planning to visit requires a visa and, if so, how to go about obtaining one. The categories of visas include

- تأشيرة الطالب (ta'.*shī*.rat aṭ.*ṭā*.lib) (*student visa*)
- تأشيرة العمل (ta'.*shī*.rat al.'*a*.mal) (*work visa*)
- تأشيرة السائح (ta'.*shī*.rat as.*sā*.'iḥ) (*tourist visa*)
- تأشيرة الأسرة (ta'.*shī*.rat al.'*us*.rah) (*family visa*)

In order to determine which نوع (naw') (*type*) of visa you need and how to go about getting one, you should contact the قنصلية (qun.ṣu.*liy*.yah) (*consulate*) of your سفارة (si.*fā*.rah) (*embassy*). If possible, arrange to speak with a موظف القنصلية (mu.*waẓ*.ẓaf al.qun.ṣu.*liy*.yah) (*consular officer*); he or she should be able to provide you with all the معلومات (ma'.lū.*māt*) (*information*) you need about visas.

Talkin' the Talk

Alan stops by the State Department and speaks to an officer to get information about traveling to the Middle East.

Alan: سأسافر إلى الشرق الأوسط وأحتاج إلى معلومات عن السفر.
sa.'u.*sā*.fir *i*.lá ash.*sharq* al.'*aw*.saṭ wa.'aḥ.*tāj i*.lá ma'.lū.māt 'an as.*sa*.far.
I'm going to be traveling to the Middle East, and I need some travel information.

Officer: حسناً. يمكنني أن أساعدك. متى ستذهب؟
a.sa.nan. yum.*kin*.nu.ni an u.*sā*.'i.dak. *ma*.tá sa.*tadh*.hab?
Okay. I'm able to help you. When will you be going?

Alan: أريد أن أذهب في نهاية السنة.
u.*rīd* an *adh*.hab fī ni.*hā*.yat as.*sa*.nah.
I would like to go at the end of the year.

Officer: ولكم من الوقت؟
wa.li.*kamm* min al.*waqt*?
And for how long?

Alan: ثلاثة أسابيع.
tha.*lā*.thah a.sā.*bī*'.
Three weeks.

Officer: أي بلد ستزور؟
ayy *ba*.lad sa.ta.*zūr*?
Which country will you be visiting?

Alan: أريد أن أزور مصر ولبنان.
u.*rīd* an a.*zūr* miṣr wa.lub.*nān*.
I want to visit Egypt and Lebanon.

Officer: حسناً. ليس ضرورياً أن تحصل على تأشيرة لمصر.
ḥa.sa.nan. *lay*.sa ḍa.rū.*riy*.yan an *taḥ*.ṣul '*a*.lá ta'.*shī*.rah li.*miṣr*.
Okay. It's not necessary to obtain a visa for Egypt.

Alan: وللبنان؟
wa.li.lub.*nān*?
And for Lebanon?

Officer: إذا كنتَ ستزور لبنان لأكثر من أسبوع فمن الضروري أن تحصل على تأشيرة.
i.*dhā* *kun*.ta sa.ta.*zūr* lub.*nān* li.'*ak*.thar min as.*bū*' fa.*mi*.na aḍ.ḍa.*rū*.rī an *taḥ*.ṣul '*a*.lá ta'.*shī*.rah.
If you're going to visit Lebanon for more than one week, then it's necessary for you to obtain a visa.

Alan: أين يمكن أن أحصل على تأشيرة للبنان؟
ay.na *yum*.kin an *aḥ*.ṣul '*a*.lá *tā*'.*shī*.rah li.lub.*nān*?
Where can I obtain a visa for Lebanon?

Officer: في القنصلية اللبنانية. هي في وسط المدينة.
fī al.qun.ṣu.*liy*.yah al.lub.nā.*niy*.yah. *hi*.ya fī *wa*.saṭ al.ma.*dī*.nah.
At the Lebanese consulate. It's located at the center of the city.

Alan: شكراً لمساعدتك.
shuk.ran li.mu.sā.'*a*.da.tak.
Thank you for your help.

Officer: عفواً.
'*af*.wan.
You're welcome.

WORDS TO KNOW

أحتاج	aḥ.tāj	I need
بلد	ba.lad	country
بلدان	bul.dān	countries
ضروري	ḍa.rū.rī	necessary
حصل	ḥa.ṣa.la	to obtain
أكثر	ak.thar	more than
أقلّ	a.qall	less than
معلومات	ma'.lū.māt	information
مساعدة	mu.sā.'a.dah	help

WHAT'S THE DIFFERENCE BETWEEN AN EMBASSY AND A CONSULATE?

The consulate and the embassy are foreign government outposts located in a host or target country. For example, the United States has both embassies and consulates in many countries around the world. A consulate is generally located in a busy tourist destination, and its officials and employees take care of minor diplomatic tasks, such as issuing visas and sponsoring educational seminars. An embassy is usually located in a nation's capital and has a more policy-oriented approach. It's slightly less bureaucratic than a consulate, and it usually represents its country's official diplomatic stance in the host country.

A consulate is headed by a *consul,* the person in charge of issuing visas and promoting better relations with the people of a host country; in contrast, an embassy is run by an *ambassador* whose general responsibility is to make sure that diplomatic ties — on a government-to-government basis — remain strong and healthy.

If you're in a foreign country and need to ask a quick bureaucratic question (such as, "How can I extend my visa?"), you should head to the consulate. However, if something serious happens (you're put in jail, for instance), then contacting the embassy is more appropriate.

If you're an American citizen traveling abroad, to find answers to any questions you have regarding preparing your وثائق السفر (wa.*thā*.'iq as.*sa*.far) (*travel documents*) prior to your trip, visit the State Department's Bureau of Consular Affairs website at `travel.state.gov`.

Using a Travel Agency

Although you can turn to a number of different sources for information on organizing your trip, few can provide you with the degree of top-notch service and personal attention that a travel agent can provide.

A good travel agent can recommend the most suitable places for your trip and provide you with logistical information and assistance to make your trip a success. A travel agent can provide you with information concerning:

- فنادق (fa.*nā*.diq) (*hotels*)
- وسائل المواصلات (wa.*sā*.'il al.mu.wā.ṣa.*lāt*) (*modes of transportation*)

- طائرات (ṭa.'i.*rāt*) (*airplanes*)
- سيارات (say.yā.*rāt*) (*cars*)
- حافلات (ḥā.fi.*lāt*) (*buses*)
- حجوزات (ḥu.jū.*zāt*) (*reservations*)
- تنزيلات (tan.zī.*lāt*) (*discounts*)
- تنزيلات المجموعات (tan.zī.*lāt* al.maj.mū.*'āt*) (*group discounts*)

For example, the travel agent can tell you about discounts that you're eligible for if you're traveling in a مجموعة (maj.*mū*.'ah) (*group*) or special rates you can obtain on transportation.

Many travel agents provide special rates and packages that include not only airfare but also hotel discounts. Here are some travel packages you should ask about:

- ليلة ويومان (*lay*.lah wa.yaw.*mān*) (*one night and two days*)
- ليلتان وثلاثة أيام (lay.la.*tān* wa.tha.*lā*.thah ay.*yām*) (*two nights and three days*)
- ست ليال وسبعة أيام (*sit* la.*yāl* wa.*sab*.'ah ay.*yām*) (*six nights and seven days*)

When reviewing information from your travel agent, keep a lookout for the following deals:

- بالفندق. (bil.*fun*.duq.) (*Hotel is included.*)
- بزيارة المدينة. (bi.zi.*yā*.rat al.ma.*dī*.nah.) (*Sightseeing around the city is included.*)
- بالفطور والغداء. (bil.fu.*ṭūr* wal.gha.*dā'*.) (*Breakfast and lunch are included.*)
- بالفندق والطيران. (bil.*fun*.duq waṭ.ṭa.ya.*rān*.) (*Hotel and airfare are included.*)

FUN & GAMES

Name the items in Arabic.

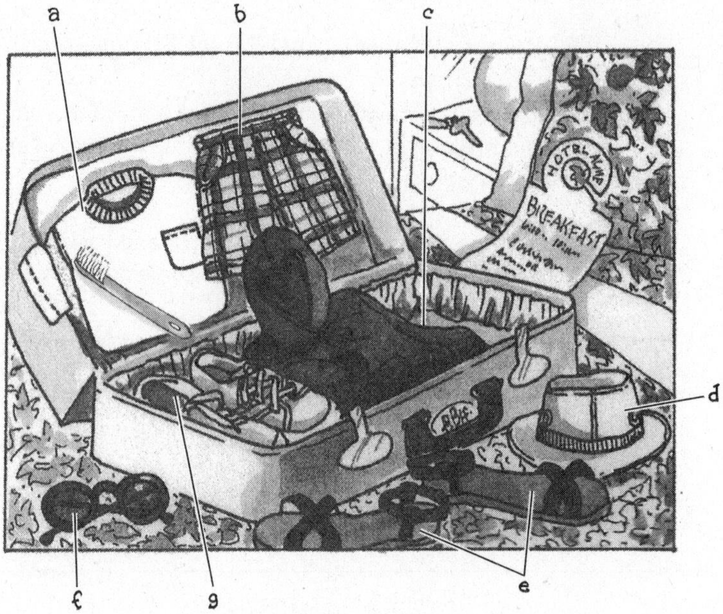

A. ____________________

B. ____________________

C. ____________________

D. ____________________

E. ____________________

F. ____________________

G. ____________________

The answers are in Appendix C.

the bank

» Understanding ATM commands

» Changing your currency

Chapter 15

Dealing with Money in a Foreign Land

Money (المال) (al.*māl)* is an essential part of everyday life. Whether you're in a foreign country or at home, having access to money is necessary in order to do the things you need to do — buy food, buy clothes, pay rent, go to the movies, and so on. Because very few activities in this world are مجاناً (maj.*jā*.nan) (*for free*), in this chapter you discover the Arabic terminology you need to manage your financial life. Specifically, I tell you how to open and maintain a bank account, how to withdraw money from the bank as well as from an automated teller machine (ATM), and how to exchange currency in case you travel to different countries.

REMEMBER

You can listen to all the Talkin' the Talk dialogues featured in this chapter. Go to `www.dummies.com/go/arabicfd` and click on the dialogue you want to hear.

Going to the Bank

The source of money is the مصرف (*maṣ*.raf) (*bank*); conveniently another word for "bank" in Arabic is البنك (al.*bank*) or simply بنك (bank). In this section, you become familiar with some of the items you find and transactions that take place at the bank. Here are some common terms associated with the bank:

- فلوس (fu.*lūs*) (*cash/physical currency*)
- نقود (nu.*qūd*) (*money/coins*)
- عملة ('*um*.lah) (*coin*)
- أوراق مالية (aw.*rāq* mā.*ly*.yah) (*money/banknotes*)
- بطاقة اعتماد (bi.*ṭā*.qat i'.ti.*mād*) (*credit card*)
- بطاقات اعتماد (bi.ṭā.*qāt* i'.ti.*mād*) (*credit cards*)
- بطاقة الاستلاف (bi.*ṭā*.qat al.'is.ti.*lāf*) (*debit card*)
- شيك (shīk) (*check*)
- شيكات (shī.*kāt*) (*checks*)
- حساب مصرفي (ḥi.*sāb maṣ*.ra.fī) (*bank account*)

Opening a bank account

One of the most important things you may do in a bank is to open a حساب مصرفي (ḥi.*sāb* *maṣ*.ra.fī) (*bank account*). Depending on your current financial situation and your future economic needs, you may open different types of حسابات مصرفية (ḥi.sā.*bāt* maṣ.ra.*fiy*.yah) i.sā.bāt (*bank accounts*). Here are some of the types of accounts that you may inquire about:

- حساب مصرفي عادي (ḥi.*sāb*.*maṣ*.ra.fī '*ā*.dī) (*checking account*)
- حساب توفير (ḥi.*sāb* taw.*fīr*) (*savings account*)
- حساب للتوفير والتقاعد (ḥi.*sāb* lil.taw.*fīr* wat.ta.*qā*.'ud) (*retirement savings account*)
- حساب مصرفي للطلاب (ḥi.*sāb* *maṣ*.ra.fī liṭ.ṭul.*lāb*) (*student checking account*)

After you determine which type is right for you, you're ready to talk to the أمين المصرف (a.*mīn* al.*maṣ*.raf) (*bank teller*) (M) or the أمينة المصرف (a.*mī*.nat al.*maṣ*.raf) (*bank teller*) (F) to open your account. The teller may ask you to step into his or her مكتب (*mak*.tab) (*office*) in order to ensure your خصوصية (khu.ṣū.*ṣiy*.yah) (*privacy*), because فتح (fatḥ) (*opening*) an account needs to be done securely.

Talkin' the Talk

Said has recently moved to a new city to attend college. One of the first things he does as he's settling into his new hometown is go to the bank to open an account. Sarah, a bank teller, helps Said decide which bank account meets his needs.

Sarah: صباح الخير. كيف يمكن أن أساعدك اليوم؟
ṣa.*bāḥ* al.*khayr*. *kay*.fa *yum*.kin an u.*sā*.'i.dak al.*yawm?*
Good morning. How may I help you today?

Said: صباح النور, أريد أن أفتح حساباً مصرفياً.
ṣa.*bāḥ* an.*nūr*, u.*rīd* an *af*.taḥ ḥi.*sā*.ban maṣ.ra.*fiy*.yan.
Good morning, I would like to open a bank account.

Sarah: حسناً, يمكن أن أساعدك. تفضل من فضلك إلى مكتبي.
ḥa.sa.nan, *yum*.kin an u.*sā*.'i.dak. ta.*fa*.ḍal min fad.lik *i*.lá *mak*.ta.bī.
Great, I'll be able to help you with that. Please come in to my office.

Said: ممتاز, شكراً.
mum.*tāz*, *shuk*.ran.
Excellent, thank you.

Sarah: أي نوع من الحسابات المصرفية تحبّ؟
ayy naw' min al.ḥi.sā.*bāt* al.maṣ.ra.*fiy*.yah tu.*ḥibb?*
What type of bank account would you like?

Said: ما أنواع الحسابات المصرفية عندكم؟
mā an.*wā'* al.ḥi.sā.*bāt* al.maṣ.ra.*fiy*.yah '*in*.da.kum?
What types of bank accounts do you have?

Sarah: عندنا أنواع مختلفة. عندنا حساب مصرفي عادي وحساب مصرفي للتوفير وحساب مصرفي للطلاب. هل أنت طالب؟
'*in*.da.nā an.*wā'* mukh.*ta*.li.fah. '*in*.da.nā ḥi.*sāb* *maṣ*.ra.fī '*ā*.dī wa.ḥi.*sāb* *maṣ*.ra.fī lil.taw.*fir* wa.ḥi.*sāb* *maṣ*.ra.fī liṭ.ṭul.*lāb*. hal *an*.ta *ṭā*.lib?
We have different types. We have regular checking accounts, savings accounts, and bank accounts for students. Are you a student?

Said: نعم, أنا طالب.
na.'am, *a*.nā *ṭā*.lib.
Yes, I'm a student.

Sarah: أظن أن الحساب المصرفي للطلاب سيناسبك.
a.*ẓunn an*.na al.ḥi.*sāb* al.*maṣ*.ra.fī liṭ.ṭul.*lāb* sa.yu.*nā*.si.buk.
I believe that the student checking account will suit you well.

Said: ما الفرق بين الحساب المصرفي العادي والحساب المصرفي للطلاب؟
mā al.*farq bay*.na al.ḥi.*sāb* al.*maṣ*.ra.fī al.'*ā*.dī wal.ḥi.*sāb* al.*maṣ*.ra.fī liṭ.ṭul.*lāb*?
What's the difference between a regular checking account and a student checking account?

Sarah: إذا أردتَ أن تفتح حساباً مصرفياً عادياً يجب أن يكون عندك ألف درهم في الحساب. ولكن يمكن أن تفتح حساباً مصرفياً للطلاب بإيداع خمس مائة درهم فقط.
i.*dhā* a.*rad*.ta an *taf*.taḥ ḥi.*sā*.ban maṣ.ra.*fiy*.yan '*ā*.di.yan *ya*.jib an ya.*kūn* '*in*.dak alf *dir*.ham fī al.ḥi.*sāb*. wa.*lā*.kin *yum*.kin an *taf*.taḥ ḥi.*sā*.ban maṣ.ra.*fiy*.yan liṭ.ṭul.*lāb* bi.'ī.*dā*' khams *mā*.'at *dir*.ham *fa*.qaṭ.
If you want to open a regular checking account, you need a minimum deposit of one thousand dirhams. However, you may open a student checking account with only five hundred dirhams.

Said: وهل هناك فرق آخر بينهما؟
wa.*hal* hu.*nā*.ka farq *ā*.khar bay.*na*.hu.mā?
And is there any other difference between the two?

Sarah: نعم. الفرق الآخر هو أن الحساب المصرفي العادي له فائدة ثلاثة في المائة ولكن الحساب المصرفي للطلاب له فائدة أربعة في المائة.
na.'am. al.*farq* al.'*ā*.khar *hu*.wa *an*.na al.ḥi.*sāb* al.maṣ.ra.*fī* al.'*ā*.dī *la*.hu *fā*.'i.dah tha.*lā*.thah fīl.*mā*.'ah wa.*lā*.kin al.ḥi.*sāb* al.maṣ.ra.*fī* liṭ.ṭul.*lāb la*.hu *fā*.'i.dah *ar*.ba.'ah fīl.*mā*.'ah.
Yes. The other difference is that the regular checking account yields three percent interest while the student checking account yields four percent interest.

Said: شكراً. أريد أن أفتح حساباً مصرفياً للطلاب.
shuk.ran, u.*rīd* an *af*.taḥ ḥi.*sā*.ban maṣ.ra.*fiy*.yan liṭ.ṭul.*lāb*.
Thank you. I would like to open a student checking account.

WORDS TO KNOW		
يفتح	yaf.taḥ	he opens
مكتب	mak.tab	office
نوع	naw'	type
أنواع	an.wā'	types
يناسب	yu.nā.sib	to suit (be suitable)
فرق	farq	difference
إيداع	ī.dā'	deposit
فقط	fa.qaṭ	only
آخر	ā.khar	other
فائدة	fā.'i.dah	interest rate
في المائة	fīl.mā.'ah	percentage

Presenting your ID

After you decide which account is right for you, you need to take care of some initial paperwork. You must present a number of وثائق (wa.*thā*.'iq) (*documents*) and then answer a few أسئلة (*as*.'i.lah) (*questions*). Here are some of the documents you should have with you when you want to open an account:

- البطاقة الشخصية (al.bi.*ṭā*.qah ash.shakh.*ṣiy*.yah) (*personal identification card*)
- رخصة القيادة (*rukh*.ṣat al.qi.*yā*.dah) (*driver's license*)
- جواز السفر (jaw.*wāz* as.*sa*.far) (*passport*)
- بطاقة تعريف الطالب (bi.*ṭā*.qat ta'.*rīf* aṭ.*ṭā*.lib) (*student identification card*)
- بطاقة الأمن الاجتماعي (bi.*ṭā*.qat al.'*amn* al.'ij.ti.*mā*.'ī) (*social security card*)

Providing your contact info

After you establish your identity by presenting various personal identification cards, the bank teller will probably ask you for some more documents, so that he or she can process your application. For example, he may ask for your

العنوان الحالي (al.'un.*wān* al.*ḥā*.lī) (*current address*) or your العنوان السابق (al.'un.*wān* as.*sā*.biq) (*former address*). Of course, in order to prove that you actually do live where you say you live, the teller may ask you for a رسالة (ri.*sā*.lah) (*letter*) addressed to you at your current address.

Filling out the forms

After you provide the documents that the teller requests, you usually receive an استمارة الطلب (is.ti.*mā*.rat aṭ.*ṭa*.lab) (*application form*) to fill out. Here are some items you're likely to find on this application form:

- الاسم الأول (al.*'ism* al.*'aw*.wal) (*first name*)
- لقب العائلة (*la*.qab al.*'ā*.'i.lah) (*last name/family name*)
- تاريخ الميلاد (*tā*.rīkh al.*mī*.lād) (*date of birth*)
- مكان الميلاد (ma.*kān* al.*mī*.lād) (*place of birth*)
- المهنة (al.*mih*.nah) (*occupation*)
- مكان العمل (ma.*kān* al.*'a*.mal) (*employer*)
- السيرة المهنية (as.*sī*.rah al.mi.ha.*niy*.yah) (*work history*)
- نوع الحساب (naw' al.ḥi.*sāb*) (*type of account*)
- رقم الهاتف (raqm al.*hā*.tif) (*telephone number*)

After you fill out the application form, the teller will ask for your إمضاء (im.*ḍā'*) (*signature*) on the document. When you finish with all the paperwork and have successfully opened your bank account, you're ready to start using it!

Talkin' the Talk

Jennifer is filling out a new bank account application. Adam, the bank manager, helps her with the application form.

Adam: ما أسمكِ الأول؟
mā is.mu.ki al.*'aw*.wal?
What's your first name?

Jennifer: جينيفر.
Jennifer.
Jennifer.

Adam: وما لقب العائلة؟
wa.*mā la*.qab al.'ā.'i.lah?
And what's your last name?

Jennifer: جونز.
Jones.
Jones.

Adam: ما تاريخ ميلادك؟
mā tā.*rī*.kh mī.*lā*.du.ki?
What's your date of birth?

Jennifer: الأول من يناير سنة ألف وتسع مائة وثمانين.
al.'*aw*.wal min ya.*nā*.yir *sa*.nat alf wa.tis' *mā*.'ah wa.tha.mā.*nīn*.
January 1, 1980.

Adam: ما مهنتكِ؟
mā mih.*na*.tu.ki?
What's your occupation?

Jennifer: أنا ممرضة.
a.nā mu.*mar*.ri.ḍah.
I'm a nurse.

Adam: وأين تعملين؟
wa.'*ay*.na ta'.ma.*līn?*
And where do you work?

Jennifer: أنا أعمل في المستشفى.
a.nā *a*'.mal fīl.mus.*tash*.fá.
I work at the hospital.

Adam: شكراً. نحن اقتربنا من النهاية.
shuk.ran. *naḥ*.nu iq.ta.rab.*nā* min an.ni.*hā*.yah.
Thank you. We're almost finished.

Jennifer: رائع.
rā.'i'.
Great.

Adam: أريد إمضاءكِ هنا.
u.*rīd* im.*ḍā*.'a.ki *hu*.nā.
I'd like your signature right here.

Jennifer: طبعاً.
ṭa.ba.'an.
Of course.

Adam: شكراً. مرحباً بك في مصرف العرب.
shuk.ran. *mar*.ḥa.ban *bi*.ki fī *maṣ*.rif al.'*a*.rab.
Thank you. Welcome to Arab Bank.

Jennifer: شكراً.
shuk.ran.
Thank you.

WORDS TO KNOW

ما هو	mā hu.wa	what is
ما	mā	what
مدير المصرف	mu.dīr al.maṣ.raf	bank manager (M)
مديرة المصرف	mu.dī.rat al.maṣ.raf	bank manager (F)
يوم	yawm	day
شهر	shahr	month
سنة	*sa*.nah	year
ممرضة	mu.mar.riḍ.ah	nurse (F)
مستشفى	mus.tash.fá	hospital
نهاية	ni.hā.yah	finish/ending
الاعتماد	al.'i'.ti.mād	credit

Open season on the verb "to open"

You can't open an account, or anything else for that matter, if you don't know how to conjugate the verb فتح (*fa*.ta.ḥa) (*opened*) in both past and present tenses. Here is the verb "to open" in the past tense:

Form	Pronunciation	English
أنا فتحتُ	*a*.nā fa.*taḥ*.tu	I opened
أنتَ فتحتَ	*an*.ta fa.*taḥ*.ta	You opened (MS)
أنتِ فتحتِ	*an*.ti fa.*taḥ*.ti	You opened (FS)
هو فتحَ	*hu*.wa *fa*.ta.ḥa	He opened
هي فتحتْ	*hi*.ya *fa*.ta.ḥat	She opened
نحن فتحنا	*naḥ*.nu fa.*taḥ*.nā	We opened
أنتم فتحتم	*an*.tum fa.*taḥ*.tum	You opened (MP)
أنتنّ فتحتنّ	an.*tun*.na fa.taḥ.*tun*.na	You opened (FP)
هم فتحوا	*hum* *fa*.ta.ḥū	They opened (MP)
هنّ فتحنّ	*hun*.na fa.*taḥ*.na	They opened (FP)
أنتما فتحتما	an.*tu*.mā fa.taḥ.*tu*.mā	You opened (dual/M/F)
هما فتحا	*hu*.mā *fa*.ta.ḥa	They opened (dual/M)
هما فتحتا	*hu*.mā fa.ta.*ḥa*.tā	They opened (dual/F)

To conjugate this verb in the present tense, you use the يفتح (*yaf*.taḥ):

Form	Pronunciation	English
أنا أفتح	*a*.nā *af*.taḥ	I am opening
أنتَ تفتح	*an*.ta *taf*.taḥ	You are opening (MS)
أنتِ تفتحين	*an*.ti taf.ta.*ḥīn*	You are opening (FS)
هو يفتح	*hu*.wa *yaf*.taḥ	He is opening
هي تفتح	*hi*.ya *taf*.taḥ	She is opening
نحن نفتح	*naḥ*.nu *naf*.taḥ	We are opening
أنتم تفتحون	*an*.tum taf.ta.*ḥūn*	You are opening (MP)
أنتنّ تفتحنّ	an.*tun*.na taf.*taḥ*.na	You are opening (FP)

Form	Pronunciation	English
هم يفتحون	*hum* yaf.ta.*ḥūn*	They are opening (MP)
هنّ يفتحن	*hun*.na yaf.*taḥ*.na	They are opening (FP)
أنتما تفتحان	an.*tu*.mā taf.ta.*ḥān*	You are opening (dual/M/F)
هما يفتحان	*hu*.mā yaf.ta.*ḥān*	They are opening (dual/M)
هما تفتحان	*hu*.mā taf.ta.*ḥān*	They are opening (dual/F)

Making deposits and withdrawals

After you open your account, the two most basic transactions you'll probably make are

- إيداع (ī.*dā'*) (*deposit*)
- سحب (saḥb) (*withdrawal*)

To make a deposit, you may deposit into your account by using a شيك (shīk) (*check*) or فلوس (fi.*lūs*) (*cash*). You may go to the bank teller to make the deposit or do it yourself at an ATM, if your bank allows that. Similarly, you may perform a withdrawal by either going to the teller or by using the ATM.

Using the ATM

In recent years, the number of ATMs located around the world has mushroomed, and in places like New York City, you can't walk half a block without spotting one. Whether you're in the United States, the Middle East, or other countries or regions of the world, there's a good chance that you'll use an ATM to withdraw money. This section covers the terminology you encounter at an ATM to help make this a smooth and efficient transaction.

Most ATMs accept all sorts of cards, whether they're issued by the same bank that operates the ATM terminal or not. However, some ATMs charge you a رسم (rasm) (*fee*). In addition, most ATMs accept both credit cards and debit cards.

Although most ATMs let you choose the language you want to conduct your transaction in, you should still be aware of ATM-related commands and phrases in Arabic:

- أدخل البطاقة. (*ad*.khil al.bi.*ṭā*.qah.) (*Insert the card.*)
- أدخل الرقم السري. (*ad*.khil ar.*ra*.qam as.*sir*.rī.) (*Enter the PIN/secret number.*)
- سحب. (saḥb) (*cash withdrawal*)
- أدخل المبلغ. (*ad*.khil al.*mab*.lagh.) (*Enter the amount.*)
- تأكد من المبلغ. (ta.*'ak*.kad min al.*mab*.lagh.) (*Confirm the amount.*)
- اسحب المبلغ. (*is*.ḥab al.*mab*.lagh.) (*Take the cash.*)
- هل تريد إيصالا؟ (*hal* tu.*rīd* ī.*ṣā*.lan?) (*Do you want a receipt?*)
- خذ الإيصال. (*khudh* al.'ī.*ṣāl*.) (*Take the receipt.*)
- تحقق من الرصيد. (ta.*ḥaq*.qaq min ar.ra.*ṣīd*.) (*Check the balance.*)
- حول الأموال. (*ḥaw*.wil al.'am.*wāl*.) (*Transfer the money.*)
- اسحب البطاقة من فضلك. (*is*.ḥab al.bi.*ṭā*.qah min *faḍ*.lik.) (*Please remove the card.*)

Exchanging Currency

If you're traveling to a foreign دولة (*daw*.lah) (*country*), you won't get very far if you don't have the right عملة (*'um*.lah) (*currency*). Of course, you can rely on الشيكات السياحية (ash.shī.*kāt* as.si.yā.*ḥiy*.yah) (*traveler's checks*), but you may find that carrying currency is more convenient. You can exchange currency at a number of different places. If you like to plan in advance, then stopping by the bank before your سفر (*sa*.far) (*trip*) is a good idea. Otherwise, you can go to a مكتب الصرف (*mak*.tab aṣ.*ṣarf*) (*exchange desk*) located at the مطار (ma.*ṭār*) (*airport*).

TIP

You're likely to get better exchange rates in your home country at your local bank than at an airport in a foreign country. If you're visiting a foreign country and need to change money, then the best way for you to exchange currencies is to go to a reputable bank of international renown and make your transactions there.

Getting to know the currencies around the world

In order to exchange your money, you need to be familiar with the different types of currencies you're dealing with. The following lists feature some of the most common currencies grouped by specific regions around the world.

The following currencies are used in the Middle East:

- Algeria: الدينار الجزائري (ad.dī.*nār* al.ja.*zā*.'ir.ī) (*Algerian dinar*)
- Bahrain: الدينار البحريني (ad.dī.*nār* al.baḥ.*ray*.nī) (*Bahraini dinar*)
- Egypt: الجنيه المصري (al.ju.*nayh* al.*miṣ*.rī) (*Egyptian pound*)
- Iraq: الدينار العراقي (ad.dī.*nār* al.'i.*rā*.qī) (*Iraqi dinar*)
- Jordan: الدينار الأردني (ad.dī.*nār* al.'*ur*.du.nī) (*Jordanian dinar*)
- Kuwait: الدينار الكويتي (ad.dī.*nār* al.ku.*way*.tī) (*Kuwaiti dinar*)
- Lebanon: الليرة اللبنانية (al.*lī*.rah al.lub.nā.*niy*.yah) (*Lebanese lira*)
- Libya: الدينار الليبي (ad.dī.*nār* al.*lī*.bī) (*Libyan dinar*)
- Morocco: الدرهم المغربي (ad.*dir*.ham al.*magh*.ri.bī) (*Moroccan dirham*)
- Oman: الريال العماني (ar.ri.*yāl* al.'u.*mā*.nī) (*Omani riyal*)
- Qatar: الريال القطري (ar.ri.*yāl* al.*qa*.ṭa.rī) (*Qatari riyal*)
- Saudi Arabia: الريال السعودي (ar.ri.*yāl* as.sa.'*ū*.dī) (*Saudi riyal*)
- Syria: الليرة السورية (al.*lī*.rah as.sū.*riy*.yah) (*Syrian lira*)
- Tunisia: الدينار التونسي (ad.dī.*nār* at.*tū*.ni.sī) (*Tunisian dinar*)
- United Arab Emirates (UAE): الدرهم الإماراتي (ad.*dir*.ham al.'i.mā.*rā*.tī) (*Emirate dirham*)
- Yemen: الريال اليمني (ar.ri.*yāl* al.*ya*.ma.nī) (*Yemeni riyal*)

In North America, you find the following currencies:

- Canada: الدولار الكندي (ad.dū.*lār* al.*ka*.na.dī) (*Canadian dollar*)
- Mexico: البيسو المكسيكي (al.*bī*.sū al.mik.*sī*.kī) (*Mexican peso*)
- United States: الدولار الأمريكي (ad.dū.*lār* al.'am.*rī*.kī) (*American dollar*)

Only two currencies are used in Europe:

- European Union (EU): اليورو (al.*yū*.rū) (*Euro*)
- United Kingdom: **الجنيه** الإسترليني (al.ju.*nayh* al.'is.tir.*lī*.nī) (*British pound*)

The following currencies are used in Asia and Australia:

- Australia: الدولار الأسترالي (ad.dū.*lār* al.'us.tu.*rā*.lī) (*Australian dollar*)
- China: اليوان الصيني (al.yū.*wān* aṣ.*ṣī*.nī) (*Chinese yuan*)
- Japan: الين الياباني (al.*yin* al.yā.*bā*.nī) (*Japanese yen*)
- South Korea: الون الكوري (al.*wun* al.*kū*.rī) (*Korean won*)

Making exchanges

Knowing the names of the currencies is only the first step toward exchanging the currency you hold into the one you need. The following list of questions can help you facilitate this exchange at the bank:

- أين مكتب الصرف؟ (*ay*.na *mak*.tab aṣ.*ṣarf*?) (*Where is the exchange desk?*)
- هل مكتب الصرف قريب من هنا؟ (hal *mak*.tab aṣ.*ṣarf* qa.*rīb* min *hu*.nā?) (*Is the exchange desk close to here?*)
- متى يفتح مكتب الصرف؟ (*ma*.tá *yaf*.taḥ *mak*.tab aṣ.*ṣarf*?) (*When does the exchange desk open?*)
- ما هي أسعار العملة اليوم؟ (mā *hi*.ya. as.'*ār* al.'*um*.lah al.*yawm*?) (*What is today's exchange rate?*)
- هل سيكون سعرالعملة أحسن غداً؟ (hal sa.ya.*kūn* si'r al.'*um*.lah *aḥ*.san *gha*.dan?) (*Will the exchange rate be better tomorrow?*)
- هل هناك رسوم لصرف العملة؟ (hal hu.*nā*.ka ru.*sūm* li.*ṣarf* al.'*um*.lah?) (*Is there a fee for exchanging money?*)
- أريد أن أحول دولارات إلى دراهم. (u.*rīd* an u.*ḥaw*.wil dū.lā.*rāt* *i*.lá da.*rā*.him.) (*I would like to exchange dollars into dirhams.*)
- كم من دينار لمائة دولار؟ (*kam* dī.*nār* li.*mā*.'at *dū*.lār?) (*How many dinars for one hundred dollars?*)

Here are some answers you may hear from the أمين مكتب الصرافة (a.*mīn mak*.tab aṣ.ṣi.*rā*.fah) (*exchange desk representative*):

- مكتب الصرافة يفتح الساعة الثامنة صباحاً. (*mak*.tab aṣ.ṣi.*rā*.fah *yaf*.taḥ as.*sā*.'ah ath.*thā*.mi.nah ṣa.*bā*.ḥan.) (*The exchange desk opens at eight o'clock in the morning.*)
- نعم، نحول دولارات إلى دراهم. (*na*.'am nu.*ḥaw*.wil dū.lā.*rāt i*.lá da.*rā*.him.) (*Yes, we exchange dollars into dirhams.*)
- سعر العملة اليوم مثل سعر العملة أمس. (si'r al.*'um*.lah al.*yawm* mithl si'r al.*'um*.lah ams.) (*Today's exchange rate is the same as yesterday's exchange rate.*)
- نحن نقبل دولارات فقط. (*naḥ*.nu *naq*.bal du.lā.*rāt fa*.qaṭ.) (*We only accept dollars.*)
- نحن نقبل نقوداً فقط. (*naḥ*.nu *naq*.bal nu.*qū*.dan *fa*.qaṭ.) (*We only accept cash.*)
- مائة دولار تساوي ألف ريال. (*mā*.'at *dū*.lār tu.*sā*.wī alf ri.*yāl*.) (*One hundred dollars equals one thousand riyals.*)
- هناك رسم عشرة دولارات لكل تحويل. (hu.*nā*.ka rasm *'ash*.rat dū.lā.*rāt* li.*kul* taḥ.*wīl*.) (*There is a ten dollar fee for every transaction.*)
- مكتب الصرافة داخل المصرف. (*mak*.tab aṣ.ṣi.*rā*.fah *dā*.khil al.*maṣ*.raf.) (*The exchange desk is inside the bank.*)

Talkin' the Talk

Sam stops by a currency exchange desk to exchange dollars into dirhams. The exchange desk teller helps him with this transaction.

Sam: هل يمكن أن تحول دولارات إلى دراهم؟
hal *yum*.kin an tu.*ḥaw*.wil dū.lā.*rāt i*.lá da.*rā*.him?
Is it possible for you to exchange dollars into dirhams?

Teller: طبعاً.
ṭa.ba.'an.
Of course.

Sam: حسناً. أريد أن أحول ألف دولار إلى دراهم.
ḥa.sa.nan. u.*rīd* an u.*ḥaw*.wil alf dū.*lār i*.lá da.*rā*.him.
Good. I would like to exchange one thousand dollars into dirhams.

Teller: رائع. يمكن أن أساعدك.
rā.'i'. *yum*.kin an u.sā.*'i*.dak.
Great. I'll be able to help you with that.

Sam: أولًا, هل يمكن أن تقول لي ما سعر العملة اليوم؟
aw.wa.lan, hal *yum*.kin an ta.*qūl* lī ma si'r al.*'um*.lah al.*yawm?*
First, can you tell me today's exchange rate?

Teller: سعر العملة اليوم دولار لكل عشرة دراهم.
si'r al.*'um*.lah al.yawm dū.*lār* li.*kul* *'ash*.rat da.*rā*.him.
Today's exchange rate is one dollar equals ten dirhams.

Sam: إذن ألف دولار تساوي عشرة آلاف درهم؟
i.*dhan* alf dū.*lār* tu.*sā*.wī *'ash*.rat ā.*lāf* *dir*.ham?
Therefore one thousand dollars equals ten thousand dirhams?

Teller: صحيح.
ṣa.*ḥīḥ*.
That's correct.

Sam: حسناً. حول لي من فضلك ألف دولار إلى عشرة آلاف درهم.
ḥa.sa.nan *ḥaw*.wil lī min *faḍ*.lik alf dū.*lār* *i*.lá *'ash*.rat ā.*lāf* *dir*.ham.
Good. Please exchange one thousand dollars into ten thousand dirhams.

Teller: فوراً.
faw.ran.
Right away.

WORDS TO KNOW

تحول	tu.ḥaw.wil	you exchange (M)
تحولين	tu.ḥaw.wi.līn	you exchange (F)
ألف	alf	thousand
يساوي	yu.sā.wī	equals (M)
تساوي	tu.sā.wī	equals (F)
صحيح	ṣa.ḥīḥ	correct

FUN & GAMES

Match the Arabic statements and questions you would use or hear at a bank with their English equivalents.

1. أي نوع من الحسابات المصرفية تحبّ؟
2. أريد أن أفتح حساباً مصرفياً للطلاب.
3. أريد إمضاءك هنا.
4. ما الفرق بين الحساب المصرفي العادي والحساب المصرفي للطلاب؟
5. رائع. يمكن أن أساعدك.

A. I would like to open a student checking account.

B. Great. I'll be able to help you with that.

C. What type of bank account would you like?

D. I'd like your signature right here.

E. What's the difference between a regular checking account and a student checking account?

» Catching taxis, buses, and trains

Chapter 16

Getting Around: Planes, Trains, and Automobiles

When it comes to getting around the block, the city, or the world, you have a lot of different modes of نقل (naql) (*transportation*) to choose from. And making the right choice for you is extremely important, particularly if you're traveling in a foreign country. Modes of transportation differ from region to region and country to country, so being aware of subtle differences between the transportation methods you're used to and those you discover when you're traveling abroad is essential.

In this chapter, I tell you, in Arabic, not only how to use all major transportation methods but also how to navigate a Middle Eastern city using these modes of transport.

REMEMBER

You can listen to all the Talkin' the Talk dialogues featured in this chapter. Go to `www.dummies.com/go/arabicfd` and click on the dialogue you want to hear.

Traveling by Plane

One of the most common methods of transportation is flying in a طائرة (*ṭā.*'i.rah) (*airplane*). The airplane is probably the best method of transportation to help you get to a distant location in the least amount of time. Chances are if you want to go to a different country, you'll take an airplane. The following sections focus on how to make your plane travels a bit smoother with helpful Arabic vocabulary.

Making reservations

The first step in air travel is making a حجز (ḥajz) (*reservation*) and buying a تذكرة السفر (*tadh*.ki.rat as.*sa*.far) (*plane ticket*). You may purchase your ticket the traditional way, by simply visiting your وكيل أسفار (wa.*kīl* as.*fār*) (*travel agent*). However, in this technological age, more and more people choose to bypass the travel agent in favor of online travel agents. Even though you get more personalized service from an in-person travel agent, you can probably get better deals by ordering your plane tickets online. If you're not sure where you want to go, the travel agent may be able to suggest destinations to suit your specific traveling needs. But if you know exactly where you want to go, using an online travel agent is probably more appropriate.

TIP

One of the potential pitfalls of going through online travel agents — particularly if you use a specialized broker that focuses on specific global destinations, such as the Middle East — is making sure that the online site is reputable. In order to not get fooled, I recommend you use one of the more established online travel agents.

Talkin' the Talk

Sophia calls her travel agent, Ahmed, to make an airline reservation.

Sophia: أهلًا وسهلًا أحمد. أنا صوفيا.
ah.lan wa.*sah*.lan *aḥ*.mad. *a*.nā *ṣūf*.yā.
Hi, Ahmed. This is Sophia.

Ahmed: أهلًا صوفيا. كيف يمكن أن أساعدك؟
ah.lan *ṣūf*.yā. *kay*.fa *yum*.kin an u.*sā*.'i.dik?
Hi, Sophia. How may I help you?

Sophia: أريد أن أذهب إلى الدار البيضاء مع أمي للعطلة.
u.*rīd* an *adh*.hab *i*.lá ad.*dār* al.bay.*ḍā'* *ma*.'a *um*.mī lil.'*uṭ*.lah.
I would like to go to Casablanca for the holidays with my mother.

Ahmed: رائع! هذه فكرة ممتازة. ومتى تريدان أن تذهبا؟
rā.'i'! *hā*.dhi.hi *fik*.rah mum.*tā*.zah. wa.*ma*.tá tu.rī.*dān* an *tadh*.ha.*bā*?
Excellent! That's a great idea. And when would you like to go?

Sophia: نريد أن نذهب يوم السبت.
nu.*rīd* an *nadh*.hab yawm as.*sabt*.
We would like to go on Saturday.

Ahmed: ممتاز. في أي ساعة؟
mum.*tāz*. fī ayy *sā*.'ah?
Excellent. At what time?

Sophia: هل هناك طيران الساعة الخامسة؟
hal hu.*nā*.ka ṭay.*rān* as.*sā*.'ah al.*khā*.mi.sah?
Are there any flights at 5:00?

Ahmed: نعم.
na.'am.
Yes.

Sophia: حسناً. سنأخذ تذكرتين من فضلك.
ḥa.sa.nan sa.*na'*.khudh tadh.ki.ra.*tayn* min *faḍ*.lik.
Good. We'll take two tickets, please.

Ahmed: هل تريدان مقاعد بجوار النافذة أو بجوار الممر؟
hal tu.rī.*dān* ma.*qā*.'id bi.ji.*wār* an.*nā*.fi.dhah aw bi.ji.*wār* al.ma.*mar*?
Would you like window or aisle seats?

Sophia: مقاعد بجوار النافذة من فضلك.
ma.*qā*.'id bi.ji.*wār* an.*nā*.fi.dhah min *faḍ*.lik.
Window seats, please.

Ahmed: عندي تذكرتان لمقعدين بجوار النافذة لراكبتين لدار البيضاء يوم السبت الساعة الخامسة.
'*in*.dī tadh.ki.ra.*tān* li.miq.'a.*dayn* bi.ji.*wār* an.*nā*.fi.dhah li.*rā*.ki.ba.tayn li.*dār* al.bay.*ḍā'* yawm as.*sabt* as.*sā*.'ah al.*khā*.mi.sah.
I have two tickets for window seats for two passengers to Casablanca on Saturday at 5:00.

Sophia: ممتاز!

mum.*tāz*!

Excellent!

Ahmed: رحلة سعيدة!

riḥ.lah sa.*'ī*.dah!

Have a nice trip!

Sophia: شكراً!

shuk.ran!

Thank you!

WORDS TO KNOW

عطلة	'uṭ.lah	holiday/vacation
تذكرة	tadh.ki.rah	ticket
تذكرتين	tadh.ki.ra.tayn	two tickets
تذاكر	ta.dhā.kir	tickets (three or more)
مقعد	miq.'ad	seat
مقعدين	miq.'a.dayn	seats (two)
مقاعد	ma.qā.'id	seats (three or more)
ممر	ma.mar	aisle
نافذة	nā.fi.dhah	window
رحلة	riḥ.lah	flight
سفر	sa.far	traveling
مسافر	mu.sā.fir	traveler (M)
مسافرة	mu.sā.fi.rah	traveler (F)
مسافرون	mu.sā.fi.rūn	travelers (M)
مسافرات	mu.sā.fi.rāt	travelers (F)

Getting some legwork out of the verb "to travel"

GRAMMATICALLY SPEAKING

If there's one verb you need to be familiar with relating to travel, it's the verb سافر (*sā*.fa.ra), which conveniently means "to travel." Even though this verb has four consonants instead of the usual three, it's nevertheless considered to be a regular verb because the fourth consonant, the ألف (alif), is actually a consonant that acts as a long vowel elongating the سين (siin). (For more on regular verbs, flip to Chapter 2.) So سافر is conjugated in the past tense and the present tense the same way as most other regular verbs. Here is the verb سافر in the past tense form:

Form	Pronunciation	English
أنا سافرتُ	*a*.nā sā.*far*.tu	I traveled
أنتَ سافرتَ	*an*.ta sā.*far*.ta	You traveled (MS)
أنتِ سافرتِ	*an*.ti sā.*far*.ti	You traveled (FS)
هو سافر	*hu*.wa *sā*.fa.ra	He traveled
هي سافرتْ	*hi*.ya *sā*.fa.rat	She traveled
نحن سافرنا	*naḥ*.nu sā.*far*.nā	We traveled
أنتم سافرتم	*an*.tum sā.*far*.tum	You traveled (MP)
أنتنّ سافرتنّ	an.*tun*.na sā.far.*tun*.na	You traveled (FP)
هم سافروا	hum *sā*.fa.rū	They traveled (MP)
هنّ سافرنّ	*hun*.na sā.*far*.na	They traveled (FP)
أنتما سافرتما	an.*tu*.mā sā.far.*tu*.mā	You traveled (dual/M/F)
هما سافرا	*hu*.mā sā.fa.*rā*	They traveled (dual/M)
هما سافرتا	*hu*.mā sā.fa.ra.*tā*	They traveled (dual/F)

Use the form يسافر (*yu*.sā.fir) to conjugate "traveling" in the present tense:

Form	Pronunciation	English
أنا أسافر	*a*.nā u.*sā*.fir	I am traveling
أنتَ تسافر	*an*.ta tu.*sā*.fir	You are traveling (MS)
أنتِ تسافرين	*an*.ti tu.sā.fi.*rīn*	You are traveling (FS)
هي يسافر	*hu*.wa yu.*sā*.fir	He is traveling
هي تسافر	*hi*.ya tu.*sā*.fir	She is traveling
نحن نسافر	*naḥ*.nu nu.*sā*.fir	We are traveling
أنتم تسافرون	*an*.tum tu.sā.fi.*rūn*	You are traveling (MP)
أنتنّ تسافرنّ	an.*tun*.na tu.sā.*fir*.na	You are traveling (FP)
هم يسافرون	hum yu.sā.fi.*rūn*	They are traveling (MP)
هنّ يسافرنّ	*hun*.na yu.sā.*fir*.na	They are traveling (FP)
أنتما تسافران	an.*tu*.mā tu.sā.fi.*rān*	You are traveling (dual/M/F)
هما يسافران	*hu*.mā yu.sā.fi.*rān*	They are traveling (dual/M)
هما تسافران	*hu*.mā tu.sā.fi.*rān*	They are traveling (dual/F)

Registering at the airport

With a plane ticket, you're ready to head off to the مطار (ma.*ṭār*) (*airport*) and board the airplane. But before you actually get on the plane, you need to take care of a few logistical things. First, you must present your جواز السفر (jaw.*wāz* as.*sa*.far) (*passport*) and your ticket at the airport تسجيل (tas.*jīl*) (*registration*) desk, which is located in the صالة المطار (*ṣā*.lat al.ma.*ṭār*) (*airport terminal*). Second, you must also answer some أسئلة (*as*.'i.lah) (*questions*) about your trip and your أمتعة (*am*.ti.'ah) (*luggage*).

REMEMBER

Unlike in English and other Romance languages, the Arabic language contains two forms of plural: the plural form for two things and the plural form for three or more things. Arabic uses these two distinct plural forms to distinguish between a pair of things, and three or more things.

Talkin' the Talk

At the airport, Zayneb is registering her luggage.

Attendant: كم عدد الأمتعة التي معك؟
kam '*a*.dad al.'*am*.ti.'ah al.*la*.tī *ma*.'ik?
How many pieces of luggage do you have?

Zayneb: معي ثلاثة: حقيبتان ومحفظة واحدة.
ma.'ī tha.*lā*.thah: ḥa.qī.ba.*tān* wa.*maḥ*.fa.ẓah *wā*.ḥi.dah.
I have three: two suitcases and a briefcase.

Attendant: كم عدد الأمتعة التي ستسجلينها؟
kam '*a*.dad al.'*am*.ti.'ah al.*la*.tī sa.tu.saj.ji.*lī*.na.hā?
How many pieces of luggage are you going to check?

Zayneb: سأسجل الحقيبتين وسآخذ المحفظة معي في الطائرة.
sa.'u.*saj*.jil al.ḥa.*qī*.ba.tayn wa.sa.'*ā*.khudh al.*maḥ*.fa.dhah *ma*.'ī fī aṭ.*ṭā*.'i.rah.
I'm going to register the two suitcases, and I will take the briefcase with me on the plane.

Attendant: ممتاز. هل ملأت الأمتعة بنفسك؟
mum.*tāz* hal ma.*la*'.ti al.'*am*.ti.'ah bi.*naf*.sik?
Okay. Did you pack your bags by yourself?

Zayneb: نعم.
na.'am.
Yes.

Attendant: لم يملأ شخص آخر الأمتعة؟
lam *yam*.la' shakhṣ *ā*.khar al.'*am*.ti.'ah?
No one else packed the bags?

Zayneb: لا. ملأتها بنفسي.
lā. ma.*la*'.tu.hā bi.*naf*.sī.
No. By myself.

Attendant: هل كل شيء في الأمتعة ملكك؟
hal kul shay' fī al.'*am*.ti.'ah *mil*.kik?
Is everything in the bags yours?

Zayneb: نعم.
na.'am.
Yes.

Attendant: هل كانت الأمتعة معك طوال الوقت؟
hal *kā*.nat al.'*am*.ti.'ah *ma.*'a.ki ṭu.*wāl* al.*waqt?*
Have you had the bags in your possession at all times?

Zayneb: نعم.
na.'am.
Yes.

Attendant: شكراً. رحلة سعيدة.
shuk.ran. *riḥ*.lah sa.'*ī*.dah.
Thank you. Have a nice flight.

Zayneb: شكراً.
shuk.ran.
Thank you.

WORDS TO KNOW

أمتعة	am.ti.'ah	luggage
حقيبة	ḥa.qī.bah	suitcase
حقيبتين	ha.qī.ba.tayn	two suitcases
حقائب	ha.qā.'ib	suitcases (three or more)
محفظة	maḥ.fa.ẓah	briefcase
محفظتين	maḥ.fa.ẓah.tayn	two briefcases
محافظ	ma.ḥā.fiẓ	briefcases (three or more)
يسجل	yu.saj.jil	to register
معي	ma.'ī	with me
ملأ	ma.la.'a	to fill/pack
شخص	shakhṣ	individual

آخر	<u>ā</u>.khar	other
بنفسي	bi.<u>naf</u>.sī	by myself
تأشيرة	ta'.<u>shī</u>.rah	visa
بوابة	baw.<u>wā</u>.bah	gate

Boarding the plane

So you're ready to board the airplane. After you check your luggage and present your boarding pass and your passport to the airline attendant, be sure to follow all تعليمات (ta'.lī.*māt*) (*instructions*) very carefully. Stay in the صف (ṣaf) (*line*) with your fellow ركاب (ruk.*kāb*) (*passengers*), and follow any requests made by airport officials.

When you reach the بوابة (baw.*wā*.bah) (*gate*) and board the plane, present your boarding pass to the مضيف الطائرة (mu.*ḍīf* aṭ.*ṭā*.'i.rah) (*flight attendant*), who will point you to your مقعد (*miq*.'ad) (*seat*). The following terms are related to the plane and your flight:

- راكب (*rā*.kib) (*passenger*)
- ركاب (ruk.*kāb*) (*passengers*)
- مضيف (mu.*ḍīf*) (*attendant*) (M)
- مضيفة (mu.*ḍī*.fah) (*attendant*) (F)
- طيار (ṭay.*yār*) (*pilot*) (M)
- طيارة (ṭay.*yā*.rah) (*pilot*) (F)
- غرفة القيادة (*ghur*.fat al.qi.*yā*.dah) (*cockpit*)
- حمام (ḥam.*mām*) (*bathroom*)
- الحمام مشغول (al.ḥam.*mām* mash.*ghūl*) (*bathroom occupied*)
- الدرجة الأولى (ad.*da*.ra.jah al.'*ū*.lá) (*first class*)
- درجة رجال الأعمال (*da*.ra.jat ri.*jāl* al.'a'.*māl*) (*business class*)
- الدرجة الاقتصادية (ad.*da*.ra.jah al.iq.ti.ṣā.*diy*.yah) (*economy class*)
- سرعة (*sur*.'ah) (*speed*)

» ارتفاع (ir.ti.*fā'*) (*altitude*)

» انطلاق (in.ṭi.*lāq*) (*take off*)

» وصول (wu.*ṣūl*) (*arrival*)

A brief departure on the verb "to arrive"

GRAMMATICALLY SPEAKING

A helpful verb to know when you're traveling is وصل (*wa*.ṣa.la) (*to arrive*). (You can also use the verb وصل to express "to arrive," "to land," or "to come.") Even though وصل has three consonants and therefore should fall into the mold of regular verb forms, it's nevertheless classified as an irregular verb. It's irregular because it includes the consonant واو (wāw); verbs with واو are classified as irregular because their present forms are radically different from the regular present verb forms. As a result, whereas the past form of the verb "arrive" follows a regular pattern, the present doesn't.

Here's the verb وصل conjugated in the past tense:

Form	Pronunciation	English
أنا وصلتُ	*a*.nā wa.*ṣal*.tu	I arrived
أنتَ وصلتَ	*an*.ta wa.*ṣal*.ta	You arrived (MS)
أنتِ وصلتِ	*an*.ti wa.*ṣal*.ti	You arrived (FS)
هو وصل	*hu*.wa *wa*.ṣa.la	He arrived
هي وصلتْ	*hi*.ya *wa*.ṣa.lat	She arrived
نحن وصلنا	*naḥ*.nu wa.*ṣal*.nā	We arrived
أنتم وصلتم	*an*.tum wa.*ṣal*.tum	You arrived (MP)
أنتنّ وصلتنّ	an.*tun*.na wa.ṣal.*tun*.na	You arrived (FP)
هم وصلوا	hum *wa*.ṣa.lū	They arrived (MP)
هنّ وصلنّ	*hun*.na wa.*ṣal*.na	They arrived (FP)
أنتما وصلتما	an.*tu*.mā wa.ṣal.*tu*.mā	You arrived (dual/M/F)
هما وصلا	*hu*.mā *wa*.ṣa.lā	They arrived (dual/M)
هما وصلتا	*hu*.mā wa.ṣa.*la*.tā	They arrived (dual/F)

Use the irregular form يصل (*ya*.ṣil) to conjugate "arriving" in the present tense:

Form	Pronunciation	English
أنا أصل	*a*.nā *a*.ṣil	I am arriving
أنتَ تصل	*an*.ta *ta*.ṣil	You are arriving (MS)
أنتِ تصلين	*an*.ti ta.ṣi.*līn*	You are arriving (FS)
هو يصل	*hu*.wa *ya*.ṣil	He is arriving
هي تصل	*hi*.ya *ta*.ṣil	She is arriving
نحن نصل	*naḥ*.nu *na*.ṣil	We are arriving
أنتم تصلون	*an*.tum ta.ṣi.*lūn*	You are arriving (MP)
أنتنّ تصلنّ	an.*tun*.na ta.*ṣil*.na	You are arriving (FP)
هم يصلون	hum ya.ṣi.*lūn*	They are arriving (MP)
هنّ يصلنّ	*hun*.na ya.*ṣil*.na	They are arriving (FP)
أنتما تصلان	an.*tu*.mā ta.ṣi.*lān*	You are arriving (dual/M/F)
هما يصلان	*hu*.mā ya.ṣi.*lān*	They are arriving (dual/M)
هما تصلان	*hu*.mā ta.ṣi.*lān*	They are arriving (dual/F)

Going through immigration and customs

When your plane lands and you arrive at your chosen destination, you have to deal with the هجرة (*hij*.rah) (*immigration*) and جمارك (ja.*mā*.rik) (*customs*) officials. In recent years, airports have established more stringent requirements on مسافرون (mu.sā.fi.*rūn*) (*travelers*), so be prepared to answer a number of questions regarding the details and purpose of your trip. Here are some common questions these officials may ask you:

- ما اسمك؟ (mā *is*.muk?) (*What's your name?*)
- كم عمرك؟(kam *'um*.rak?) (*How old are you?*)
- أين تسكن؟ (*ay*.na tas.*kun*?) (*Where do you live?*)
- ما هي مهنتك؟ (mā *hi*.ya mih.*na*.tuk?) (*What do you do?*)
- ما مدة سفرك؟ (mā *mud*.dat *sa*.fa.rak?) (*How long is your trip?*)

- ؟ما هدف سفرك (mā *ha*.daf *sa*.fa.rak?) (*What's the purpose of your trip?*)
- ؟أين ستسكن مدة السفر (*ay*.na sa.*tas*.kun *mud*.dat as.*sa*.far?) (*Where will you be staying during the trip?*)
- ؟هل تسافر لوحدك (hal tu.*sā*.fir li.*waḥ*.dak?) (*Are you traveling alone?*)

REMEMBER

Provide clear and accurate answers to these questions. Providing false statements to an official from immigration or customs is a serious offense, so make sure you're truthful throughout the questioning.

CULTURAL WISDOM

If you're visiting a Muslim country, check with your travel agent or consular official about restrictions certain countries may have regarding bringing particular items into the country. For example, if you're traveling to Saudi Arabia, you can't bring alcohol with you into the country. If you're a woman, you may have to wear specific clothing, such as the حجاب (ḥi.*jāb*) (*veil*) in order to comply with local religious laws, which is the case at least for the Kingdom of Saudi Arabia, for example. You want to be certain you are aware of all the rules and laws before you face someone from immigration or customs.

Talkin' the Talk

Jennifer has just landed at the Mohammed V Airport in Casablanca, Morocco, and she answers some questions at the immigration booth.

Officer: .تقدمي من فضلك
ta.*qad*.da.mī min *faḍ*.lik.
Step forward, please.

Jennifer: .أهلًا يا سيدي
ah.lan yā *say*.yi.dī.
Hello, sir.

Officer: .جواز السفر من فضلك
jaw.*wāz* as.*sa*.far min *faḍ*.lik.
Your passport, please.

Jennifer: .ها هو
hā *hu*.wa.
Here it is.

Officer: ؟الجنسية
al.jin.*siy*.yah?
Nationality?

Jennifer: أمريكية.
am.rī.*kiy*.yah.
American.

Officer: تاريخ الميلاد؟
tā.*rīkh* al.mī.*lād*?
Date of birth?

Jennifer: 1980
sa.nat alf wa.tis' *mā*.'ah wa.tha.mā.*nīn*.
1980.

Officer: ما هدف سفرك؟
mā *ha*.daf *sa*.fa.rik?
What's the purpose of your trip?

Jennifer: أنا سائحة.
a.nā *sā*.'i.ḥah.
I'm a tourist.

Officer: أين ستسكنين مدة سفرك؟
ay.na sa.tas.ku.*nīn* *mud*.dat *sa*.fa.rik?
Where will you be staying during the trip?

Jennifer: فندق بوشنتوف.
fun.duq bū.shan.*tūf*.
The Bouchentouf Hotel.

Officer: ما هو تاريخ الخروج؟
mā *hu*.wa tā.*rīkh* al.khu.*rūj*?
When is your date of departure?

Jennifer: عشرين يونيو.
'ish.*rīn* *yūn*.yū.
June 20.

Officer: شكراً. مرحباً في المغرب.
shuk.ran *mar*.ḥa.ban fī al.*magh*.rib.
Thank you. Step forward, please.

Jennifer: شكراً!
shuk.ran!
Thank you!

WORDS TO KNOW

جنسية	jin.siy.yah	nationality
تاريخ الميلاد	tā.rīkh al.mī.lād	date of birth
هدف	ha.daf	purpose/goal
تاريخ	tā.rīkh	date
خروج	khu.rūj	exit/departure
دخول	du.khūl	entry
سياحة	si.yā.ḥah	tourism
سائح	sā.'iḥ	tourist (M)
سائحة	sā.'i.ḥah	tourist (F)
مهاجر	mu.hā.jir	immigrant (M)
مهاجرة	mu.hā.ji.rah	immigrant (F)
مهاجرون	mu.hā.ji.rūn	immigrants (M)
مهاجرات	mu.hā.ji.rāt	immigrants (F)

Getting through the immigration post puts you one step closer to leaving the airport and discovering the wonders of the exotic country you're visiting! After your interview with the immigration official, you may proceed to pick up your luggage. You may use the help of a حمال (ḥam.*māl*) (*baggage handler/porter*), or you may simply use a عربة (*'a*.ra.bah) (*cart*) to haul your own luggage.

Before you actually leave the airport, you must go through customs. Use the following phrases when speaking with customs officials:

- لا شيء للإعلان. (lā shay' lil.'i'.*lān.*) (*Nothing to declare.*)
- معي شيء للإعلان. (*ma.*'ī shay' lil.'i'.*lān.*) (*I have something to declare.*)

TIP

Check with your travel agent, consular officer, or embassy official to find out about any products or restrictions imposed by countries you're traveling to. You should know what's prohibited from entering or leaving a specific country because the consequences of not knowing may be quite high. In addition, certain countries have limits on the amount of cash you can bring in and take out. Knowing these currency restrictions is equally important.

Talkin' the Talk

Before leaving the airport, Hassan needs to stop by the customs department.

Officer: هل عندك شيء للإعلان؟
hal *'in*.dak shay' lil.'i'.*lān*?
Do you have anything to declare?

Hassan: لا.
lā.
No.

Officer: ماذا في الحقيبة؟
mā.dhā fīl.ḥa.*qī*.bah?
What's inside the suitcase?

Hassan: ملابسي.
ma.*lā*.bi.sī.
My clothes.

Officer: إفتح الشنطة من فضلك.
if.taḥ as.*shan*.ṭah min *faḍ*.lik.
Open the suitcase, please.

Hassan: طبعاً. تفضل.
ṭa.ba.'an. ta.*fa*.ḍal.
Certainly. Here you go.

Officer: شكراً. يمكن أن تخرج الآن.
shuk.ran. *yum*.kin an *takh*.ruj al.'*ān*.
Thank you. You may proceed now.

WORDS TO KNOW

داخل	dā.khil	inside
خارج	khā.rij	outside
إفتح	if.taḥ	open (command form)

Getting Around on Land

Major metropolitan areas and most small towns have a number of transportation methods you can choose from. Table 16-1 lists some of the most common forms of transportation you're likely to use.

TABLE 16-1 Major Forms of Transportation

Arabic	Pronunciation	Translation
سيارة اجرة	say.*yā*.rat *uj*.rah	taxi
حافلة	*ḥā*.fi.lah	bus
قطار	qi.*ṭār*	train
مترو الأنفاق	*mit*.rū al.'an.*fāq*	subway
سفينة	sa.*fī*.nah	ship
سيارة	say.*yā*.rah	car
سيارة للإيجار	say.*yā*.rah lil.'ī.jār	rental car
دراجة	dar.*rā*.jah	bicycle
دراجة نارية	dar.*rā*.jah nā.*riy*.yah	motorcycle

Hailing a taxi

If you're in a large or medium-sized city and need to get from one location to another quickly and relatively inexpensively, then hailing a taxi is probably the best option for you. When hailing a cab in a foreign country, keep the following advice in mind:

- **Make sure that the taxi you hail is fully licensed and authorized by the local agencies to operate as a taxi.** A number of companies operate illegal taxis and take advantage of unsuspecting tourists — make sure you're not one of them! Usually, most legitimate taxi operators have licensing information on display somewhere inside the cab or even on the car's exterior.
- **Be aware that most taxis that run to and from the airport charge a flat rate.** Inquire about the flat rate before you get into the taxi.
- **If you're in the city, make sure the taxi سائق (*sā.'iq*) (*driver*) turns on the عداد ('ad.*dād*) (*meter*).** A common occurrence is that a driver forgets (either accidentally or intentionally) to turn on the meter and ends up charging you, the passenger, an exorbitant amount of money for a short ride.

In most Arab and Middle Eastern countries, tipping the driver isn't required. However, I'm sure the driver won't argue if you decide to give him a little tip!

Talkin' the Talk

Larry hails a taxi in downtown Casablanca.

Driver: أين تريد أن تذهب؟
ay.na tu.*rīd* an *tadh*.hab?
Where do you want to go?

Larry: إلى الفندق.
i.lá al.*fun*.duq.
To the hotel.

Driver: ما اسم الفندق؟
mā ism al.*fun*.duq?
What's the name of the hotel?

Larry: فندق مريم.
fun.duq *mar*.yam.
Hotel Myriam.

Driver: حسناً. تفضل.
ḥa.sa.nan. ta.*fa*.ḍal.
Okay. Come in.

The taxi arrives at the hotel.

Driver: وصلنا إلى الفندق.
wa.*ṣal*.nā *i*.lá al.*fun*.duq.
We've arrived at the hotel.

Larry: كم؟
kam?
How much?

Driver: عشرين درهم.
'ish.*rīn dir*.ham.
Twenty dirhams.

Larry: تفضل. احتفظ بالباقي.
ta.*fa*.al. iḥ.*ta*.fiẓ bil.*bā*.qī.
Here you go. Keep the change.

Driver: شكراً جزيلًا!
shuk.ran ja.*zī*.lan!
Thank you very much!

WORDS TO KNOW

احتفظ	iḥ.ta.fiẓ	keep (command form)
باقي	bā.qī	change (money)
الأجرة	al.'uj.rah	fare
عداد	'ad.dād	counter/meter

Taking a bus

The حافلة (*ḥā*.fi.la) (*bus*) is a convenient mode of transportation whether you're traveling across town or across the country. If you're in a city and traveling within city limits, taking the bus is a good option because it usually costs less than a taxi. If you're traveling across the country, not only is taking a bus an economical option, but you also get to enjoy the beautiful scenery up close and personal!

Most حافلات (hā.fi.*lāt*) (*buses*) accept prepaid تذاكر (ta.*dhā*.kir) (*tickets*). If you frequently take the bus, refill your bus pass regularly. Otherwise, if you only take a bus occasionally, you'll be glad to know that most buses also accept فلوس (fi.*lūs*) (*cash*) as long as it's small bills. Here are some common terms you may need or encounter if you decide to take a bus:

- تذكرة الحافلة (*tadh*.ka.rat al.*ḥā*.fi.lah) (*bus ticket*)
- محطة الحافلة (ma.*ḥaṭ*.ṭat al.*ḥā*.fi.lah) (*bus station/bus stop*)
- سائق الحافلة (*sā*.'iq al.*ḥā*.fi.lah) (*bus driver*)
- توقيت الحافلة (taw.*qīt* al.*ḥā*.fi.lah) (*bus schedule*)

TIP

If you want to say "every" as in "every day" or "every hour," all you do is add the word كل (*kul*) (*every*) before the noun that describes the time you're referring to. For example:

- كل يوم (kul yawm) (*every day*)
- كل ساعة (kul *sā*.'ah) (*every hour*)
- كل نصف ساعة (kul niṣf *sā*.'ah) (*every half-hour*)
- كل ربع ساعة(kul rub' *sā*.'ah) (*every 15 minutes*)

Talkin' the Talk

Malika is waiting at the bus stop. She's trying to figure out which bus to take, so she asks a fellow commuter for information.

Malika: عفواً, هل هذه الحافلة تذهب إلى وسط المدينة؟
'af.wan, hal *hā*.dhi.hi al.*ḥā*.fi.lah *tadh*.hab *i*.lá *wa*.saṭ al.ma.*dī*.nah?
Excuse me, does this bus go downtown?

Commuter: لا. هذه الحافلة تذهب إلى خارج المدينة.
lā. *hā*.dhi.hi al.*ḥā*.fi.lah *tadh*.hab *ī*.lá *khā*.rij al.ma.*dī*.nah.
No. This bus goes outside of the city.

Malika: أي حافلة تذهب إلى وسط المدينة؟
ayy *ḥā*.fi.lah *tadh*.hab *i*.lá *wa*.saṭ al.ma.*dī*.nah?
Which bus goes downtown?

Commuter: الحافلة رقم عشرة.
al.*ḥā*.fi.lah raqm *'ash*.rah.
Bus number 10.

Malika: متى ستصل الحافلة رقم عشرة؟
ma.tá sa.*ta*.ṣil al.*ḥā*.fi.lah raqm *'ash*.rah?
When does bus number 10 arrive?

Commuter: بعد عشرين دقيقة.
ba'd 'ish.*rīn* da.*qī*.qah.
In 20 minutes.

Malika: شكراً.
shuk.ran.
Thank you.

Commuter: عفواً.
'*af*.wan.
You're welcome.

Boarding a train

The قطار (qi.*ṭār*) (*train*) is a popular alternative if you're looking for transportation that's convenient, fast, and affordable, and allows you to do a little sightseeing while you're on the go. When you board the train, be ready to provide your pass to the train attendant. Although boarding most trains doesn't require a بطاقة شخصية (bi.*ṭā*.qah shakh.*ṣiy*.yah) (*personal ID card*), you should be ready to present one if an attendant asks you for it.

Talkin' the Talk

Fatima is purchasing a ticket at the train station.

Fatima: أريد تذكرة لمراكش.
u.*rīd tadh*.ki.rah li.mur.*rā*.kush.
I would like a ticket to Marrakech.

Clerk: ذهاب فقط أو ذهاب وإياب؟
dhi.*hāb fa*.qaṭ aw di.*hāb* wa.'i.*yāb*?
One-way or round-trip?

Fatima: ذهاب فقط من فضلك.

dhi.*hāb* *fa*.qaṭ min *faḍ*.lik.

One-way, please.

Clerk: تفضل.

ta.*fa*.ḍal.

Here you go.

Fatima: شكراً. متى ينطلق القطار؟

shuk.ran *ma*.tá yan.*ṭa*.liq al.qi.*ṭār?*

Thank you. When does the train leave?

Clerk: القطار ينطلق بعد نصف ساعة من الرصيف رقم خمسة.

al.qi.*ṭār* yan.*ṭa*.liq *ba'*.da niṣf *sā*.'ah min ar.ra.*ṣīf* raqm *kham*.sah.

The train leaves in a half-hour from platform number 5.

Fatima: شكراً.

shuk.ran.

Thank you.

WORDS TO KNOW

ذهاب فقط	dhi.hāb fa.qaṭ	one-way trip
ذهاب وإياب	dhi.hāb wa.'i.yāb	round-trip
رصيف	ra.*ṣīf*	platform

FUN & GAMES

Identify the following modes of transportation in Arabic:

1.  ______________________

2.  ______________________

3. 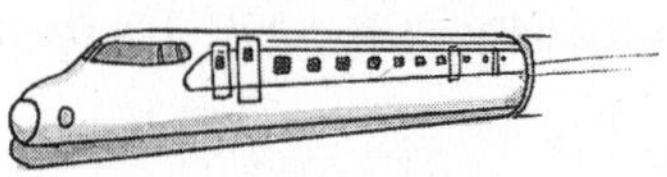 ______________________

4.  ______________________

5.  ______________________

Illustrations by Elizabeth Kurtzman

The answers are in Appendix C.

» Reserving your room

» Checking in and out

Chapter 17
Finding a Place to Stay

Picking the right فندق (*fun*.duq) (*hotel*) for you and your family or friends can sometimes make or break your رحلة (*riḥ*.lah) (*trip*). During a عطلة (*'uṭ*.lah) (*vacation*), the hotel is your home away from home — it's where you get up in the morning and sleep at night, and it can serve as a base for you to regroup before facing daily adventures. So choosing the hotel that's right for you is very important.

In this chapter, I show you the ins and outs of choosing the right hotel to meet your travel, budgetary, and personal needs. You find out how to inquire about specific aspects of the hotel (such as available amenities and proximity to the city center), how to make a room reservation and check into your room, how to interact with the hotel staff, and, last but not least, how to successfully check out of your hotel room! You find out everything you ever wanted to know about hotel life and more!

REMEMBER

You can listen to all the Talkin' the Talk dialogues featured in this chapter. Go to `www.dummies.com/go/arabicfd` and click on the dialogue you want to hear.

Choosing the Right Accommodations

When choosing the right hotel, you need to consider a number of factors. First and foremost, you must figure out what kind of hotel you want to stay in. With so many options to choose from, how do you know which one is right for you? Here are some details to consider:

» أين (*ay*.na) (*where*)

» ثمن (*tha*.man) (*price*)

» غرفة (*ghur*.fah) (*room*)

» مساحة الغرفة (mi.*sā*.ḥat al.*ghur*.fah) (*room size*)

» نوع الغرفة (naw' al.*ghur*.fah) (*room type*)

» خدمة الغرفة (*khid*.mat al.*ghur*.fah) (*room service*)

» سكن (*sa*.kan) (*accommodations*)

Of course, you have many other factors to consider, but these are some of the more popular ones. Not only do you need to find the right hotel, one that perhaps includes such مرافق (ma.*rā*.fiq) (*amenities*) as a مسبح (*mas*.baḥ) (*swimming pool*) or a مطعم (*maṭ*.'am) (*restaurant*), but you also need to make sure you find the right room. After all, that's where you'll spend most of your private time.

An important factor to think about when finding a hotel is its مساحة (mi.*sā*.ḥah) (*size*). For example, if you're traveling alone, a غرفة لشخص واحد (*ghur*.fah li.*shakhṣ* *wā*.ḥid) (*single room*) is more appropriate than a غرفة لسخصين (*ghur*.fah li.shakh.*ṣayn*) (*double room*). When inquiring about a hotel, you may need to use the following terms:

» سرير (sa.*rīr*) (*bed*)

» حمام (ḥam.*mām*) (*toilet*)

» شرفة (*shur*.fah) (*balcony*)

» تلفزيون (ti.li.fiz.*yūn*) (*television*)

» طابق (*ṭā*.biq) (*floor/level*)

GRAMMATICALLY SPEAKING

To create a possessive noun in the English language, you usually use an apostrophe, such as "the girl's cat" or "the woman's house." It's the same in Arabic, except that you reverse the word order — you use an indefinite noun followed by a definite noun, as in مساحة الغرفة. الغرفة (a definite noun because it contains the definite article prefix **al-**) means "the room," and مساحة (an undefined noun) means "size." So when you read or hear مساحة الغرفة, you automatically know that the غرفة is the possessor acting on the مساحة (*size*) to express the "room's size" or, literally, "the size of the room."

Talkin' the Talk

Sarah is planning a trip and wants to find the right hotel for her visit. She calls one of the local hotels to inquire about its facilities.

Desk clerk: فندق البركة.
fun.duq al.*ba*.ra.kah.
Al-Baraka Hotel.

Sarah: مساء الخير. أريد أن أعرف إذا كان عندكم غرف متاحة.
ma.*sā'* al.*khayr*. u.*rīd* an *a'*.rif i.*dhā* *kā*.na *'in*.da.kum *ghu*.raf mu.*tā*.ḥah.
Good evening. I would like to know whether you have any rooms available.

Desk clerk: لحظة.
laḥ.ẓah.
One moment.

Sarah: طبعاً.
ṭa.ba.'an.
Certainly.

Desk clerk: نعم عندنا غرف متاحة. ما نوع الغرفة التي تريدين؟
na.'am *'in*.da.nā *ghu*.raf mu.*tā*.ḥah. mā naw' al.*ghur*.fah al.*la*.tī tu.rī.*dīn?*
Yes, we have rooms available. What type of room would you like?

Sarah: هل عندكم غرف لسخصين؟
hal *'in*.da.kum *ghu*.raf li.shakh.*ṣayn?*
Do you have any double rooms?

Desk clerk: نعم.
na.'am.
Yes.

Sarah: كم سرير في هذه الغرفة؟
kam sa.*rīr* fī *hā*.dhi.hi al.*ghur*.fah?
How many beds are in this room?

Desk clerk: اثنان.
ith.*nān*.
Two.

Sarah: وكم نافذة في الغرفة؟
wa.*kam nā*.fi.dhah fī al.*ghur*.fah?
And how many windows are in the room?

Desk clerk: ثلاث نوافذ. هذه الغرفة مشمسة.
tha.*lāth* na.*wā*.fidh. *hā*.dhi.hi al.*ghur*.fah *mush*.mi.sah.
Three windows. This room gets plenty of sunlight.

Sarah: حسناً. وهل فيها شرفة؟
ḥa.sa.nan. wa.*hal fī*.hā *shur*.fah?
Okay. And does it have a balcony?

Desk clerk: نعم, فيها شرفة تطل على الشاطئ.
na.'am, *fī*.hā *shur*.fah tu.*ṭil* '*a*.lá ash.*shā*.*ṭi*'.
Yes, it has a balcony that overlooks the beach.

Sarah: ممتاز! سأخذ هذه الغرفة.
mum.*tāz*! sa.'*ā*.khudh *hā*.dhi.hi al.*ghur*.fah.
Excellent! I'll take this room.

WORDS TO KNOW

غرف	ghu.raf	rooms
متاحة	mu.tā.ḥah	available (F)
نافذة	nā.fi.dhah	window
شمس	shams	sun
شاطئ	shā.ṭi'	beach

Discussing minor room details

I don't know about you, but before I reserve a hotel room, I want to find out as much as possible about what's actually inside the room. Your friends, like mine, may call it obsessive-compulsive, but I want to know everything about the room, down to the last detail, such as the kind of bathroom, what channels the TV receives, and even the number of pillows I can expect to find on the bed!

Talkin' the Talk

Amine calls Hotel Salam to inquire about the room he's reserving.

Amine: هل هذه الغرفة لشخص واحد أو لشخصين؟
hal *hā*.dhi.hi al.*ghur*.fah li.*shakhṣ* *wā*.ḥid aw li.shakh.*ṣayn?*
Is this a single room or a double room?

Desk clerk: هذه غرفة لشخص واحد.
hā.dhi.hi al.*ghur*.fah li.*shakhṣ* *wā*.ḥid.
This is a single room.

Amine: وفي أي طابق هذه الغرفة؟
wa.*fī* ayy *ṭā*.biq *hā*.dhi.hi al.*ghur*.fah?
And on what floor is this room located?

Desk clerk: في الطابق الخامس.
fī aṭ.*ṭā*.biq al.*khā*.mis.
On the fifth floor.

Amine: الغرفة فيها حمام, أليس كذلك؟
al.*ghur*.fah *fī*.ha ḥam.*mām*, a.*lay*.sa ka.*dhā*.lik?
The room comes with a bathroom, correct?

Desk clerk: نعم يا سيدي.
na.ʻam yā *say*.yi.dī.
Yes, sir.

Amine: هل هناك دوش وبانيو في الحمّام؟
hal hu.*nā*.ka dūsh wa.*bān*.yū fī al.ḥam.*mām*?
Is there a shower and a bathtub in the bathroom?

Desk clerk: فيها دوش فقط.
fī.hā dūsh *fa*.qaṭ.
It only comes with a shower.

Amine: حسناً. وهل هناك خزانة في الغرفة؟
ḥa.sa.nan. wa.*hal* hu.*nā*.ka kha.*zā*.nah fī al.*ghur*.fah?
Okay. And is there a safe in the room?

Desk clerk: نعم. وعندنا خزانة في مكتب الاستقبال أيضاً.
na.'am. wa.'*in*.da.nā khi.*zā*.nah fī *mak*.tab al.'is.tiq.
bāl ay.ḍan.
Yes. And we have a safe in the reception desk as well.

Amine: سؤال أخير: هل في الغرفة مكواة ملابس؟
su.'*āl* a.*khīr:* hal fī al.*ghur*.fah mik.*wāt* ma.*lā*.bis?
One final question: Does the room come equipped with a clothes iron?

Desk clerk: نعم، وإذا أردت، يمكن أن تعطي ملابسك لمشرفة الغرفة للغسل.
na.'am, wa.'*i*.dhā a.*rad*.ta, *yum*.kin an tu'.*ṭī* ma.*lā*.bi.sak li.mush.*ri*.fat al.*ghur*.fah lil.*ghasl*.
Yes, and if you'd like, you may give your clothes to the room's staff attendant for dry cleaning.

WORDS TO KNOW

حمّام	ḥam.māmbathroom	
دوش	dūsh	shower
بانيو	ban.yū	bathtub
مرحاض	mir.ḥāḍ	toilet
مغسلة	magh.sa.lah	sink
منشفة	min.sha.fah	towel
مرآة	mir.'āh	mirror
سرير	sa.rīr	bed

وسادة	wi.sā.dah	pillow
دثار	di.thār	blanket
مكواة الملابس	mik.wāt al.ma.lā.bis	clothes iron
مصباح	miṣ.bāḥ	lamp
هاتف	hā.tif	phone
تلفزيون	ti.li.fiz.yūn	TV
مذياع	midh.yā‘	radio
خزانة	khi.zā.nah	safe deposit box
نافذة	nā.fi.dhah	window
مشرفة الغرفة	mush.ri.fat al.ghur.fah	room staff attendant

Getting to know direct object pronouns

GRAMMATICALLY SPEAKING

Direct object pronouns ascribe possession to a particular individual or group of individuals, as in "his room," "her cat," or "their house." In Arabic, instead of using a separate possessive word such as "his," "her," or "their," you add a possessive direct object pronoun suffix to the noun to which you're ascribing possession.

For example, if you want to say "his room" in Arabic, you take the noun for "room" (غرفة) and add the direct object pronoun suffix corresponding to "his," which is the suffix ـه (hu). So "his room" in Arabic is غرفته (ghur.*fa*.tu.hu). Note that because غرفة is a feminine singular noun, it automatically ends in تاء مربوطة (tā' mar.*bū*.ṭah) — the silent "t" located at the end of every feminine singular noun — and you must also add a ضمة (*ḍam*.mah) — the "u" sound (u) — to the end of the word before placing the suffix ـه (hu). So instead of saying غرفه (ghur.*fa*.hu), you say غرفته.

If you want to say "her room," follow the same rule except that instead of adding the masculine possessive suffix ـه, you add the feminine possessive suffix ها. Hence, "her room" is غرفتها (ghur.*fa*.tu.hā). This rule applies to all singular possessive direct object pronouns, but you must pay close attention when using the possessive suffix in the plural form. For example, to say "their room," you must first determine the gender of "their" — whether it's masculine plural or feminine plural; the plural possessive suffix is gender-defined, meaning it changes based on the gender. "Their room" in the masculine is غرفتهم (ghur.*fa*.tu.hum) (هم [-hum] is the masculine plural possessive suffix). Alternatively, "their room" in the feminine is غرفتهنّ (ghur.fa.tu.*hun*.na) — (you add the feminine plural possessive suffix هنّ [-*hun*.na]).

Table 17-1 contains all direct object pronoun possessive suffixes, so feel free to turn to this table whenever you're looking to add a possessive suffix to a particular noun but aren't sure which possessive suffix to use.

TABLE 17-1 **Direct Object Pronoun Possessive Suffixes**

Personal Pronoun	English	Possessive Suffix	Possessive Suffix Arabic	English
أنا	my	-i	ي	mine
أنتَ	you (MS)	-ka	كَ	your (MS)
أنتِ	you (FS)	-ki	كِ	your (FS)
هو	he/him	-uh	ـه	his
هي	she/her	-hā	ـها	hers
نحن	we/us	-nā	ـنا	ours
أنتم	you (MP)	-kum	ـكم	your (MP)
أنتنّ	you (FP)	-*kun*.na	ـكنّ	your (FP)
هم	they (MP)	-hum	ـهم	their (MP)
هنّ	they (FP)	-*hun*.na	ـهنّ	their (FP)
أنتما	you (dual)	-*ku*.mā	ـكما	your (dual)
هما	they (dual)	-*hu*.mā	ـهما	their (dual)

REMEMBER

The dual form هما is generally gender-neutral, meaning that there's a هما in both the feminine and the masculine. However, in the construction of direct object pronoun suffixes, you use the same possessive suffix هما regardless of the gender.

Making a Reservation

After you identify the right hotel with the right accommodations and room, you're ready to make a حجز (ḥajz) (*reservation*). Before you do, though, you have a few considerations to make, such as the duration of your stay, the number and type of room you're reserving, the number of people staying, and the cost to stay at the hotel. This section explores all these elements in-depth so that you can be prepared to make a smooth reservation and secure the best accommodations for your trip!

Figuring out the price

Price is an important factor to think about before you make your reservation. Fortunately, there are many accommodations options to suit every ميزانية (mī.zā.*niy.*yah) (*budget*). If you can afford it, making a reservation in a فندق فاخر (*fun.*duq *fā.*khir) (*luxury hotel*) is nice. These five-star hotels tend to have all sorts of accommodations, and you're sure to get the star treatment from the hotel staff; a luxury hotel almost guarantees a great experience. If you're a طالب (*ṭā.*lib) (*student*) or someone with a limited budget, staying at a دار الطلبة (dār aṭ.*ṭa.*la.bah) (*youth hostel*) is a more affordable option. Hostels tend to have very basic accommodations, such as communal bathrooms and shared living space, but are fine if you're not planning to spend that much وقت (waqt) (*time*) in the hotel.

When making your reservation, be sure to inquire about any special تخفيضات (takh.fī.*ḍāt*) (*discounts*) that the hotel may offer. Here are some discounts you can ask about:

- تخفيضات المجموعات (takh.fī.*ḍāt* al.maj.mū.*'āt*) (*group discounts*)
- تخفيضات الفصول (takh.fī.*ḍāt* al.fu.*ṣūl*) (*seasonal discounts*)

When you inquire about the ثمن, ask about any عروض خاصة ('u.*rūḍ khāṣ.*ṣah) (*special travel packages*) that the hotel may offer, such as local sightseeing expeditions. Many hotels now offer these kinds of packages in addition to basic room and board accommodations. If you don't ask, you may miss out on a good deal!

Talkin' the Talk

Omar wants to make a reservation at Hotel Ramadan. He asks the operator about the price of the rooms and about any applicable discounts.

Omar: كم ثمن الغرفة لشخص واحد لمدة ليلة واحدة؟
kam *tha*.man al.*ghur*.fah li.*shakhṣ wā*.ḥid li.*mud*.dat *lay*.lah *wā*.ḥi.dah?
How much is a single room for one night?

Operator: مائة وخمسون درهماً لليلة واحدة.
mā.'ah wa.kham.*sūn* dir.*ha*.man li.*lay*.lah *wā*.ḥi.dah.
One hundred and fifty dirhams for one night.

Omar: وكم ثمن غرفة لشخصين لمدة ليلة واحدة؟
wa.*kam tha*.man *ghur*.fah li.shakh.*ṣayn* li.*mud*.dat *lay*.lah *wā*.ḥi.dah?
And how much is a double room for one night?

Operator: مائتا درهم لليلة.
mā.'a.tā *dir*.ham lil.*lay*.lah.
Two hundred dirhams for the night.

Omar: طيّب. أريد غرفة لشخص واحد لمدة أسبوع.
ṭay.yib. u.*rīd ghur*.fah li.*shakhṣ wā*.ḥid li.*mud*.dat us.*bū*'.
Okay. I'd like a single room for one week.

Operator: ممتاز!
mum.*tāz*!
Excellent!

Omar: هل عندكم أي تخفيضات فصلية؟
hal '*in*.da.kum ayy takh.fī.*ḍāt* faṣ.*liy*.yah?
Do you have any seasonal discounts?

Operator: نعم.
na.'am.
Yes.

Omar: وما هي هذه التنزيلات؟
wa.*mā hi*.ya *hā*.dhi.hi at.tan.zī.*lāt*?
And what are these discounts?

Operator: إذا بقيتَ لمدة عشرة أيام, سيكون الثمن مائة وعشرين درهماً بدلاً من مائة وخمسين لليلة.
i.*dhā* ba.*qay*.ta li.*mud*.dat *'ash*.rat ay.*yām* sa.ya.*kūn* ath.*tha*.man *mā*.'ah wa.'ish.*rīn dir*.ha.man *ba*.da.lan min *mā*.'ah wa.kham.*sīn* lil.*lay*.lah.
If you stay in the room for ten days, the price goes down to one hundred and twenty dirhams per night instead of one hundred and fifty dirhams.

Omar: أريد ان أفكّر أكثر في هذا. سأكلمك بعد قليل.
u.*rīd* an u.*fak*.kir *ak*.thar fī *hā*.dhā. sa.'u.kal.*li*.muk *ba'*.da qa.*līl*.
I'd like to think about it a little bit longer. I'll call you back in a little while.

Omar thinks about the discount and then calls back the operator.

Omar: طيّب. أريد غرفة واحدة لمدة عشرة أيام.
ṭay.yib. u.*rīd ghur*.fah *wā*.ḥi.dah li.*mud*.dat *'ash*.raṭ ay.*yām*.
Okay. I'd like a single room for ten days.

Operator: رائع. هل ستدفع نقداً أو بشيك أو ببطاقة ائتمان؟
rā.'i'. hal sa.*tad*.fa' *naq*.dan aw bi.*shīk* aw bi.bi.*ṭā*.qat i'.ti.*mān?*
Great. Will you be paying by cash, check, or credit card?

Omar: ببطاقة ائتمان.
bi.bi.*ṭā*.qat i'.ti.*mān*.
By credit card.

WORDS TO KNOW

مدة	mud.dah	period/duration
دراهم	da.rā.him	dirhams (Moroccan currency)
مائة	mā.'ah	one hundred
مائتا	mā.'a.tā	two hundred
أسبوع	us.bū'	week

أسابيع	a.sā.bī'	weeks
تخفيضات	takh.fī.ḍāt	discounts
يوم	yawm	day
أيام	ay.yām	days
بقي	ba.qi.ya	he stayed
بقيت	ba.qay.ta	you stayed
بـ	bi	with
قليل	qa.līl	a short while
دفع	da.fa.'a	he paid
تدفع	tad.fa'	you pay
نقداً	naq.dan	cash
شيك	shīk	check
بطاقة ائتمان	bi.ṭā.qat i'.ti.mān	credit card

Indicating the length of your stay

Making sure you get the room you want when you need it is as important as sticking to your hotel budget. Securing a reservation can be difficult, particularly during the موسم الأعياد (*maw*.sim al.'a'.*yād*) (*holiday season*); therefore, it's advisable you make your reservation ahead of schedule so that you're assured to get the hotel you want during the مدة (*mud*.dah) (*period*) of your choosing.

TIP

In order to say you're going to stay at the فندق "for a period of" so much time, use the following formula: لمدة (li.*mud*.dat) followed by the duration of your stay. For example, to say you're staying "for a period of a week," say لمدة أسبوع (li.*mud*.dat us.*bū*'). Here are some other examples:

- لمدة يوم (li.*mud*.dat yawm) (*for a period of one day*)
- لمدة شهر (li.*mud*.dat shahr) (*for a period of one month*)
- لمدة أسبوعين (li.*mud*.dat us.bū.'*ayn*) (*for a period of two weeks*)

» لمدة خمسة أيام (li.*mud*.dat *kham*.sat ay.*yām*) (*for a period of five days*)

» لمدة أسبوع ونصف (li.*mud*.dat us.*bū'* wa.*niṣf*) (*for a period of one and a half weeks*)

To say that you're staying from one date until another date, use the prepositions من (min) (*from*) and إلى (*i*.lá) (*until*). For example, if you're staying "from Monday until Thursday," you say من الاثنين إلى الخميس (min al.'ith.*nayn i*.lá al.kha.*mīs*). Here are some other examples:

» من الأربعاء إلى الأحد (min al.'ar.ba.*'ā' i*.lá al.*'a*.ḥad) (*from Thursday until Sunday*)

» من عشرين يوليو إلى ثلاثين يوليو (min 'ish.*rīn yul*.yū *i*.lá tha.lā.*thīn yul*.yū) (*from July 20 until July 30*)

» من أغسطس إلى سبتمبر (min u.*ghus*.ṭus *i*.lá sib.*tam*.bir) (*from August until September*)

REMEMBER

The verb for "to stay" is بقي (*ba*.qi.ya) in the past tense and يبقى (*yab*.qá) in the present tense. To put a فعل (fi'l) (*verb*) in the مستقبل (mus.*taq*.bal) (*future*), all you do is add the prefix **sa-** to the فعل in the present tense. For example, to communicate "I will stay for a period of one week," you say سأبقى لمدة أسبوع (sa.*'ab*.qá li.*mud*.dat us.*bū'*).

Talkin' the Talk

Reda calls the Hotel Marrakech to make a room reservation.

Reda: هل عندك غرفة لسخصين؟
hal *'in*.dak *ghur*.fah li.shakh.*ṣayn?*
Are there any double rooms?

Clerk: نعم, عندنا غرفة متاحة لشخصين.
na.'am, *'in*.da.nā *ghur*.fah mu.*tā*.ḥah li.shakh.*ṣayn*.
Yes, we have one double room available.

Reda: هل هذه الغرفة متاحة في عطلة نهاية السنة؟
hal *hā*.dhi.hi al.*ghur*.fah mu.*tā*.ḥah fī *'uṭ*.lat ni.*hā*.yat as.*sa*.nah?
Is this room available during the end of year holiday?

Clerk: الفندق مشغول جداً في هذه المدة ولكن هذه الغرفة مازالت متاحة.
al.*fun*.duq mash.*ghūl jid*.dan fī *hā*.dhi.hi al.*mud*.dah wa.*lā*. kin *hā*.dhi.hi al.*ghur*.fah mā.*zā*.lat mu.*tā*.ḥa.
This is a very busy period, but this room is still available.

Reda: رائع! اريد هذه الغرفة لمدة أسبوع.
rā.'i'! u.*rīd hā*.dhi.hi al.*ghur*.fah li.*mud*.dat us.*bū*'.
Great! I'd like this room for a period of one week.

Clerk: طيّب. ما تواريخ الحجز بالضبط؟
ṭay.yib. *mā* ta.wā.*rīkh* al.*ḥajz* bil.*ḍabṭ*?
Okay. And what are the exact dates for the reservation?

Reda: من الأول من ديسمبر إلى السابع من ديسمبر.
min al.'*aw*.wal min dī.*sam*.bir *i*.lá as.*sā*.bi' min dī.*sam*.bir.
From December 1 until December 7.

WORDS TO KNOW		
متاحة	mu.tā.ḥah	available (F)
متاح	mu.tāḥ	available (M)
عطلة	'uṭ.lah	holidays
سنة	sa.nah	year
نهاية	ni.hā.yah	end
مشغولة	mash.ghū.lah	busy (F)
مشغول	mash.ghūl	busy (M)
بالضبط	bil.ḍabṭ	exactly
لكن	lā.kin	but

Subjecting you to subjunctive verbs

GRAMMATICALLY SPEAKING

يريد (yu.*rīd*) is a special kind of verb — called subjunctive — that means "want to." Other verbs that fall into this category include يجب (*ya*.jib) (*have to*), يستطيع (yas. ta.*ṭī*') (*able to*), and يحبّ (yu.*ḥibb*) (*like*). Unlike other types of verbs, these four verbs fall into the main subjunctive category, which means that they're conjugated in only one tense.

For example, here is the verb يريد conjugated in the subjunctive form:

Form	Pronunciation	English
أنا أريد	*a*.nā u.*rīd*	I want
أنتَ تريد	*an*.ta tu.*rīd*	You want (MS)
أنتِ تريدين	*an*.ti tu.rī.*dīn*	You want (FS)
هو يريد	*hu*.wa yu.*rīd*	He wants
هي تريد	*hi*.ya tu.*rīd*	She wants
نحن نريد	*naḥ*.nu nu.*rīd*	We want
أنتم تريدون	*an*.tum tu.rī.*dūn*	You want (MP)
أنتنّ تريدنّ	an.*tun*.na tu.*rīd*.na	You want (FP)
هم يريدون	hum yu.rī.*dūn*	They want (MP)
هنّ يريدنّ	*hun*.na yu.*rīd*.na	They want (FP)
أنتما تريدان	an.*tu*.mā tu.rī.*dān*	You want (dual/M/F)
هما يريدان	*hu*.mā yu.rī.*dān*	They want (dual/M)
هما تريدان	*hu*.mā tu.rī.*dān*	They want (dual/F)

In English, when you use a subjunctive verb to describe an action, you always follow the verb with the preposition "to." For example, you say "I want to watch movies" or "I like to eat chocolate"; you would never say "I want watch movies" or "I like eat chocolate." Not only is it not proper English, but dropping the "to" doesn't really make that much sense. The same rule applies in Arabic: When you use a subjunctive verb to describe an action, you always add the preposition "to," which is pronounced (an) in Arabic.

To illustrate the subjunctive verbs in action, here are some examples:

- أحب أن أذهب إلى المكتبة. (u.*ḥibb* an *adh*.hab *i*.lá al.*mak*.ta.bah) (*I like to go to the library.*)
- أستطيع أن أعمل الواجب غدًا. (as.ta.*ṭī'* an *a'*.mal al.*wā*.jib *gha*.dan) (*I'm able to do the homework for tomorrow.*)
- يجب أن تقرأ الكتاب . (*ya*.jib an *taq*.ra' al.ki.*tāb*) (*You must read the book.*)

However, unlike in English where the auxiliary verb — the verb after the main verbs "have to," "like to," "able to," and "want to" — remains the same, the auxiliary verb in Arabic changes and becomes a subjunctive verb. For all intents and purposes, the subjunctive verb in this case is any verb that follows the preposition أن (an) after one of the four main verbs. So when you use one of the four main verbs followed by أن and an auxiliary verb, you must conjugate the auxiliary verb in the subjunctive form.

The subjunctive verb form is similar to the present verb tense, except that the verb endings are significantly different. For example, the present tense form of the verb كتب (*ka*.ta.ba) (*wrote*) is يكتب (*yak*.tu.bu) (*write*). The subjunctive form of يكتبُ is يكتبَ (*yak*.tu.ba), with the ضمة (*ḍam*.mah) changed to a فتحة (*fat*.ḥa). So if you wanted to say "I like to write," you would say أحب أن أكتبَ (u.*ḥib*.bu an *ak*.tu.ba) and not أحب أن أكتبُ ('u.*ḥib*.bu an *ak*.tu.bu).

To get a better sense of the subjunctive, here is the verb "to write" in the subjunctive form:

Form	Pronunciation	English
أنا أكتب	*a*.nā *ak*.tu.ba	I write
أنتَ تكتب	*an*.ta *tak*.tu.ba	You write (MS)
أنتِ تكتبي	*an*.ti tak.*tu*.bī	You write (FS)
هو يكتب	*hu*.wa *yak*.tu.ba	He writes
هي تكتب	*hi*.ya *tak*.tu.ba	She writes
نحن نكتب	*naḥ*.nu *nak*.tu.ba	We write
أنتم تكتبوا	*an*.tum tak.*tu*.bū	You write (MP)
أنتنّ تكتبنّ	*an*.tun.na tak.*tub*.na	You write (FP)
هم يكتبوا	hum yak.*tu*.bū	They write (MP)
هنّ يكتبنّ	*hun*.na yak.*tub*.na	They write (FP)
أنتما تكتبا	an.*tu*.mā tak.*tu*.bā	You write (dual/M/F)
هما يكتبا	*hu*.mā yak.*tu*.bā	They write (dual/M)
هما تكتبا	*hu*.mā tak.*tu*.bā	They write (dual/F)

Notice that whereas most of the endings in the subjunctive form change, a few remain the same. These are the personal pronouns whose endings remain the same in both the subjunctive and the present tense environments — أنتن and هن. Also, although a majority of the endings change vowels, a few have endings that change completely: أنتِ, أنتم, هم, هما (M), and هما (F). In these endings, you actually drop the suffix. For example, أنتم تكتبون (*an*.tum tak.tu.*bū*.na) becomes أنتم تكتبوا (*an*.tum tak.*tu*.bū).

REMEMBER

Whenever you use an auxiliary verb, make sure you use the subjunctive form of that verb!

Checking In to the Hotel

When you arrive at your hotel after a long trip, probably the last thing on your mind is going through the formalities of checking in. You probably just want to go up to your room, jump into bed, and relax for a little while. To help relieve the annoyance of check-in time, this section covers all the necessary words and phrases to help you check in to your room as smoothly as possible.

If you already have a reservation, ask the موظف الاستقبال (mu.*waẓ*.ẓaf al.'is.tiq.*bāl*) (*desk clerk*) for more معلومات (ma'.lū.*māt*) (*information*) regarding your room. If you don't have a reservation, you can inquire about room متاحة (mu.*tā*.ḥah) (*availability*) at the front desk.

Here are some important terms you may need during check-in:

- مفتاح (mif.*tāḥ*) (*key*)
- مفتاح الغرفة (mif.*tāḥ* al.*ghur*.fah) (*room key*)
- أمتعة (*am*.ti.'ah) (*luggage*)
- حقيبة (ḥa.*qī*.bah) (*suitcase*)
- محفظة (*maḥ*.fa.ẓah) (*briefcase*)
- طابق (*ṭā*.biq) (*floor*)
- مصعد (*miṣ*.'ad) (*elevator*)
- استقبال (is.tiq.*bāl*) (*reception*)
- مكتب الاستقبال (*mak*.tab al.'is.tiq.*bāl*) (*reception desk*)
- موظف الاستقبال (mu.*waẓ*.ẓaf al.'is.tiq.*bāl*) (*desk clerk*) (M)
- موظفة الاستقبال (mu.*waẓ*.ẓa.fat al.'is.tiq.*bāl*) (*desk clerk*) (F)

» بواب (baw.*wāb*) (*concierge*) (M)

» بوابة (baw.*wā*.bah) (*concierge*) (F)

When interacting with the hotel staff, the following key phrases are likely to come in handy:

» هل الفطور مع الغرفة؟ (hal al.fu.*ṭūr ma*.'a al.*ghur*.fah?) (*Is breakfast with the room?*)

» متى يبدأ الفطور؟ (*ma*.tá *yab*.da' al.fu.*ṭūr?*) (*When does breakfast begin?*)

» متى ينتهي الفطور؟ (*ma*.tá yan.*ta*.hī al.fu.*ṭūr?*) (*When does breakfast end?*)

» هل هناك رسائل لي؟ (hal hu.*nā*.ka ra.*sā*.'il lī?) (*Are there any messages for me?*)

» أريد مكالمة إيقاظ الساعة السابعة. (u.*rī.d* mu.kā.*la*.mat ī.*qāẓ* as.*sā*.'ah as.*sā*.bi.'ah.) (*I would like a wake-up call at seven o'clock.*)

Talkin' the Talk

Frank arrives at Hotel Casablanca and begins checking in to his room.

Frank: أهلًا. عندي حجز لغرفة لشخص واحد لمدة أسبوع بدايةً من اليوم.
ah.lan. '*in*.dī ḥajz li.*ghur*.fah li.*shakhṣ wā*.ḥid li.*mud*.dat us.*bū*' bi.*dā*.ya.tan min al.*yawm*.
Hi. I have a reservation for a single room for one week beginning today.

Clerk: طيّب. ما اسمك؟
ṭay.yib mā is.*muk?*
Okay. What's your name?

Frank: فرانك عبد الله.
Frank 'abd *al*.lah.
Frank Abdallah.

Clerk: دقيقة من فضلك.
da.qī.*qah* min *faḍ*.lik.
One minute, please.

The clerk checks the reservation log.

Clerk: مرحباً بك سيد عبد الله! غرفتك في الطابق السادس.
mar.ḥa.ban *bi*.ka *say*.yid 'abd *al*.lah! ghur.*fa*.tuk fī aṭ.*ṭā*.biq as.*sā*.dis.
Welcome, Mr. Abdallah! Your room is located on the sixth floor.

Frank: شكراً.
shuk.ran.
Thank you.

Clerk: ها هو المفتاح. هل معك أمتعة؟
hā *hu*.wa al.mif.*tāḥ*. hal *ma*.'ak *am*.ti.'a?
Here is your room key. Do you have any luggage?

Frank: نعم, معي ثلاث حقائب.
na.'am *ma*.'ī tha.*lāth* ḥa.*qā*.'ib.
Yes, I have three suitcases.

Clerk: طيّب. الحمال سيساعدك إلى الغرفة.
ṭay.yib. al.ḥam.*māl* sa.yu.*sā*.'i.duk *i*.lá al.*ghur*.fah.
Okay. The baggage handler will help you to your room.

Frank: جيد. وأين المصعد؟
jay.yid wa.'*ay*.na al.*miṣ*.'ad?
Good. And where is the elevator?

Clerk: إلى اليسار.
i.lá al.ya.*sār*.
To your left.

Frank: شكراً.
shuk.ran.
Thank you.

Checking Out of the Hotel

After your nice stay at the hotel, it's time for المغادرة (al.mu.*ghā*.da.rah) (*checkout*). Ask the front desk clerk for the exact checkout; most hotels have a specific checkout time, such as noon, and if you go over that time by only a few minutes, some hotels will charge you for a whole extra night! It's your responsibility to know the exact checkout time and to be out of your room by then.

Before you leave the hotel, make sure you get all your belongings from your room, and take care of the فاتورة (fā.*tū*.rah) (*bill*). Some common extra charges to watch out for include

- فاتورة الهاتف (fā.*tū*.rat al.*hā*.tif) (*telephone bill*)
- فاتورة التلفزيون (fā.*tū*.rat at.ti.li.fiz.*yūn*) (*TV pay-per-view bill*)
- فاتورة الطعام (fā.*tū*.rat aṭ.ṭa.*'ām*) (*food bill*)

When you pay the bill, get a وصل (waṣl) (*receipt*) in case you have a problem with the bill later on or can be reimbursed for your travel costs.

Talkin' the Talk

Gabrielle is ready to check out of her room.

Gabrielle: متى وقت المغادرة؟
ma.tá waqt al.mu.*ghā*.da.rah?
When is the checkout time?

Clerk: وقت المغادرة هو الساعة الواحدة.
waqt al.mu.*ghā*.da.rah *hu*.wa as.*sā*.'ah al.*wā*.ḥi.dah.
Checkout time is one o'clock.

Gabrielle: طيّب. ما هي الفاتورة النهائة؟
ṭay.yib. mā *hi*.ya al.fā.*tū*.rah an.ni.hā.'*iy*.yah?
Okay. What's the final bill?

Clerk: خمسمائة درهم.
khams.*mā*.'at *dir*.ham.
Five hundred dirhams.

Gabrielle: أريد فاتورة من فضلك.
u.*rīd* fā.*tū*.rah min *faḍ*.lik.
I'd like a receipt, please.

Clerk: طبعاً. شكراً لزيارتك وإلى اللقاء!
ṭa.ba.'an. *shuk*.ran li.zi.yā.*ra*.tak wa.'*i*.lá al.li.*qā*'!
Of course. Thank you for your visit, and we look forward to seeing you soon!

FUN & GAMES

Match the Arabic words and phrases with their English equivalents:

Arabic terms and phrases:

1. فاتورة الهاتف
2. هل عندك رسائل لي؟
3. مكتب الاستقبال
4. مرافق
5. متى وقت المغادرة؟

English terms and phrases:

A. Are there any messages for me?
B. When is the checkout time?
C. Telephone bill
D. Reception desk
E. Amenities

The answers are in Appendix C.

» Talking with a doctor

» Getting legal help

Chapter 18
Handling Emergencies

No one can deny the power of positive thinking. However, sometimes negative situations arise, and you must be able to rise to the occasion and help not only yourself but those around you if necessary. So even though remaining positive is always a good thing, you should also know how to handle negative situations if you find yourself faced with them.

Handling an emergency in your native tongue can be quite hard to begin with, given the adrenaline rush and possible feelings of panic, so dealing with a situation in a foreign language such as Arabic may seem daunting. But don't panic! In this chapter, I give you the right words, phrases, and procedures to help you overcome any emergency situation — whether medical, legal, or political — just like a native speaker.

REMEMBER

You can listen to all the Talkin' the Talk dialogues featured in this chapter. Go to `www.dummies.com/go/arabicfd` and click on the dialogue you want to hear.

Shouting Out for Help

When you're witnessing or experiencing an emergency such as a theft, a fire, or even someone having a heart attack, your first instinct is to start yelling and shouting. That's the right instinct. But you also need to be able to communicate coherently so that you can get مساعدة (mu.*sā*.'a.dah) (*help*). This section tells you which words to use to verbally express your sense of emergency in order to get the right kind of help.

Essentially, Arabic has three words that mean "help": مساعدة (mu.*sā*.ʻa.dah), معاونة (mu.*ʻā*.wa.nah), and النجدة (an.*naj*.dah). People interchangeably use all of these words to ask for help in an emergency. You can attract help by shouting النجدة (an.*naj*.dah) once, but you attract more attention when you shout the words consecutively:

» النجدة النجدة! (an.*naj*.dah an.*naj*.dah!) (*Help help!*)

» معاونة معاونة! (mu.*ʻā*.wa.nah mu.*ʻā*.wa.nah!) (*Help help!*)

You can use النجدة to call for help, but be aware that screaming it means that someone is in a severe, extremely dangerous, life-and-death situation. (If there were degrees to words for "help" — where level 3 is high, النجدة would be a level 5.)

Understanding this classification of "help" may be difficult because when you're in an emergency, you tend not to think about your situation on a scale of seriousness. Your reaction is usually, "I'm in trouble, and I need help now." The Arabic vocabulary for emergencies is structured in such a way as to differentiate between life-and-death emergencies and non–life-and-death situations.

REMEMBER

The basic rule for expressing that you need help is that if you're involved in a life-and-death situation, you should scream out النجدة. Think of النجدة as the code red of distress signals, only to be used if your life or the lives of others are in danger. For example, screaming النجدة isn't appropriate if you sprain your ankle while playing soccer. However, if you're witnessing or experiencing a drowning, a heart attack, or a suicide attempt, you should scream النجدة like this:

النجدة النجدة! (an.*naj*.dah an.*naj*.dah!) (*Help help!*)

Here are some other important words and phrases to help you cope with an emergency:

» ساعدوني! (sā.ʻi.*dū*.nī!) (*Help me!*)

» شرطة! (*shur*.ṭah!) (*Police!*)

» أحتاج طبيب! (aḥ.*tāj* ṭa.*bīb!*) (*I need a doctor!*)

» لص! (liṣ!) (*Thief!*)

» حريق! (ḥa.*rīq!*) (*Fire!*)

A little help with the verb "to help"

GRAMMATICALLY SPEAKING

The word مساعدة (mu.*sā*.ʻa.dah) (*assistance*) is derived from the verb ساعد (*sā*.ʻā.da), which means "to help." Although screaming مساعدة is an important first step to attract attention to an emergency, you also need to be able to coherently formulate a sentence in order to get the right kind of help. Use the form ساعد to conjugate the verb "to help" in the ماضي (*mā*.ḍī) (*past tense*) and يساعد (yu.*sā*.ʻid) to conjugate it in the مضارع (mu.*ḍā*.riʻ) (*present tense*). (Check out Chapter 2 for a quick reminder of the present and past tenses.)

Here's the verb "to help" conjugated in the past tense:

Form	Pronunciation	English
أنا ساعدتُ	*a*.nā sā.*'ad*.tu	I helped
أنتَ ساعدتَ	*an*.ta sā.*'ad*.ta	You helped (MS)
أنتِ ساعدتِ	*an*.ti sā.*'ad*.ti	You helped (FS)
هو ساعد	*hu*.wa *sā*.'a.da	He helped
هي ساعدتْ	*hi*.ya *sā*.'a.dat	She helped
نحن ساعدنا	*naḥ*.nu sā.*'ad*.nā	We helped
أنتم ساعدتم	*an*.tum sā.*'ad*.tum	You helped (MP)
أنتنّ ساعدتنّ	an.*tun*.na sā.'ad.*tun*.na	You helped (FP)
هم ساعدوا	hum *sā*.'a.dū	They helped (MP)
هنّ ساعدنّ	*hun*.na sā.*'ad*.na	They helped (FP)
أنتما ساعدتما	an.*tu*.mā sā.'ad.*tu*.mā	You helped (dual/F/M)
هما ساعدا	*hu*.mā sā.'a.*dā*	They helped (dual/M)
هما ساعدتا	*hu*.mā sā.'a.da.*tā*	They helped (dual/F)

Use the form يساعد to conjugate "to help" in the present tense. Recall that the present tense in Arabic describes both a habitual action, such as "I help," and an ongoing action, such as "I am helping."

Form	Pronunciation	English
أنا أساعد	*a*.nā u.*sā*.'id	I am helping
أنتَ تساعد	*an*.ta tu.*sā*.'id	You are helping (MS)
أنتِ تساعدين	*an*.ti tu.sā.'i.*dīn*	You are helping (FS)
هو يساعد	*hu*.wa yu.*sā*.'id	He is helping
هي تساعد	*hi*.ya tu.*sā*.'id	She is helping
نحن نساعد	*naḥ*.nu nu.*sā*.'id	We are helping
أنتم تساعدون	*an*.tum tu.sā.'i.*dūn*	You are helping (MP)
أنتنّ تساعدنّ	an.*tun*.na tu.sā.*'id*.na	You are helping (FP)
هم يساعدون	hum yu.sā.'i.*dūn*	They are helping (MP)
هنّ يساعدن	*hun*.na yu.sā.*'id*.na	They are helping (FP)
أنتما تساعدان	an.*tu*.mā tu.sā.'i.*dān*	You are helping (dual/M/F)
هما يساعدان	*hu*.mā yu.sā.'i.*dān*	They are helping (dual/M)
هما تساعدان	*hu*.mā tu.sā.'i.*dān*	They are helping (dual/F)

GRAMMATICALLY SPEAKING

Although Arabic has more than one word for "help," **مساعدة** is the most conjugated verb form. **معاونة** may also be conjugated using the form **عاون** in the past tense and **يعاون** in the present, but it's more of an archaic and arcane verb that isn't widely used in everyday Arabic. Because **النجدة** is more of a code word for distress, it doesn't have a verb equivalent form.

Lending a hand

Being in an emergency doesn't always mean that you're the one who needs help. You may be faced with a situation where you're actually the person who's in a position to offer help. In this case, you need to know words and phrases of an altogether different nature. The words and phrases in this section help you better respond to a situation in which you're the helper and not the one being helped.

REMEMBER

The first thing you do in such a situation is ask questions to assess the damage and determine what course of action to take:

- ماذا حدث؟ (*mā*.dhā *ḥa*.da.tha?) (*What happened?*)
- هل كل شيء بخير؟ (hal kul shay' bi.*khayr?*) (*Is everything alright?*)
- هل تريد مساعدة؟ (hal tu.*rīd* mu.*sā*.'a.dah?) (*Do you need help?*) (M)
- ما نوع المساعدة التي تريد؟ (mā naw' al.mu.*sā*.'a.dah al.*la*.tī tu.*rīd?*) (*What kind of help do you need?*) (M)
- هل تريد أن تذهب إلى المستشفى؟ (hal tu.*rīd* an *tadh*.hab *i*.lá al.mus.*tash*.fá?) (*Do you want to go to the hospital?*) (M)
- هل تريد طبيب؟ (hal tu.*rīd* ṭa.*bīb?*) (*Do you need a doctor?*) (M)

If you're in a situation in which injuries are serious and the person appears to be disoriented, then you must take further steps, such as contacting police or other first responders.

If you're ever in a situation where you need to call the police, you may say the following on the phone: أحتاج مساعدة فوراً (aḥ.*tāj* mu.*sā*.'a.dah *faw*.ran) (*I need help right away*).

Talkin' the Talk

Lamia is walking down the street when, all of a sudden, the woman walking in front of her falls on the ground. Lamia approaches the woman to see how she can be of help.

Lamia: **عفواً. هل كل شيء بخير؟**
'*af*.wan, hal kul shay' bi.*khayr?*
Excuse me. Is everything alright?

Woman: **نعم. كل شيء بخير.**
na.'am. kul shay' bi.*khayr*.
Yes. Everything is alright.

Lamia: **ماذا حدث؟**
mā.dhā *ḥa*.dath.tha?
What happened?

Woman: **لا شيء. وقعتُ.**
lā shay'. wa.*qa'*.tu.
Nothing. I fell.

Lamia: هل تريدين مساعدة؟
hal tu.rī.*dīn* mu.*sā*.'a.dah?
Do you need help?

Woman: لا شكراً. كل شيء سيكون بخير.
lā *shuk*.ran. kul shay' sa.ya.*kūn* bi.*khayr*.
No thank you. Everything will be alright.

Getting Medical Help

If you're like me, you may find that even though going to the doctor's office is necessary and important, it isn't always the most fun part of your day. But visiting the doctor is essential for each and every one of us. This section introduces you to important medical terms to help you interact effectively with medical staff.

Locating the appropriate doctor

In case of a medical urgency, your first stop should be the مستشفى (mus.*tash*.fá) (*hospital*) to see a طبيب (ṭa.*bīb*) (*doctor*). If you simply need a checkup, go see a طبيب عام (ṭa.*bīb* 'ām) (*general doctor*). If your needs are more specific, look for one of these specialist doctors:

- طبيب أسنان (ṭa.*bīb* as.*nān*) (*dentist*)
- طبيب عيون (ṭa.*bīb* 'u.*yūn*) (*ophthalmologist*)
- طبيب أقدام (ṭa.*bīb* aq.*dām*) (*orthopedist*)
- طبيب أطفال (ṭa.*bīb* aṭ.*fāl*) (*pediatrician*)

Talking about your body

Locating the right doctor is only the first step toward getting treatment. In order to interact with the doctor, you need to be able to identify your different body parts in Arabic, explaining which parts hurt and which are fine. Table 18-1 lists all your major body parts.

TABLE 18-1 Body Parts

Arabic	Pronunciation	English
جسد	*ja*.sad	body
رأس	ra's	head
فم	fam	mouth
لسان	li.*sān*	tongue
أسنان	as.*nān*	teeth
وجه	wajh	face
شعر	sha'r	hair
جلد	jild	skin
أنف	anf	nose
أذنان	u.dhu.*nān*	ears
عينان	'ay.*nān*	eyes
مخ	mukh	brain
قلب	qalb	heart
رئة	*ri*.'ah	lung
كتف	*ka*.tif	shoulder
صدر	ṣadr	chest
معدة	*ma*.'i.dah	stomach
ذراع	dhi.*rā'*	arm
يد	yad	hand
أصابع	a.*ṣā*.bi'	fingers
رجل	rijl	leg

(continued)

TABLE 18-1 ***(continued)***

Arabic	Pronunciation	English
قدم	*qa*.dam	foot
القدم	a.*sā*.bi' al.*qa*.dam	toes
ركبة	*ruk*.bah	knee
عظم	'aẓm	bone
دم	dam	blood
ظهر	ẓahr	back

Explaining your symptoms

The doctor can't provide you with the proper treatment unless you communicate the kind of pain you're experiencing. How مريض (ma.*rīḍ*) (*sick*) do you feel? Do you have a صداع (ṣu.*dā*') (*headache*)? Or perhaps a حرارة (ḥa.*rā*.rah) (*fever*)? Table 18-2 lists common symptoms.

TABLE 18-2 **Common Symptoms**

Arabic	Pronunciation	English
مرض	ma.*raḍ*	sickness
ألم	a.*lam*	ache/ailment
سعال	su.*'āl*	cough
برد	bard	cold
حرق	ḥarq	burn
رضة	raḍ.*ḍah*	bruise
ألم الظهر	a.lam aẓ.ẓahr	backache
حساسية	ḥa.sā.*siy*.ya	allergy

When you go to the doctor, he or she may ask you, ماذا يؤلمك؟ (*mā*.dhā yu'.*li*.muk) (*What hurts you?*). The most common way to respond to this question is to name the body part that hurts followed by يؤلمني (yu'.*li*.mu.nī) (*hurts me*). So when the doctor asks, "What hurts you?" you may say:

- رأسي يؤلمني. (*ra'*.sī yu'.*li*.mu.nī.) (*My head hurts me.*)
- أذناي تؤلمني. (u.dhu.*nāy*.ya tu'.*li*.mu.nī.) (*My ears hurt me.*)
- صدري يؤلمني. (*ṣad*.rī yu'.*li*.mu.nī.) (*My chest hurts me.*)
- ذراعي تؤلمني. (dhi.*rā*.'ī tu'.*li*.mu.nī.) (*My arm hurts me.*)

Getting treatment

After the doctor analyzes your symptoms, he or she is able to offer you علاج ('i.*lāj*) (*treatment*). Following the doctor's orders is important for both getting and remaining سليم (sa.*līm*) (*healthy*), so pay attention. Here are treatment-related words you may encounter:

- دواء (da.*wā'*) (*medicine*)
- صيدلية (ṣay.da.*liy*.yah) (*pharmacy*)
- عيادة ('i.*yā*.dah) (*clinic*)

Talkin' the Talk

Omar has been feeling nauseous all day long, so he decides to go see his doctor in the afternoon.

Doctor: ماذا يؤلمك؟
mā.dhā yu'.*li*.muk?
What hurts you?

Omar: رأسي يؤلمني.
ra'.sī yu'.*li*.mu.nī.
My head hurts.

Doctor: شيء آخر؟
shay' *ā*.khar?
Anything else?

Omar:	نعم. عندي حرارة. *na*.'am. '*in*.dī ḥa.*rā*.rah. *Yes. I have a fever.*
Doctor:	خذ هذا الأسبرين وستكون بخير. khudh *hā*.dhā al.as.bi.*rīn* wa.sa.ta.*kūn* bi.*khayr*. *Take this aspirin, and you will be alright.*

WORDS TO KNOW

شراب السعال	sha.rāb as.su.'āl	cough medicine
صورة أشعة	ṣū.rat a.shi.'ah	X-ray
أسبرين	as.bi.rīn	aspirin

Acquiring Legal Help

I hope you never need it, but you may have a run-in with the law and need the services of a محامي (mu.*ḥā*.mī) (*lawyer*). The lawyer has a good understanding of the قانون (qā.*nūn*) (*law*) and is in a position to help you if you're ever charged with committing a جريمة (ja.*rī*.mah) (*crime*).

TIP

If you happen to be in a foreign country and need legal representation, the best route is to contact your country's قنصلية (qun.ṣu.*liy*.yah) (*consulate*) and ask to speak to the قنصل (*qun*.ṣul) (*consul*). Because consular officers have a very good understanding of the laws of their host countries, you may be better off getting help directly from them rather than finding your own lawyer. Especially if it looks like you have to go to محكمة (*maḥ*.ka.mah) (*court*) and face a قاضي (*qā*.ḍī) (*judge*), the help a consulate can provide is invaluable.

You may also want to call your country's سفارة (si.*fā*.rah) (*embassy*) if you're in a really serious situation. Even if you're unable to talk directly to the سفير (sa.*fīr*) (*ambassador*), your embassy staff may take the appropriate steps to provide you with assistance.

FUN & GAMES

How do you say the following body parts in Arabic? Answers are in Appendix C.

Illustrations by Elizabeth Kurtzman

1. ________
2. ________
3. ________
4. ________
5. ________
6. ________
7. ________
8. ________
9. ________
10. ________
11. ________

4
The Part of Tens

IN THIS PART . . .

Discover the best ways to learn Arabic as quickly as possible.

Find out the ten greatest Arabic expressions.

Get to know the ten greatest Arabic proverbs.

» Practicing on Arabic speakers

» Getting musical

Chapter 19

Ten Ways to Pick Up Arabic Quickly

Arabic is a language that needs to be constantly spoken, heard, and practiced. Even many native speakers try to read an Arabic newspaper every day or watch a نشرة إخبارية (*nash*.rah ikh.bā.*riy*.yah) (*news broadcast*) in order to maintain their level of fluency. So to get the best grasp of the language, you should try to immerse yourself in an environment where Arabic is the prevalent language. This chapter has recommendations on some key ways to help you not only pick up Arabic, but also maintain a good degree of understanding of the language after you're comfortable with it.

Watch Arabic Television

Since the late 1990s, the Arabic audiovisual landscape has experienced a seismic shift. With the advent of satellite TV across the Arab world and the Middle East, Arab TV stations have spread across the world. Besides the well-known satellite news outlets الجزيرة (al.ja.*zī*.rah) (*The Peninsula*) and العربية (al.ʻa.ra.*biy*.yah) (*The Arabic*), there are a number of other TV stations you can watch to help you fine-tune your accent and intonation. The news channels offer valuable exposure to spoken Modern Standard Arabic, which is the Arabic used in this book. Because this version's more formal than others, watching Arabic news channels will give you a better grasp of the grammatical rules — and your Arabic will be greatly improved as a result.

Another option for Arabic TV is MBC (Middle East Broadcast Corporation), which airs movies, soap operas, and talk shows that showcase some of the local spoken dialects such as Lebanese and Egyptian. If you're in the United States, you can order Arabic channels from your local cable provider or satellite TV operator; these channels have subtitles in English so you can follow along. Believe it or not, watching TV is one of the best ways to pick up a language. Personally, I didn't start speaking English until I was 10 years old, and one of the most effective tools that helped me grasp the language was watching sitcoms like *The Simpsons.*

Use the Dictionary

The قاموس (qā.*mūs*) (*dictionary*) contains a wealth of information about Arabic words, phrases, and expressions. Simply picking up the dictionary once a day and memorizing a single word can have a huge effect on your Arabic vocabulary. After you reach fluency in reading and writing Arabic, you'll realize that vowels aren't included in most of the Arabic texts you read, such as newspapers, books, and magazines. At first, trying to read without the vocalizations takes practice, but with the help of the dictionary, you should be able to overcome this hurdle.

TIP

If reading the dictionary is simply too low-tech for your taste, go online and find a word-a-day generating program that sends you an email every morning with a new Arabic word that includes its pronunciation, meaning, etymology, and the context in which you use it. What a great way for you to build your vocabulary without actually opening the dictionary. Check out `www.ectaco.com` and `arabicpod101.com`.

Read Arabic Newspapers

The Arabic صحافة (ṣa.*ḥā*.fah) (*press*) is very vibrant and offers many different publications covering a wide array of perspectives. Newspapers across the Arab world cater to all sorts of viewpoints, from the ultra-liberal to the ultra-conservative. Reading Arabic newspapers is a good way to not only practice reading the language, but also become more familiar with the issues concerning the Arab world.

You can purchase Arabic newspapers at most major newsstands in major metropolitan areas, such as New York. Also, many Arabic newspapers now have online editions that you can access anytime, from anywhere. For more on Arabic newspapers and where to locate them, visit www.al-baab.com.

Surf the Internet

The Internet is one of the greatest inventions of all time — you have practically all the world's information at your fingertips! Plus, it's an amazing tool that can help you master Arabic quickly and efficiently. Simply visit any search engine — such as Google or Yahoo! — type the search word "Arabic," and start surfing. Or you can browse media websites, such as www.aljazeera.net. Most media sites have a Links section where you generally find a list of other websites that are similar in nature. Another wonderful resource is foreigncy.us, which includes vocabulary lists along with articles and video clips. Perusing these sites in Arabic should greatly improve your reading comprehension.

Streaming Services

The explosion of Arabic online content has been a boon to aspiring Arabic speakers the world over! As the Internet becomes more ubiquitous in our lives, so do the available choices to help us become better Arabic speakers. In recent years, streaming services online have proliferated, and they offer an excellent way for you to immerse yourself in the pleasures of Arabic speaking. Jump online and search for "Arabic streaming services," and a plethora of sites will pop up. One of my favorites, which I highly recommend, is the BBC Arabic streaming service. This is a terrific way for you to pick up new words and also stay up-to-date on current events in the Middle East and around the world!

Listen to Arabic Music

Arabic music is one of the liveliest, most melodic, and fun types of music in the world. Because Arabic music is so energetic and fun, you'll pick up new phrases and words without even realizing it! You can choose from a lot of popular Arabic musicians, including:

- الشاب خالد **Sheb Khaled** from Algeria, who plays راي (rai) music. Rai music is the equivalent of Arabic hip-hop. The singer freestyles over a musical beat or rhythm.

- فريد الأطرش **Farid al-Atrash,** also written as **Farid El-Atrache,** was a master of the عود ('ūd). The عود is a musical instrument that's similar to the guitar, but unlike a regular guitar, it has a tear-dropped shape with six sets of double strings.
- نجاة عتابو **Najat Aatabou** is a popular folk singer from Morocco.
- نانسي عجرم No list of Arabic singers would be complete without **Nancy Ajram**, perhaps the most famous Arabic pop musician in the world.

Check out any of these artists online, or go to your local music store and browse through the Middle East section for even more possibilities.

Sing Arabic Songs

Singing an أغنية (ugh.*niy*.yah) (*song*) is a fun, interactive, and effective way to pick up Arabic. Arabic songs tend to be extremely melodic and soulful, so not only will you enjoy singing a song, but you'll also encounter new vocabulary and identify some of the intonations and beats that make Arabic such a unique language.

Make Arabic-Speaking Friends

Nothing can really substitute for having human contact and human interactions. Making friends who are native or fluent Arabic speakers and carrying on conversations with them in Arabic dramatically improves your speaking and comprehension skills. After all, your friends are in a position to correct you gently and help you use the right expressions, phrases, and sentences in the appropriate contexts. Part of the challenge of picking up a language, especially one like Arabic, lies in the fact that you need to put your language skills — especially vocabulary and expressions — in the right context. Speaking with friends is the best way to do that.

Watch Arabic Movies

Watching Arabic movies can be a lot more fun than watching TV because you aren't interrupted by commercials and you generally have subtitles to follow. Most local movie stores and libraries carry popular Arabic movies on DVD, so you're sure to find something that interests you. Just be sure to get a movie with

English subtitles so that you can follow along! Popular streaming services such as Netflix also often carry a number of Arabic movies, complete with subtitles.

TIP

A movie that's worth watching is the Arabic version of *Lawrence of Arabia*. Another classic movie is *The Messenger* الرسالة (ar.ri.*sā*.lah).

Eat at a Middle Eastern Restaurant

Almost every city in the world has at least one Middle Eastern مطعم (maṭ.'*am*) (*restaurant*), so find one in your area. Eating at a Middle Eastern restaurant provides you with a safe, fun, and engaging atmosphere in which to practice your language skills by interacting with the waitstaff in Arabic. Order drinks, food, and ask questions about the food preparation in Arabic, and you'll be amazed at how much you'll improve your Arabic reading and comprehension skills. And the restaurant staff are sure to be impressed with both your skill and interest in the language!

IN THIS CHAPTER

» Welcoming someone with open arms

» Using religious expressions appropriately

» Sending your regards

Chapter 20 Ten Favorite Arabic Expressions

Arabic uses a lot of very colorful expressions and words, which is to be expected because Arabic is a very poetic language. Arabic speakers speak Arabic with a burning passion because the words, phrases, and expressions are so descriptive and conjure up strong visual images.

Linguists have studied the language in order to figure out why Arabic tends to be much more flowery and descriptive than most languages. One theory explains this phenomenon by examining the structure of the language itself; unlike in English, adjectives in Arabic always come *after* the noun. This simple linguistic construct encourages speakers to use adjectives — some would argue they're the main ingredients of poetic sentences — which in turn creates very descriptive sentences. In English, because adjectives come before the noun, you're forced to use a limited number of adjectives before you have to get to the point, the noun.

Whatever the explanation, the passion with which speakers speak Arabic is sometimes hard to translate. However, if you familiarize yourself with some common expressions that make Arabic one of the most poetic languages in the world, you can come close to capturing that spirit! The expressions I cover in this chapter help you get acquainted with popular phrases in Arabic.

مرحباً بكم

(*mar.*ḥa.ban *bi.*kum) (*Welcome to all of you!*)

This term of welcoming is extremely popular with Arabic speakers. They usually say it with a lot of zest and enthusiasm while using animated hand gestures. It's not uncommon for someone to say مرحباً بكم and then proceed to hug you or give you a kiss on the cheek. This expression is a very affectionate form of greeting someone, such as an old friend, a very special guest, or a close family relative. But the relationship doesn't necessarily have to be a close one — if you're ever invited into a Middle Eastern home for a dinner or a lunch, don't be surprised if the host jovially shouts مرحباً بكم and gives you a great big bear hug.

The shortened form of مرحباً بكم is to simply say مرحباً, which literally means "welcome." You may also say مرحباً بكَ (*mar.*ḥa.ban *bi.*ka), which is the masculine singular form of مرحباً بكم. (So you use مرحباً بكَ when greeting a male friend and مرحباً بكِ [*mar.*ḥa.ban *bi.*ki] to greet a female friend because بكِ is the feminine singular form of بكم.) Finally, if you have a very close relationship with the person you're greeting, you may even use a variation of the following expression: مرحباً يا حبيبي (*mar.*ḥa.ban yā ḥa.*bī.*bī) (*Welcome my darling* [M]) or مرحباً يا حبيبتي (*mar.*ḥa.ban yā ḥa.*bī.*ba.tī) (*Welcome my darling* [F]).

ممتاز!

(mum.*tāz*) (*Excellent!*)

This expression is used much like "excellent" is used in English: It's a way to note that something is going very well. For instance, a teacher may tell her students ممتاز if they conjugate a difficult Arabic verb in the past tense, or a fan may yell ممتاز if his hometown team scores a goal against an opponent. ممتاز is used during joyous events or as a sign of encouragement. It's a very positive word that Arabic speakers like to use because it connotes a positive attitude. If you're having a conversation with a native speaker, it's very likely that he or she will use the word a lot for the duration of the conversation. You should do the same.

الحمد لله

(al.*ḥam*.du lil.*lāh*) (*Praise to God*)

A number of expressions in the Arabic language make reference to God for a very simple reason: as a spoken language, Arabic evolved from the writings of the Quran — Islam's Holy Book — which was recorded soon after the death of the Prophet Muhammad. Muslims believe that the Quran is actually God's words transmitted by the Angel Gabriel to the Prophet Muhammad.

According to Muslim tradition and belief, the Quran is literally God's message to His followers. Therefore, a lot of references to God come directly from the Quran. Although spoken Arabic evolved from a religious language based on the Quran toward one with a more secular and everyday usage, it nevertheless retained many of its references to God. Although they're based on a direct reference to God, many of these phrases are actually used quite casually nowadays.

الحمد لله, which has very wide usage, is a part of everyday Arabic. Arabic speakers say الحمد لله after performing almost any single task, including finishing a meal, drinking water, finishing a project at work, and running an errand. The expression's extensive application goes beyond completing tasks; for example, if someone asks you, كيف الحال (kayf al.*ḥāl*?) (*How are you doing?*) you may reply الحمد لله and mean "Praise to God; I'm doing well." Because of its versatility, it's customary to hear الحمد لله quite often when native speakers are talking to each other.

إن شاء الله

(in *shā*.'a al.*lāh*) (*God willing*)

If you've ever watched Arabic speakers on Arabic TV, you've probably heard them use the expression إن شاء الله. This expression, which literally means "If God wishes it" or "If God wills it," is very popular among Arabic speakers when discussing future events. It's almost a rule that whenever someone brings up an event that will take place in the future, the expression إن شاء الله follows soon after.

For example, when someone asks you how you think you're going to do on your next exam, you say أتمنى أن أنجح إن شاء الله (a.ta.*man*.ná an *an*.jaḥ in *shā*.'a al.*lāh*) (*I hope I do well, if God wishes it*). Or if someone asks you if your sister is going to start working soon, you say ستبدأ الاثنين إن شاء الله (sa.*tab*.da' al.'ith.*nayn* in *shā*.'a al.*lāh*) (*She starts on Monday, if God wishes it*). Politicians in particular like to use this expression when someone asks them when they're going to hold elections. They say وقت قريب إن شاء الله (waqt qa.*rīb* in *shā*.'a al.*lāh*) (*Sometime soon, if God wishes it*).

مبروك!

(mab.*rūk!*) (*Congratulations!*)

The root of the word مبروك is the noun بركة (*ba*.ra.kah), which means "blessing." مبروك is used at joyous occasions, such as the birth of a baby, a wedding, a graduation ceremony, or another festive event. Though its strict interpretation is "Blessing upon you," مبروك is just like saying "Congratulations." When you say مبروك, make sure you say it with a lot of energy and enthusiasm!

بإذن الله

(bi.'*idhn* il.*lāh*) (*With God's permission*)

This expression is meant to motivate and offer support and guidance, and although this expression contains a reference to God, it's actually a lot less common than expressions such as إن شاء الله or الحمد لله. بإذن الله is used only during very special occasions, such as when one is facing serious challenges or is having difficulty in life, marriage, work, or school. Whenever someone's facing hardship, you can commonly hear him or her say سأواجه هذه الصعوبة بإذن الله (sa.'u.*wā*.jih *hā*.dhi.hi aṣ.ṣu.'ū.bah bi.'*idhn* il.*lāh*) (*I will face this difficulty, with God's permission*). You can also use بإذن الله to encourage a friend who's having troubles. You may tell her كل شيء سيكون بخير بإذن الله (kul shay' sa.ya.*kūn* bi.*khayr* bi.'*idhn* il.*lāh*) (*All will go well, with God's permission*).

بالصحة

(biṣ.*ṣaḥ*.ḥah) (*With health*)

Even though this expression literally means "with health," people don't necessarily use it in a context of encouragement or support like بإذن الله (see the preceding section). Rather, بالصحة is an appropriate thing to say after someone has finished a difficult task and can relax and enjoy himself. For example, if a friend has wrapped up writing a book, closed a big deal, or ended a difficult case, you may say to him بالصحة, which signifies that your friend will be stronger as a result of accomplishing what he's accomplished and now can rest a bit.

تحيات

(ta.*ḥiy.yāt*) (*Regards*)

تحيات is a religious term that Muslims use when they're praying. After a Muslim finishes praying, he performs the تحيات by turning once to the right and once to the left, acknowledging the two angels that Muslims believe guard each person.

In addition to its religious affiliation, Arabic speakers commonly use تحيات to send their regards. For instance, a friend may say to you سلّم على أبيك (*sal.*lim '*a.*lá a.*bīk*) (*Say hello to your father for me*). Similarly, to send your regards to a friend, you say تحيات.

مبلغ

(mu.*bal.*lagh) (*To be delivered*)

مبلغ is an expression that's similar to تحيات in that you use it to send regards. However, unlike مبلغ, تحيات is a response; that is, you use it *after* someone sends his or her regards to someone you know. So if someone says to you, سلّم على أخيك (*sal.*lim '*a.*lá 'a.*khīk*) (*Say hello to your brother for me*), you respond, مبلغ. Responding with this expression means that you acknowledge the message and thank the person for it on behalf of your sister. So make sure to only say مبلغ after someone sends his or her regards — not before!

تبارك الله

(ta.*bā.*rak al.*lāh*) (*God be exalted*)

This expression is the equivalent of "God bless you" in English; it's most commonly used among close friends or family members to congratulate each other on accomplishments, achievements, or other happy events. For instance, if a son or daughter receives a good grade on an exam, the parents say, تبارك الله. Another very popular use for this expression is to express warmth and joy toward kids.

» Seeking knowledge

» Expressing the importance of teamwork

Chapter 21

Ten Great Arabic Proverbs

Even if you've read only a few chapters of this book, you've probably figured out that Arabic is a very poetic language. One aspect of the language that reinforces its poetic nature is the use of أمثال (am.*thāl*) (*proverbs*). Proverbs play an important role in the Arabic language. If you're having a conversation with an Arabic speaker or listening to Arabic speakers converse among themselves, don't be surprised to hear proverbs peppered throughout the conversation. This chapter introduces you to some of the more common and flowery proverbs of the Arabic language.

الأمثال نور الكلام

(al.'am.*thāl* nūr al.ka.*lām*.) (*Proverbs are the light of speech.*)

The role of proverbs in Arabic is so important that there's a proverb on the importance of proverbs!

اعمل خيراً وألقه في البحر

(*i*ʿ.mal *khay*.ran wa.al.*qi*.hi fī al.*baḥr.*) (*Do a good deed and cast it into the sea.*)

Arab culture emphasizes humility and modesty. This proverb means that when you commit a charitable act, you shouldn't go around boasting about it; rather, you should "cast it into the sea" where no one can find out about it.

اطلبوا العلم من المهد إلى اللحد

(uṭ.*lu*.bū al.ʿ*ilm* min al.*mahd* i.lá al.*laḥd.*) (*Seek knowledge from the cradle to the grave.*)

العلم (al.ʿ*ilm*) (*knowledge*) is an important virtue in Arabic culture. Arabs have produced some of the greatest legal, medical, and scientific minds in history, in no small part because Arabs like to instill in their children a lifelong desire to learn and continue learning every single day of one's existence.

يد واحدة لا تصفّق

(yadd *wā*.ḥi.dah lā tu.*ṣaf*.fiq.) (*A hand by itself cannot clap.*)

This proverb, which is common in the West but originates in Arab culture, underscores the importance of teamwork, cooperation, and collaboration.

الحرباء لا يغادر شجرته حتى يكون مؤكداً على شجرة أخرى

(al.ḥir.*bā*' lā yu.*ghā*.di.ru sha.ja.*ra*.tu.hu *ḥat*.tá ya.*kū*.na mu.'ak.*ki*.dan *ʿa*.lá *sha*.ja.rah *ukh*.r.á) (*The chameleon does not leave his tree until he is sure of another.*)

This proverb stresses the importance of foresight, planning, and looking ahead. A chameleon that is mindful of predators won't change trees until it knows that it'll be safe in the next tree it goes to.

خطأ معروف أحسن من حقيقة غير معروفة

(*kha.*ṭa' *ma'*.rūf *aḥ*.san min ḥa.*qī*.qah ghayr ma'.*rū*.fah.) (*A known mistake is better than an unknown truth.*)

This metaphysical proverb has a deep meaning: It's better for you to identify and learn from a mistake than to not know a truth at all. In the debate of known versus unknown knowledge, this proverb indicates that knowing is better than not knowing, even if what you know is not an absolute truth.

السرّ مثل الحمامة: عندما يغادر يدي يطير

(as.*sirr* mithl al.ḥa.*mā*.mah: '*in*.da.mā yu.*ghā*.dir *ya*.dī ya.*ṭīr*.) (*A secret is like a dove: When it leaves my hand, it flies away.*)

A secret is meant to be kept close to your chest — in other words, you shouldn't divulge a secret. As soon as you let out a secret, it flies away and spreads around. Just as a dove won't leave unless you release it, a secret won't become known unless you divulge it.

العقل للنظر والقلب للسمع

(al.'*aql* lin.*na*.ẓar wal.*qalb* lis.*sa*.ma'.) (*The mind is for seeing, and the heart is for hearing.*)

The mind is to be used for analytical purposes: observation and analysis. The heart, on the other hand, is for emotions; you should listen and feel with your heart.

كل يوم من حياتك صفحة من تاريخك

(kul yawm min ḥa.*yā*.tak *ṣaf*.ḥah min tā.*rī*.khak.) (*Every day of your life is a page of your history.*)

You only live one life, so you should enjoy every single day. At the end, each day's experiences are what make up your history.

اللي فاتك بليلة فاتك بحيلة

(*il.*lī *fā*.tak bi.*lī*.la *fā*.tak bi.*ḥī*.lah.) (*He who surpasses [is older than] you by one night surpasses you by one idea.*)

In Arabic culture and society, maturity and respect for elders is a highly regarded virtue. This proverb reinforces the idea that elders are respected, and their counsel is often sought.

5 Appendixes

IN THIS PART . . .

Look up common words in the mini-dictionary, which includes both Arabic to English and English to Arabic.

Use the verb tables for help conjugating verbs in the past, present, and future tenses.

Check the answers to the Fun & Games exercises to see how well you did!

Appendix A

Arabic to English Mini-Dictionary

ا

أبريل (ab.*rīl*): April

الاثنين (al.'ith.*nayn*): Monday

إجاصة (i.*jā*.ṣah) F: pear

أجرة (*uj*.rah) F: fee

الأحد (al.'*a*.ḥad): Sunday

أذنين (u.dhu.*nayn*) F: two ears

الأربعاء (al.'ar.ba.'*ā*'): Wednesday

أرز (*a*.ruz) M: rice

أرقام (ar.*qām*) M: numbers

استقبال (is.tiq.*bāl*) M: reception

أسرة (*us*.rah) F: family

سبانخ (sa.bā.*nekh*) M: spinach

إسلام (is.*lām*) M: Islam

لقب الأسرة (*la*.qab al.'*us*.rah) M: last name, family name

اسم شخصي (ism *shakh*.ṣī) M: first name

أسنان (as.*nān*) F: teeth

أصدقاء (aṣ.di.*qā*') M: friends

أغسطس (u.*ghus*.ṭus): August

أكتوبر (uk.*tū*.bar): October

أفوكادو (a.fū.*kā*.dū) F: avocado

أكل (*a*.ka.la): ate

آلة (*ā*.lah) F: machine

آلة تصوير مستندات (*ā*.lat taṣ.*wīr* mus.ta.na.*dāt*) F: photocopy machine

آلة الفاكس (*ā*.lat al.*fāks*) F: fax machine

أمتعة (*am*.ti.'ah) F: luggage

انسحاب (in.si.*ḥāb*) M: withdrawal

أنف (anf) M: nose

أولئك (u.*lā*.'i.ka) MP/FP: those

أيس كريم (*a*.yis ki.*rīm*) M: ice cream

أين (*ay*.na): where

ب

باب (bāb) M: door

باذنجان (bā.dhin.*jān*) F: eggplant

برد (bard) M: cold

برق (barq) M: lightning

بازلاء (bā.zil.*lā*') F: peas

بصل (*ba*.ṣal) M: onions

بطاطا (ba.*ṭā*.ṭā) F: potato

شمام؟ (ba.*ṭīkh*) M: cantaloupe

بعد (*ba*'.da): after

بعد الظهر (*ba*'.da aẓ.*ẓuhr*): afternoon

بكم (bi.*kam*): how much

بنت (bint) F: girl

بوق (būq) M: trumpet

بيانو (bi.*yā*.nū) M: piano

بيت (bayt) M: house

بيض (bayḍ) M: eggs

ت

تاريخ الميلاد (tā.*rīkh* al.mī.*lād*) M: date of birth

تاكسي (*tāk*.sī) M: taxi

تزحلق (ta.*zaḥ*.luq) M: ice skating

تزلج (ta.*zal*.luj) M: skiing

تقاعد (ta.*qā*.ʻud) M: retirement

تكلم (ta.*kal*.la.ma): spoke

تلفزيون (ti.li.fiz.*yūn*) M: television

تلك (*til*.ka) F: that

توازن (ta.*wā*.zun) M: balance

توت (tūt) M: strawberry

ث

ثانية (*thā*.ni.yah) F: second

الثلاثاء (ath.thu.lā.*thā'*): Tuesday

ثلاجة (thal.*lā*.jah) F: refrigerator

ثلج (thalj) M: snow

ثمن (*tha*.man) M: price

ثوم محمّر (thawm mu.*ḥam*.mar) M: roasted garlic

ج

جامعة (*jā*.mi.ʻah) F: university

جبن (jubn) M: cheese

جريدة (ja.*rī*.dah) F: newspaper

جريمة (ja.*rī*.mah) F: crime

جسد (*ja*.sad) M: body

جلّابة (jal.*lā*.bah) F: Arab dress

جمباز (jum.*bāz*) M: gymnastics

الجمعة (al.*jum*.ʻah): Friday

جملة (*jum*.lah) F: sentence

جوارب (ja.*wā*.rib) F: socks

جواز السفر (jaw.*wāz* as.*sa*.far) M: passport

جواهري (ja.*wā*.hi.rī) M: jeweler

ح

حاسوب (ḥā.*sūb*) F: computer

حافلة (*ḥā*.fi.lah) F: bus

حبوب الفطور (ḥu.*būb* al.fu.*ṭūr*) M: breakfast cereal

حجز (ḥajz) M: reservation

حذاء (ḥi.*dhā'*) M: shoe

حرارة (ḥa.*rā*.rah) F: temperature

حريرة (ḥa.*rī*.rah) F: Moroccan soup

حزام (ḥi.*zām*) M: belt

حزين (ḥa.*zīn*): sad

حساء (ḥa.*sā'*) F: soup

حكم (*ḥa*.kam) M: referee

حلّاق (ḥal.*lāq*) M: barber, hairdresser

حليب (ḥa.*līb*) M: milk

حوار (ḥi.*wār*) M: conversation/dialogue

حياكة (ḥi.*yā*.kah) F: sewing

خ

خرشوف (khar.*shūf*) M: artichokes

خريف (kha.*rīf*) M: fall

خزانة (kha.*zā*.nah) F: cupboard

خس (khas) M: lettuce

خسر (*kha*.si.ra): lose

خطأ (*kha*.ṭa') M: foul; mistake

الخميس (al.kha.*mīs*): Thursday

خوخ (khawkh) M: peach

خيار (khī.*yār*) M: cucumber

د

دجاج (da.*jāj*) M: chicken

درّاجة (dar.*rā*.jah) F: bicycle

درّاجة نارية (dar.*rā*.jah nā.*riy*.yah) F: motorcycle

درجة (*da*.ra.jah) F: degree

درس (*da*.ra.sa): studied

دفتر (*daf*.tar) M: notebook

دقيقة (da.*qī*.qah) F: minute

دكّان (duk.*kān*) M: store

دلاحة (dal.*lā*.ḥah) F: watermelon

دواء (da.*wā*') M: medicine

دوش (dūsh) M: shower

ديسمبر (dī.*sam*.bir): December

ذ

ذراع (dhi.*rā*') M: arm

ذرة (*dhu*.rah) F: corn

ذلك (*dhā*.li.ka) M: that

ذهب (*dha*.ha.ba): went

ر

رئة (*ri*.'ah) F: lung

راتب (*rā*.tib) M: salary

رأس (ra's) M: head

ربيع (ra.*bī*') M: spring

رجل (rijl) F: leg

رجل الإطفاء (ra.*jul* al.'iṭ.*fā*') M: firefighter

رحلة (*riḥ*.lah) F: trip

رخصة القيادة (*rukh*.ṣat al.qi.*yā*.dah) F: driver's license

رسم (rasm) M: drawing

رطوبة (ru.*ṭū*.bah) F: humidity

رعد (ra'd) M: thunder

رقص (raqṣ) M: dancing

رقم (*ra*.qam) M: number

رقم الهاتف (*ra*.qam al.*hā*.tif) M: telephone number

ركبة (*ruk*.bah) F: knee

روبيان (rūb.*yān*) M: shrimp

ريح (*rīḥ*) F: wind

ز

زبون (zu.*būn*) M: client

زيارة (zi.*yā*.rah) F: visit

زيت (zayt) M: oil

زيت الزيتون (zayt az.zay.*tūn*) M: olive oil

زيتونة (zay.*tū*.nah) F: an olive

س

ساعة (*sā*.'ah) F: hour

سباحة (si.*bā*.ḥah) F: swimming

سباق السيارات (si.*bāq* as.say.yā.*rāt*) M: car racing

السبت (as.*sabt*): Saturday

سبتمبر (sib.*tam*.bir): September

سحابة (sa.*ḥā*.bah) M: cloud

سحب (*su*.ḥub) F: clouds

ساخن (*sā*.khin): hot

سروال (sir.*wāl*) M: pants

سرير (sa.*rīr*) M: bed

سفر (*sa*.far) M: travel

سفينة (sa.*fī*.nah) F: ship

سكّر (*suk*.kar) M: sugar

سكن (*sa*.kan) M: accommodations

سكّين (sik.*kīn*) M: knife

سليم (sa.*līm*): healthy

سمك (*sa*.mak) M: fish

سؤال (su.*'āl*) M: question

السيرة المهنية (as.*sī*.rah al.mi.ha.*niy*.yah) M: work history/curriculum vitae

سينما (*sī*.ni.mā) F: movie theater

ش

شاهد (*shā*.ha.da): watched

شتاء (shi.*tā'*) M: winter

شرطة (*shur*.ṭah) F: police

شرفة (*shur*.fah) M: balcony

شركة (*sha*.ri.ka) F: company

شركة محاسبات (*sha*.ri.kat mu.ḥā.sa.*bāt*) F: accounting firm

شركة محاماة (*sha*.ri.kat mu.ḥā.*māh*) F: law firm

شطرنج (shaṭ.*ranj*) M: chess

شعر (shi'r) M: poetry

شفنج (shi.*fanj*) M: donuts

شمس (shams) F: sun

شنطة (*shan*.ṭah) F: suitcase

شوكة (*shaw*.kah) F: fork

شوكولات (shū.kū.*lāt*) M: chocolate

شيك (shīk) M: check

ص

صابون (ṣā.*būn*) M: soap

صباح (ṣa.*bāḥ*) M: morning

صحن (ṣaḥn) M: plate

صغير (ṣa.*ghīr*): small

صوت (ṣawt) M: sound/voice

صيدلية (ṣay.da.*līy*.yah) F: pharmacy

صيف (ṣayf) M: summer

ط

طائرة ورقية (*ṭā*.'i.rah wa.ra.*qiy*.yah) F: kite

طابق (*ṭā*.biq) M: floor/story

طبق (*ṭa*.baq) M: dish

طبل (ṭabl) M: drums

طعام (ṭa.*'ām*) M: food

طقس (ṭaqs) M: weather

طماطم (ṭa.*mā*.ṭim) F: tomatoes

ظ

ظهر (ẓahr) M: back

ظهر (ẓuhr) M: noon

ع

عاصفة (*'ā*.ṣi.fah) F: storm

عجيب ('a.*jīb*): amazing

عدس (*'a*.das) M: lentils

عريض ('a.*rīḍ*): wide

عزيمة ('a.*zī*.mah) F: determination

عسل (*'a*.sal) M: honey

عشاء ('a.*shā'*) M: dinner

العصر (al.*'aṣr*) M: late afternoon

علاج (‘i.*lāj*) M: treatment

عمال (‘um.*māl*) MP: workers

عمل (*‘a*.mal) M: work, job

عنب (*‘i*.nab) M: grapes

العنبج (al.*‘an*.baj) M: mango

عيادة (‘i.*yā*.dah) F: clinic

عيش الغراب (‘aysh al.ghu.*rāb*) M: mushrooms

عين (‘ayn) F: eye

عينين (‘ay.*nayn*) F: two eyes

غ

غداً (*gha*.dan): tomorrow

غداء (gha.*dā’*) M: lunch

غرفة (*ghur*.fah) F: room

غسول الشعر (gha.*sūl* ash.*sha‘r*) M: shampoo

غضبان (ghaḍ.*bān*): angry

غناء (ghi.*nā’*) M: singing

غول (ghūl) M: ghoul

غولف (ghūlf) M: golf

ف

فبراير (fib.*rā*.yir): February

فخار (fakh.*khār*) M: pottery

فرن (furn) M: oven

فروسية (fu.rū.*siy*.yah) F: horseback riding

فطور (fu.*ṭūr*) M: breakfast

فعل (*fa*.‘a.la): did

فلفل (*fil*.fil) M: pepper

فلوت (flūt) M: flute

فم (*fam*) M: mouth

فندق (*fun*.duq) M: hotel

فوز (fawz) M: win

فول (*fūl*) M: beans

فيلم (fīlm) M: movie

ق

قاضي (*qā*.*ḍī*) M: judge

قاموس (qā.*mūs*) M: dictionary

قبّعة (qub.*ba‘h*) F: hat

قبل (*qab*.la): before

قرأ (*qa*.ra.’a): read

بروكلي (qar.na.*bīṭ*) M: broccoli

قراءة (qi.*rā*.’ah) F: reading

قرد (qird) M: monkey

قطار (qi.*ṭār*) M: train

قف (qif): stop

قلب (qalb) M: heart

قلم جاف (*qa*.lam jāf) M: pen

قلم رصاص (*qa*.lam ra.*ṣāṣ*) M: pencil

قميص (qa.*mīṣ*) M: shirt

قنبيط (qan.*bīṭ*) M: cauliflower

قهوة (*qah*.wah) F: coffee

قوس (qaws) M: bow

قوس قزح (qaws *qu*.zaḥ) M: rainbow

ك

كأس (ka’s) M: glass

كبير (ka.*bīr*): big

كتاب (ki.*tāb*) M: book

كتب (*ka*.ta.ba): wrote

كرة (*ku*.rah) F: ball

كرة السلة (ku.rat as.*sal*.lah) F: basketball

الكرة الطائرة (al.*ku*.rah aṭ.*ṭā*.’i.rah) F: volleyball

كرة القدم (*ku*.rat al.*qa*.dam) F: soccer

كرسي (*kur*.sī) M: chair

كعك (ka'k) M: cake

كعك الشوكولات (ka'k ash.shū.kū.*lāt*) M: chocolate cake

كلب (kalb) M: dog

كلمة (*ka*.li.mah) F: word

كم (kam): how many

كمان (ka.*mān*) F: violin

كوب (kūb) M: tumbler/cup

كؤوس (ku.*'ūs*) F: glasses (cups)

كيف (*kay*.fa): how

ل

لاعب (*lā*.'ib) M: player

لاعبة (*lā*.'i.bah) F: player

لحم (laḥm) M: meat

لحم البقر (laḥm al.*ba*.qar) M: beef

لحم العجل (laḥm al.*'ijl*) M: veal

لحم الغنم (laḥm al.*gha*.nam) M: lamb

لسان (li.*sān*) M: tongue

لغة (*lu*.ghah) F: language

لماذا (li.*mā*.dhā): why

ليلة (*lay*.lah) F: night

ليمون (lay.*mūn*) M: lemon

ليمون مالح (lay.*mūn mā*.liḥ) M: lime

ليمون هندي (lay.*mūn hin*.dī) M: grapefruit

م

ماذا (*mā*.dhā): what

مارس (*mā*.ris): March

مال (māl) M: money

مايو (*mā*.yū): May

معدة (*ma*.'i.dah) F: stomach

مباراة (mu.bā.*rāh*) F: game

متى (*ma*.tā): when

متحف (*mat*.ḥaf) M: museum

محامي (mu.*ḥā*.mī) M: lawyer

محفظة (*maḥ*.fa.ẓah) F: briefcase

محكمة (*maḥ*.ka.mah) F: court

مخبز (*makh*.baz) M: bakery

مدرسة (*mad*.ra.sah) F: school

مدة (*mud*.dah) F: period of time

مدينة (ma.*dī*.nah) F: city

مرافق (ma.*rā*.fiq) F: amenities

مرآة (mir.*'āh*) F: mirror

مرحاض (mir.*ḥāḍ*) M: toilet

مريض (ma.*rīḍ*): sick

مساعدة (mu.*sā*.'a.dah) F: help, assistance

مساء (ma.*sā'*) M: evening

مسبح (*mas*.baḥ) M: swimming pool

مستخدم (mus.*takh*.dim) M: employer

مسجد (*mas*.jid) M: mosque

مشبك أوراق (*mash*.bak aw.*rāq*) M: paper clip

مصرف (*maṣ*.raf) M: bank

مصرفي (*maṣ*.ra.fī) M: banker

مصعد (*miṣ*.'ad) M: elevator

مطعم (*maṭ*.'am) M: restaurant

مطر (*ma*.ṭar) M: rain

معجنات (mu.'aj.ja.*nāt*) F: pastries

معطف (*mi'*.ṭaf) M: coat

معلومة (ma'.*lū*.mah) F: information

معمل (*ma'*.mal) M: laboratory

مغسلة (*magh*.sa.lah) F: sink

مفتاح (mif.*tāḥ*) M: key

مكان الميلاد (ma.*kān* al.mī.*lād*) M: place of birth

مكتب سياحة (*mak*.tab si.*yā*.ḥah) M: travel agency

مكتبة (*mak*.ta.bah) F: bookstore, library

ملابس (ma.*lā*.bis) F: clothes

ملابس رياضية (ma.*lā*.bis ri.yā.*ḍiy*.yah) M: sports uniform

ملح (milḥ) M: salt

ملعب (*mal*.ʻab) M: stadium

ملعقة (*mil*.ʻa.qah) F: spoon

ممحاة (mim.*ḥāh*) F: eraser

من (man): who

منديل (min.*dīl*) M: napkin

منزل (*man*.zil) M: house

مهنة (*mih*.nah) F: job, profession

ن

نتيجة (na.*tī*.jah) F: score

نقد (naqd) M: currency

نقل (naql) M: transportation

نور (nūr) M: light

نوع الحساب (nawʻ al.ḥi.*sāb*) M: type of account

نوفمبر (nū.*fam*.bir): November

نوم (nawm) M: sleep

ه

هاتف (*hā*.tif) M: telephone

هذا (*hā*.dhā) M: this

هذه (*hā*.dhi.hi) F: this

هليون (hil.*yūn*) M: asparagus

هواية (hu.*wā*.yah) F: hobby

هؤلاء (hā.'u.*lā*.'i) MP/FP: these

و

وديعة (wa.*dī*.ʻah) F: deposit

ورق عنب (*wa*.raq ʻ*i*.nab) M: stuffed vine leaves

ورق اللعب (*wa*.raq al.*la*.ʻib) M: playing cards

ولد (*wa*.lad) M: boy

ي

يأكل (*ya'*.kul): to eat

يد (yad) F: hand

يدرس (*yad*.rus): to study

يذهب (*yadh*.hab): to go

يرجع (*yar*.jiʻ): to return

يسكن (*yas*.kun): to live

يعرف (*ya*ʻ.rif): to know

يفتح (*yaf*.taḥ): to open

يفعل (*yaf*.ʻal): to do

يقرأ (*yaq*.ra'): to read

يكتب (*yak*.tub): to write

يناير (ya.*nā*.yir): January

يوليو (*yūl*.yū): July

يوم (yawm) M: day

يونيو (*yūn*.yū): June

English-to-Arabic Mini-Dictionary

A

accommodations: سكن (*sa*.kan) M

accounting firm: شركة محاسبات (*sha*.ri.kat mu.ḥā.sa.*bāt*) F

after: بعد (*ba*ʻ.da)

afternoon: بعد الظهر (*ba*ʻ.da aẓ.*ẓuhr*)

amazing: عجيب (ʻa.*jīb*)

amenities: مرافق (ma.*rā*.fiq) F

angry: غضبان (ghaḍ.*bān*)

April: أبريل (ab.*rīl*)

Arab dress: جلّابة (jal.*lā*.bah) F

arm: ذراع (dhi.*rā*ʻ) M

artichokes: خرشوف (khar.*shūf*) M

asparagus: هليون (hil.*yūn*) M

ate: أكل (*a*.ka.la)

August: أغسطس (u.*ghus*.ṭus)

avocado: أفوكادو (a.fū.*kāt*) F

B

back: ظهر (ẓahr) M

bakery: مخبز (*makh*.baz) F

balance: توازن (ta.*wā*.zun) M

balcony: شرفة (*shur*.fah) M

ball: كرة (*ku*.rah) F

bank: مصرف (*maṣ*.raf) M

banker: مصرفي (*maṣ*.ra.fī) M

barber: حلّاق (ḥal.*lāq*) M

basketball: كرة السلة (ku.rat as.*sal*.lah) F

beans: فول (fūl) M

bed: سرير (sa.*rīr*) M

beef: لحم البقر (laḥm al.*ba*.qar) M

before: قبل (*qab*.la)

belt: حزام (ḥi.*zām*) M

bicycle: درّاجة (dar.*rā*.jah) F

big: كبير (ka.*bīr*)

body: جسد (*ja*.sad) M

book: كتاب (ki.*tāb*) M

bow: قوس (qaws) M

boy: ولد (*wa*.lad) M

breakfast: فطور (fu.*ṭūr*) M

breakfast cereal: حبوب الفطور (ḥu.*būb* al.fu.*ṭūr*) M

briefcase: محفظة (*maḥ*.fa.ẓah) F

broccoli: بروكلي (qar.na.*bīṭ*) M

bus: حافلة (*ḥā*.fi.lah) F

C

cake: كعك (ka'k) M
cantaloupe: بطيخ (baṭ.*ṭīkh*) M
car racing: سباق السيارات (si.*bāq* as.say.ya.*rāt*) M
cards: ورق اللعب (*wa*.raq al.*la*.'ib) M
cauliflower: قنبيط (qan.*bīṭ*) M
chair: كرسي (*kur*.sī) M
check: شيك (shīk) M
cheese: جبن (jubn) M
chess: شطرنج (shaṭ.*ranj*) M
chicken: دجاج (da.*jāj*) M
chocolate: شوكولات (shū.kū.*lāt*) M
chocolate cake: كعك الشوكولات (ka'k ash.shū.kū.*lāt*) M
city: مدينة (ma.*dī*.nah) F
client: زبون (zu.*būn*) M
clinic: عيادة ('i.*yā*.dah) F
clothes: ملابس (ma.*lā*.bis) F
cloud: سحابة (sa.*ḥā*.bah) M
clouds: سحب (*su*.ḥub) M
coat: معطف (*mi*'.ṭaf) M
coffee: قهوة (*qah*.wah) F
cold: برد (bard)
company: شركة (*sha*.ri.ka) F
computer: حاسوب (ḥā.*sūb*) F
conversation/dialogue: حوار (ḥi.*wār*) M
corn: ذرة (*dhu*.rah) F
court: محكمة (*maḥ*.ka.mah) F
crime: جريمة (ja.*rī*.mah) F
cucumber: خيار (khi.*yār*) M
cupboard: خزانة (kha.*zā*.nah) F
currency: نقد (naqd) M

D

dancing: رقص (raqṣ) M
date of birth: تاريخ الميلاد (tā.*rīkh* al.mī.*lād*) M
day: يوم (yawm) M
December: دسمبر (dī.*sam*.bir)
degree: درجة (*da*.ra.jah) F
deposit: وديعة (wa.*dī*.'ah) F
determination: عزيمة ('a.*zī*.mah) F
dictionary: قاموس (qā.*mūs*) M
did: فعل (*fa*.'a.la)
dinner: عشاء ('a.*shā'*) M
dish: طبق (*ṭa*.baq)
do: يفعل (*yaf*.'al)
dog: كلب (kalb) M
donuts: شفنج (shi.*fanj*) M
door: باب (bāb) M
drawing: رسم (rasm) M
dress: فستان (fus.*tān*) M
driver's license: رخصة القيادة (*rukh*.ṣat al.qi.*yā*.dah) F
drums: طبل (ṭabl) M

E

ears: أذنين (u.dhu.*nayn*) M
eat: يأكل (*ya'*.kul)
eggplant: باذنجان (bā.dhin.*jān*) F
eggs: بيض (bayḍ) M
elevator: مصعد (*miṣ*.'ad) M
employer: مستخدم (mus.*takh*.dim) M
eraser: ممحاة (mim.*ḥāh*) F
evening: مساء (ma.*sā'*) M

eye: عين (‘ayn) F

eyes: عينان (‘ay.*nayn*) M

F

factory: مصنع (*maṣ*.na‘) M

fall: خريف (kha.*rīf*)

family: أسرة (*us*.rah) F

fax machine: آلة الفاكس (*ā*.lat al.*fāks*) F

February: فبراير (fib.*rā*.yir)

fee: أجرة (*uj*.rah) F

firefighter: رجل الإطفاء (ra.*jul* al.’iṭ.*fā’*) M

first name: اسم شخصي (ism *shakh*.ṣī) M

fish: سمك (*sa*.mak) M

floor: طابق (*ṭā*.biq) M

flute: فلوت (flūt) M

food: طعام (ṭa.*‘ām*)

fork: شوكة (*shaw*.kah) F

foul/mistake: خطأ (*kha*.ṭa’) M

Friday: الجمعة (al.*jum*.‘ah)

friends: أصدقاء (aṣ.di.*qā’*) M

G

game: مباراة (mu.bā.*rāh*) F

ghoul: غول (ghūl) M

girl: بنت (bint) F

glass: كأس (ka’s) M

glasses (cups): كؤوس (ku.*’ūs*) F

glue: صمغ (ṣamgh) M

go: يذهب (*yadh*.hab)

golf: غولف (al.ghūlf) M

grapefruit: ليمون هندي (lay.*mūn hin*.dī) M

grapes: عنب (‘*i*.nab) M

guitar: قيثارة (qī.*thā*.rah) F

gymnastics: جمباز (jum.*bāz*) M

H

hand: يد (yad) F

hat: قبعة (qub.*ba‘h*) F

head: رأس (ra’s) M

healthy: سليم (sa.*līm*)

heart: قلب (qalb) M

help: مساعدة (mu.*sā*.‘a.dah) F

hobby: هواية (hu.*wā*.yah) F

home: بيت (bayt) M

honey: عسل(‘*a*.sal) M

horseback riding: فروسية (fu.rū.*siy*.yah) F

hot: ساخن (*sā*.khin)

hotel: فندق (*fun*.duq) M

hour: ساعة (*sā*.‘ah) F

house: منزل (*man*.zil) M

how: كيف (*kay*.fa)

how many: كم (kam)

how much: بكم (bi.*kam*)

humidity: رطوبة (ru.*ṭū*.bah) F

I

ice cream: أيس كريم (*a*.yis ki.*rīm*) M

ice skating: تزحلق (ta.*zaḥ*.luq) M

included: متضمن (mu.ta.*ḍam*.man)

Islam: إسلام (is.*lām*)

J

January: يناير (ya.*nā*.yir)
jeweler: جواهري (ja.*wā*.hi.rī) M
job: مهنة (*mih*.nah) F
judge: قاضي (*qā*.ḍī) M
July: يوليو (*yūl*.yū)
June: يونيو (*yūn*.yū)

K

key: مفتاح (mif.*tāḥ*) M
kite: طائرة ورقية (*ṭā*.'i.rah wa.ra.*qiy*.yah) F
knee: ركبة (*ruk*.bah) F
knife: سكّين (sik.*kīn*) M
know: يعرف (*ya*'.rif)

L

lamb: لحم الغنم (laḥm al.*gha*.nam) M
language: لغة (*lu*.ghah) F
last name: لقب الأسرة (*la*.qab al.'*us*.rah) M
late afternoon: العصر (al.'*aṣr*)
law firm: شركة محاماة (*sha*.ri.kat mu.ḥā.*māh*) F
lawyer: محامي (mu.*ḥā*.mī)
leg: رجل (rijl) F
lemon: ليمون (lay.*mūn*) M
lentils: عدس ('*a*.das) M
lettuce: خس (khas) M
library: مكتبة (*mak*.ta.bah) F
light: نور (nūr) M
lightning: برق (barq) M
lime: ليمون مالح (lay.*mūn mā*.liḥ) M
live: يسكن (*yas*.kun)
lose: خسر (*kha*.si.ra)
luggage: أمتعة (*am*.ti.'ah) F
lunch: غداء (gha.*dā*') M
lung: رئة (*ri*.'ah) F

M

machine: آلة (*ā*.lah) F
mango: العنبج (al.'*an*.baj) M
March: مارس (*mā*.ris)
May: مايو (*mā*.yū)
meat: لحم (laḥm) M
medicine: دواء (da.*wā*') M
milk: حليب (ḥa.*līb*) M
minute: دقيقة (da.*qī*.qah) F
mirror: مرآة (mir.'*āh*) F
Monday: الاثنين (al.'ith.*nayn*)
money: مال (māl) M
monkey: قرد (qird) M
morning: صباح (ṣa.*bāḥ*) M
Moroccan soup: حريرة (ḥah.*rī*.rah) F
mosque: مسجد (*mas*.jid) M
motorcycle: درّاجة نارية (dar.*rā*.jah nā.*riy*.yah) F
mouth: فم (*fam*) M
movie: فيلم (fīlm) M
movie theater: سينما (*sī*.ni.mā) F
museum: متحف (*mat*.ḥaf) M
mushrooms: عيش الغراب ('aysh al.ghu.*rāb*) M

N

napkin: منديل (min.*dīl*) M
newspaper: جريدة (ja.*rī*.dah) F
night: ليلة (*lay*.lah) F
noon: ظهر (ẓuhr)
nose: أنف (anf) M
notebook: دفتر (*daf*.tar) M
November: نوفمبر (nū.*fam*.bir)
number: رقم (*ra*.qam) M
numbers: أرقام (ar.*qām*) F

O

October: أكتوبر (uk.*tū*.bar)
oil: زيت (zayt) M
olive: زيتونة (zay.*tū*.nah) F
olive oil: زيت الزيتون (zayt az.zay.*tūn*) M
onions: بصل (*ba*.ṣal) M
open: يفتح (*yaf*.tah)
oven: فرن (furn) M

P

pants: سروال (sir.*wāl*) M
paper clip: مشبك أوراق (*mash*.bak aw.*rāq*) M
passport: جواز السفر (jaw.*wāz* as.*sa*.far) M
pastries: معجنات (mu.ʻaj.ja.*nāt*) F
peach: خوخ (khawkh) M
pear: إجاصة (i.*jā*.ṣah) M
peas: بازلاء (bā.zil.*lā'*) F
pen: قلم جاف (*qa*.lam jāf) M
pencil: قلم رصاص (*qa*.lam ra.*ṣāṣ*) M
pepper: فلفل (*fil*.fil) M
period: مدة (*mud*.dah) F
pharmacy: صيدلية (ṣay.da.*līy*.yah) F
photocopy machine: آلة تصوير مستندات (ā.lat taṣ.*wīr* mus.ta.na.*dāt*) F
piano: بيانو (bi.*yā*.nū) M
place of birth: مكان الميلاد (ma.*kān* al.mī.*lād*) M
plate: صحن (ṣaḥn) M
player: لاعب (*lā*.ʻib) M
player: لاعبة (*lā*.ʻi.bah) F
poetry: شعر (shiʻr) M
police: شرطة (*shur*.ṭah) F
potato: بطاطا (ba.*ṭā*.ṭā) F
pottery: فخار (fakh.*khār*) M
price: ثمن (*tha*.man) M
profession: مهنة (*mih*.nah) F

Q

question: سؤال (su.*'āl*) M

R

rain: مطر (*ma*.ṭar) M
rainbow: قوس قزح (qaws *qu*.zaḥ) M
read: يقرأ (*yaq*.ra')
reading: قراءة (qi.*rā*.'ah) F
reception: استقبال (is.tiq.*bāl*) M
referee: حكم (*ḥa*.kam) M
refrigerator: ثلاجة (thal.*lā*.jah) F
reservation: حجز (ḥajz) M
restaurant: مطعم (*maṭ*.ʻam) M

retirement: تقاعد (ta.*qā*.'ud) M

return: يرجع (*yar*.ji')

rice: أرز (*a*.ruz) M

roasted garlic: ثوم محمّر (thawm mu.*ḥam*.mar) M

room: غرفة (*ghur*.fah) F

S

sad: حزين (ḥa.*zīn*)

salary: راتب (*rā*.tib) M

salt: ملح (milḥ) M

Saturday: السبت (as.*sabt*)

saxophone: ساكسافون (sāk.sā.*fūn*) M

school: مدرسة (*mad*.ra.sah) F

score: نتيجة (na.*tī*.jah) F

second: ثانية (*thā*.ni.yah) F

sentence: جملة (*jum*.lah) F

September: سبتمبر (sib.*tam*.bir)

shampoo: غسول الشعر (gha.*sūl* ash.*sha*'r) M

ship: سفينة (sa.*fī*.nah) F

shirt: قميص (qa.*mīṣ*) M

shoe: حذاء (ḥi.*dhā*') M

shower: دوش (dūsh) F

shrimp: روبيان (rūb.*yān*) M

sick: مريض (ma.*rīḍ*)

singing: غناء (ghi.*nā*')

sink: مغسلة (*magh*.sa.lah) F

skiing: تزلج (ta.*zal*.luj) M

sleep: نوم (nawm) M

small: صغير (ṣa.*ghīr*)

snow: ثلج (thalj) M

soap: صابون (*ṣā*.*būn*) M

soccer: كرة القدم (*ku*.rat al.*qa*.dam) F

socks: جوارب (ja.*wā*.rib) F

sound: صوت (ṣawt) M

soup: حساء (ḥa.*sā*') F

spinach: سبانخ (sa.bā.*nekh*) M

spoke: تكلم (ta.*kal*.lam)

spoon: ملعقة (*mil*.'a.qah) F

spring: ربيع (ra.*bī*') M

stadium: ملعب (*mal*.'ab) M

stomach: معدة (*ma*.'i.dah) F

stop: قف (qif)

store: دكان (duk.*kān*) M

storm: عاصفة ('*ā*.ṣi.fah) F

strawberry: توت (tūt) M

studied: درس (*da*.ra.sa)

study: يدرس (*yad*.rus)

stuffed vine leaves: ورق عنب (*wa*.raq '*i*.nab) M

sugar: سكر (*suk*.kar) M

suitcase: شنطة (*shan*.ṭah) F

summer: صيف (ṣayf) M

sun: شمس (shams) F

Sunday: الأحد (al.'*a*.ḥad)

swimming: سباحة (si.*bā*.ḥah) F

swimming pool: مسبح (*mas*.baḥ) M

T

taxi: تاكسي (*tāk*.sī) M

teeth: أسنان (as.*nān*) F

telephone: هاتف (*hā*.tif) M

telephone number: رقم الهاتف (*ra*.qam al.*hā*.tif) M

television: تلفزيون (ti.li.fiz.*yūn*) M

temperature: حرارة (ḥa.*rā*.rah) F

tennis: تنس (*ti*.nis) F

that: تلك (*til*.ka) F

that: ذلك (*dhā*.li.ka) M

these: هؤلاء (hā.'u.*lā*.'i) MP/FP

this: هذا (*hā*.dhā) M

this: هذه (*hā*.dhi.hi) F

those: أولئك (u.*lā*.'i.ka) MP/FP

thunder: رعد (ra'd) M

Thursday: الخميس (al.kha.*mīs*)

toilet: مرحاض (mir.*ḥāḍ*) M

tomatoes: طماطم (ṭa.*mā*.ṭim) F

tomorrow: غداً (*gha*.dan)

tongue: لسان (li.*sān*) M

toothbrush: فرشاة أسنان (fur.*shāt* as.*nān*) F

train: قطار (qi.*ṭār*) M

transportation: نقل (naql)

travel agency: مكتب لسياحة (*mak*.tab si.*yā*.ḥah) M

treatment: علاج ('i.*lāj*) M

trip: رحلة (*riḥ*.lah) M

trumpet: بوق (būq) M

Tuesday: الثلاثاء (ath.thu.lā.*thā*')

tumbler/cup: كوب (kūb) M

type of account: نوع الحساب (naw' al.ḥi.*sāb*) M

U

uniforms, sportsware: ملابس رياضية (ma.*lā*.bis ri.yā.*ḍiy*.yah) M

university: جامعة (*jā*.mi.'ah) F

V

vacation/trip: رحلة (*riḥ*.lah) F

veal: لحم العجل (laḥm al.'*ijl*) M

violin: كمان (ka.*mān*) F

visit: زيارة (zi.*yā*.rah) F

volleyball: الكرة الطائرة (al.*ku*.rah aṭ.*ṭā*.'i.rah) F

W

watched: شاهد (*shā*.ha.da)

watermelon: دلاحة (dal.*lā*.ḥah) F

weather: طقس (ṭaqs) M

Wednesday: الأربعاء (al.'ar.ba.'*ā*')

went: ذهب (*dha*.ha.ba)

what: ماذا (*mā*.dhā)

when: متى (*ma*.tā)

where: أين (*ay*.na)

who: من (man)

why: لماذا (li.*mā*.dhā)

wide: عريض ('a.*rīḍ*)

win: فوز (fawz) M

wind: ريح (*rīḥ*) F

winter: شتاء (shi.*tā*')

withdrawal: انسحاب (in.si.*ḥāb*) M

word: كلمة (*ka*.li.mah) F

work: عمل ('*a*.mal) M

work history: السيرة المهنية (as.*sī*.rah al.mi.ha.*niy*.yah) F

workers: عمال ('um.*māl*) M

write: يكتب (*yak*.tub)

wrote: كتب (*ka*.ta.ba)

Appendix B
Verb Tables

Regular Arabic Verbs in the Past Tense

كتب (*ka*.ta.ba) (*wrote*)

Form	Pronunciation	English
أنا كتبتُ	*a*.nā ka.*tab*.tu	I wrote
أنتَ كتبتَ	*an*.ta ka.*tab*.ta	You wrote (M)
أنتِ كتبتِ	*an*.ti ka.*tab*.ti	You wrote (F)
هو كتب	*hu*.wa *ka*.ta.ba	He wrote
هي كتبت	*hi*.ya *ka*.ta.bat	She wrote
نحن كتبنا	*naḥ*.nu ka.*tab*.nā	We wrote
أنتم كتبتم	*an*.tum ka.*tab*.tum	You wrote (MP)
أنتنّ كتبتنّ	an.*tun*.na ka.tab.*tun*.na	You wrote (FP)
هم كتبوا	hum *ka*.ta.bū	They wrote (MP)
هنّ كتبنّ	*hun*.na ka.*tab*.na	They wrote (FP)
أنتما كتبتما	an.*tu*.mā ka.tab.*tu*.mā	You wrote (dual/M/F)
هما كتبا	*hu*.mā *ka*.ta.bā	They wrote (dual/M)
هما كتبتا	*hu*.mā ka.ta.*ba*.tā	They wrote (dual/F)

درس (*da*.ra.sa) (*studied*)

Form	Pronunciation	English
أنا درستُ	*a*.nā da.ras.tu	I studied
أنتَ درستَ	*an*.ta da.*ras*.ta	You studied (M)
أنتِ درستِ	*an*.ti da.*ras*.ti	You studied (F)
هو درس	*hu*.wa *da*.ra.sa	He studied
هي درست	*hi*.ya *da*.ra.sat	She studied
نحن درسنا	*naḥ*.nu da.*ras*.nā	We studied
أنتم درستم	*an*.tum da.*ras*.tum	You studied (MP)
أنتنّ درستنّ	an.*tun*.na da.ras.*tun*.na	You studied (FP)
هم درسوا	hum *da*.ra.sū	They studied (MP)
هنّ درسنّ	*hun*.na da.*ras*.na	They studied (FP)
أنتما درستما	an.*tu*.mā da.ras.*tu*.mā	You studied (dual/M/F)
هما درسا	*hu*.mā *da*.ra.sā	They studied (dual/M)
هما درستا	*hu*.mā da.ra.*sa*.tā	They studied (dual/F)

أكل (*a*.ka.la) (*ate*)

Form	Pronunciation	English
أنا أكلتُ	*a*.nā a.*kal*.tu	I ate
أنتَ أكلتَ	*an*.ta a.*kal*.ta	You ate (M)
أنتِ أكلتِ	*an*.ti a.*kal*.ti	You ate (F)
هو أكل	*hu*.wa *a*.ka.la	He ate
هي أكلت	*hi*.ya *a*.ka.lat	She ate
نحن أكلنا	*naḥ*.nu a.*kal*.nā	We ate
أنتم أكلتم	*an*.tum a.*kal*.tum	You ate (MP)

Form	Pronunciation	English
أنتنّ أكلتنّ	an.*tun*.na a.kal.*tun*.na	You ate (FP)
هم أكلوا	hum *a*.ka.lū	They ate (MP)
هنّ أكلنّ	*hun*.na a.*kal*.na	They ate (FP)
أنتما أكلتما	an.*tu*.mā a.kal.*tu*.mā	You ate (dual/M/F)
هما أكلا	*hu*.mā *a*.ka.lā	They ate (dual/M)
هما أكلتا	*hu*.mā a.ka.*la*.tā	They ate (dual/F)

Regular Arabic Verbs in the Present Tense

يكتب (*yak*.tu.bu) (*write*)

Form	Pronunciation	English
أنا أكتب	*a*.nā *ak*.tub	I am writing
أنتَ تكتب	*an*.ta *tak*.tub	You are writing (M)
أنتِ تكتبين	*an*.ti tak.tu.*bīn*	You are writing (F)
هو يكتب	*hu*.wa *yak*.tub	He is writing
هي تكتب	*hi*.ya *tak*.tub	She is writing
نحن نكتب	*naḥ*.nu *nak*.tub	We are writing
أنتم تكتبون	*an*.tum tak.tu.*būn*	You are writing (MP)
أنتنّ تكتبنّ	an.*tun*.na tak.*tub*.na	You are writing (FP)
هم يكتبون	hum yak.tu.*būn*	They are writing (MP)
هنّ يكتبنّ	*hun*.na yak.*tub*.na	They are writing (FP)
أنتما تكتبان	an.*tu*.mā tak.tu.*bān*	You are writing (dual/M/F)
هما يكتبان	*hu*.mā yak.tu.*bān*	They are writing (dual/M)
هما تكتبان	*hu*.mā tak.tu.*bān*	They are writing (dual/F)

سردي (*yad*.ru.su) (*study*)

Form	Pronunciation	English
أنا أدرس	*a*.nā *ad*.rus	I am studying
أنتَ تدرس	*an*.ta *tad*.rus	You are studying (M)
أنتِ تدرسين	*an*.ti tad.ru.*sīn*	You are studying (F)
هو يدرس	*hu*.wa *yad*.rus	He is studying
هي تدرس	*hi*.ya *tad*.rus	She is studying
نحن ندرس	*naḥ*.nu *nad*.rus	We are studying
أنتم تدرسون	*an*.tum tad.ru.*sūn*	You are studying (MP)
أنتنّ تدرسنّ	an.*tun*.na tad.*rus*.na	You are studying (FP)
هم يدرسون	hum yad.ru.*sūn*	They are studying (MP)
هنّ يدرسنّ	*hun*.na yad.*rus*.na	They are studying (FP)
أنتما تدرسان	an.*tu*.mā tad.ru.*sān*	You are studying (dual/M/F)
هما يدرسان	*hu*.mā yad.ru.*sān*	They are studying (dual/M)
هما تدرسان	*hu*.mā tad.ru.*sān*	They are studying (dual/F)

لكأي (*ya'*.ku.lu) (*eat*)

Form	Pronunciation	English
آكل	*a*.nā *ā*.kul	I am eating
أنتَ تأكل	*an*.ta *ta'*.kul	You are eating (M)
أنتِ تأكلين	*an*.ti ta'.ku.*līn*	You are eating (F)
هو يأكل	*hu*.wa *ya'*.kul	He is eating
هي تأكل	*hi*.ya *ta'*.kul	She is eating
نحن نأكل	*naḥ*.nu *na'*.kul	We are eating
أنتم تأكلون	*an*.tum ta'.ku.*lūn*	You are eating (MP)

Form	Pronunciation	English
أنتنّ تأكلنّ	an.*tun*.na ta'.*kul*.na	You are eating (FP)
هم يأكلون	hum ya'.ku.*lūn*	They are eating (MP)
هنّ يأكلنّ	*hun*.na ya'.*kul*.na	They are eating (FP)
أنتما تأكلان	an.*tu*.mā ta'.ku.*lān*	You are eating (dual/M/F)
هما يأكلان	*hu*.mā ya'.ku.*lān*	They are eating (dual/M)
هما تأكلان	*hu*.mā ta'.ku.*lān*	They are eating (dual/F)

Regular Arabic Verbs in the Future Tense

سيكتب (sa.*yak*.tu.bu) (*will write*)

Form	Pronunciation	English
أنا سأكتب	*a*.nā sa.'*ak*.tub	I will write
أنتَ ستكتب	*an*.ta sa.*tak*.tub	You will write (M)
أنتِ ستكتبين	*an*.ti sa.tak.tu.*bīn*	You will write (F)
هو سيكتب	*hu*.wa sa.*yak*.tub	He will write
هي ستكتب	*hi*.ya sa.*tak*.tub	She will write
نحن سنكتب	*naḥ*.nu sa.*nak*.tub	We will write
أنتم ستكتبون	*an*.tum sa.tak.tu.*būn*	You will write (MP)
أنتنّ ستكتبنّ	an.*tun*.na sa.tak.*tub*.na	You will write (FP)
هم سيكتبون	hum sa.yak.tu.*būn*	They will write (MP)
هنّ سيكتبنّ	*hun*.na sa.yak.*tub*.na	They will write (FP)
أنتما ستكتبان	an.*tu*.mā sa.tak.tu.*bān*	You will write (dual/M/F)
هما سيكتبان	*hu*.mā sa.yak.tu.*bān*	They will write (dual/M)
هما ستكتبان	*hu*.mā sa.tak.tu.*bān*	They will write (dual/F)

سيدرس (sa.*yad*.ru.su) (*will study*)

Form	Pronunciation	English
أنا سأدرس	*a*.nā sa.'*ad*.rus	I will study
أنتَ ستدرس	*an*.ta sa.*tad*.rus	You will study (M)
أنتِ ستدرسين	*an*.ti sa.tad.ru.*sīn*	You will study (F)
هو سيدرس	*hu*.wa sa.*yad*.rus	He will study
هي ستدرس	*hi*.ya sa.*tad*.rus	She will study
نحن سندرس	*naḥ*.nu sa.*nad*.rus	We will study
أنتم ستدرسون	*an*.tum sa.tad.ru.*sūn*	You will study (MP)
أنتنّ ستدرسنّ	an.*tun*.na sa.tad.*rus*.na	You will study (FP)
هم سيدرسون	hum sa.yad.ru.*sūn*	They will study (MP)
هنّ سيدرسنّ	*hun*.na sa.yad.*rus*.na	They will study (FP)
أنتما ستدرسان	an.*tu*.mā sa.tad.ru.*sān*	You will study (dual/M/F)
هما سيدرسان	*hu*.mā sa.yad.ru.*sān*	They will study (dual/M)
هما ستدرسان	*hu*.mā sa.tad.ru.*sān*	They will study (dual/F)

سيأكل (sa.*ya'*.ku.lu) (*will eat*)

Form	Pronunciation	English
أنا سآكل	*a*.nā sa.'*ā*.kul	I will eat
أنتَ ستأكل	*an*.ta sa.*ta'*.kul	You will eat (M)
أنتِ ستأكلين	*an*.ti sa.ta'.ku.*līn*	You will eat (F)
هو سيأكل	*hu*.wa sa.*ya'*.kul	He will eat
هي ستأكل	*hi*.ya sa.*ta'*.kul	She will eat
نحن سنأكل	*naḥ*.nu sa.*na'*.kul	We will eat
أنتم ستأكلون	*an*.tum sa.ta'.ku.*lūn*	You will eat (MP)

Form	Pronunciation	English
أنتنّ ستأكلنّ	an.*tun*.na sa.ta'.*kul*.na	You will eat (FP)
هم سيأكلون	hum sa.ya'.ku.*lūn*	They will eat (MP)
هنّ سيأكلنّ	*hun*.na sa.ya'.*kul*.na	They will eat (FP)
أنتما ستأكلان	an.*tu*.mā sa.ta'.ku.*lān*	You will eat (dual/M/F)
هما سيأكلان	*hu*.mā sa.ya'.ku.*lān*	They will eat (dual/M)
هما ستأكلان	*hu*.mā sa.ta'.ku.*lān*	They will eat (dual/F)

Irregular Arabic Verbs in the Past Tense

باع (*bā*.'a) (*sold*)

Form	Pronunciation	English
أنا بعتُ	*a*.nā *bi'*.tu	I sold
أنتَ بعتَ	*an*.ta *bi'*.ta	You sold (M)
أنتِ بعتِ	*an*.ti *bi'*.ti	You sold (F)
هو باع	*hu*.wa *bā*.'a	He sold
هي باعت	*hi*.ya *bā*.'at	She sold
نحن بعنا	*naḥ*.nu *bi'*.nā	We sold
أنتم بعتم	*an*.tum *bi'*.tum	You sold (MP)
أنتن بعتن	an.*tun*.na bi'.*tun*.na	You sold (FP)
هم باعوا	hum *bā*.'ū	They sold (MP)
هن بعن	*hun*.na *bi'*.na	They sold (FP)
أنتما بعتما	an.*tu*.mā bi'.*tu*.mā	You sold (dual/M/F)
هما باعا	*hu*.mā *bā*.'ā	They sold (dual/MP)
هما باعتا	*hu*.mā *bā*.'a.tā	They sold (dual/F)

اشترى (ish.*ta*.rā) (*bought*)

Form	Pronunciation	English
أنا اشتريتُ	*a*.nā ish.ta.*ray*.tu	I bought
انتَ اشتريتَ	*an*.ta ish.ta.*ray*.ta	You bought (M)
أنتِ اشتريتِ	*an*.ti ish.ta.*ray*.ti	You bought (F)
هو اشترى	*hu*.wa ish.*ta*.rá	He bought
هي اشترتْ	*hi*.ya ish.*ta*.rat	She bought
نحن اشترينا	*naḥ*.nu ish.ta.*ray*.nā	We bought
أنتم اشتريتم	*an*.tum ish.ta.*ray*.tum	You bought (MP)
أنتنّ اشتريتنّ	an.*tun*.na ish.ta.ray.*tun*.na	You bought (FP)
هم اشتروا	hum ish.*ta*.rū	They bought (MP)
هنّ اشترينّ	*hun*.ṇa ish.ta.*ray*.na	They bought (FP)
انتما اشتريتما	an.*tu*.mā ish.ta.ray.*tu*.mā	You bought (dual/M/F/MP/FP)
هما اشتريا	*hu*.mā ish.*ta*.ra.yā	They bought (dual/M)
هما اشترتا	hu.mā ish.*ta*.ra.tā	They bought (dual/F)

زار (*zā*.ra) (*visited*)

Form	Pronunciation	English
أنا زرتُ	*a*.nā *zur*.tu	I visited
انتَ زرتَ	*an*.ta *zur*.ta	You visited (M)
أنتِ زرتِ	*an*.ti *zur*.ti	You visited (F)
هو زار	*hu*.wa *zā*.ra	He visited
هي زارتْ	*hi*.ya *zā*.rat	She visited
نحن زرنا	*naḥ*.nu *zur*.nā	We visited
أنتم زرتم	*an*.tum *zur*.tum	You visited (FP)

Form	Pronunciation	English
أنتنّ زرتنّ	an.*tun*.na zur.*tun*.na	You visited (MP)
هم زاروا	hum *zā*.rū	They visited (MP)
هنّ زرنّ	*hun*.na *zur*.na	They visited (FP)
أنتما زرتما	an.*tu*.mā zur.*tu*.mā	You visited (dual/M/F)
هما زارا	*hu*.mā *zā*.rā	They visited (dual/M)
هما زارتا	*hu*.mā zā.*ra*.tā	They visited (dual/F)

Irregular Arabic Verbs in the Present Tense

يبيع (ya.*bī'*u) (*sell*)

Form	Pronunciation	English
أنا أبيع	*a*.nā a.*bī'*	I am selling
أنتَ تبيع	*an*.ta ta.*bī'*	You are selling (M)
أنتِ تبيعين	*an*.ti ta.bī.*'īn*	You are selling (F)
هو يبيع	*hu*.wa ya.*bī'*	He is selling
هي تبيع	*hi*.ya ta.*bī'*	She is selling
نحن نبيع	*naḥ*.nu na.*bī'*	We are selling
أنتم تبيعون	*an*.tum ta.bī.*'ūn*	You are selling (MP)
أنتنّ تبعنّ	an.*tun*.na ta.*bi'*.na	You are selling (FP)
هم يبيعون	hum ya.bī.*'ūn*	They are selling (MP)
هنّ يبعنّ	*hun*.na ya.*bi'*.na	They are selling (FP)
أنتما تبيعان	an.*tu*.mā ta.bī.*'ān*	You are selling (dual/M/F)
هما يبيعان	*hu*.mā ya.bī.*'ān*	They are selling (dual/M)
هما تبيعان	*hu*.mā ta.bī.*'ān*	They are selling (dual/F)

يرتشي (*yash*.ta.rī) (*buy*)

Form	Pronunciation	English
أنا أشتري	*a*.nā *ash*.ta.rī	I am buying
أنتَ تشتري	*an*.ta *tash*.ta.rī	You are buying (M)
أنتِ تشترين	*an*.ti tash.ta.*rīn*	You are buying (F)
هو يشتري	*hu*.wa *yash*.ta.rī	He is buying
هي تشتري	*hi*.ya *tash*.ta.rī	She is buying
نحن نشتري	*naḥ*.nu *nash*.ta.rī	We are buying
أنتم تشترون	*an*.tum tash.ta.*rūn*	You are buying (MP)
أنتنّ تشترينّ	an.*tun*.na tash.ta.*rīn*	You are buying (FP)
هم يشترون	hum yash.ta.*rūn*	They are buying (MP)
هنّ يشترينّ	*hun*.na yash.ta.*rī*.na	They are buying (FP)
أنتما تشتريان	an.*tu*.mā tash.ta.ri.*yān*	You are buying (dual/M/F)
هما يشتريان	*hu*.mā yash.ta.ri.*yān*	They are buying (dual/M)
هما تشتريان	*hu*.mā tash.ta.ri.*yān*	They are buying (dual/F)

روزي (ya.*zū*.ru) (*visit*)

Form	Pronunciation	English
أنا أزور	*a*.nā a.*zūr*	I am visiting
أنتَ تزور	*an*.ta ta.*zūr*	You are visiting (M)
أنتِ تزورين	*an*.ti ta.zū.*rīn*	You are visiting (F)
هو يزور	*hu*.wa ya.*zūr*	He is visiting
هي تزور	*hi*.ya ta.*zūr*	She is visiting
نحن نزور	*naḥ*.nu na.*zūr*	We are visiting
أنتم تزورون	*an*.tum ta.zū.*rūn*	You are visiting (MP)

Form	Pronunciation	English
أنتنّ تزرنّ	an.*tun*.na ta.*zur*.na	You are visiting (FP)
هم يزورون	hum ya.zū.*rūn*	They are visiting (MP)
هنّ يزرنّ	*hun*.na ya.*zur*.na	They are visiting (FP)
أنتما تزوران	an.*tu*.mā ta.zū.*rān*	You are visiting (dual/M/F)
هما يزوران	*hu*.mā ya.zū.*rān*	They are visiting (dual/M)
هما تزوران	*hu*.mā ta.zū.*rān*	They are visiting (dual/F)

Irregular Arabic Verbs in the Future Tense

عبىسى (sa.ya.*bī*.'u) (*will sell*)

Form	Pronunciation	English
أنا سأبيع	*a*.nā sa.'a.*bī'*	I will sell
أنتَ ستبيع	*an*.ta sa.ta.*bī'*	You will sell (M)
أنتِ ستبيعين	*an*.ti sa.ta.bī.*'īn*	You will sell (F)
هو سيبيع	*hu*.wa sa.ya.*bī'*	He will sell
هي ستبيع	*hi*.ya sa.ta.*bī'*	She will sell
نحن سنبيع	*naḥ*.nu sa.na.*bī'*	We will sell
أنتم ستبيعون	*an*.tum sa.ta.bī.*'ūn*	You will sell (MP)
أنتنّ ستبعنّ	an.*tun*.na sa.ta.*bi'*.na	You will sell (FP)
هم سيبيعون	hum sa.ya.bī.*'ūn*	They will sell (MP)
هنّ سيبعنّ	*hun*.na sa.ya.*bi'*.na	They will sell (FP)
أنتما ستبيعان	an.*tu*.mā sa.ta.bī.*'an*	You will sell (dual/M/F)
هما سيبيعان	*hu*.mā sa.ya.bī.*'ān*	They will sell (dual/M)
هما ستبيعان	*hu*.mā sa.ta.bī.*'ān*	They will sell (dual/F)

يرتشسى (sa.ya.sh.*ta*.ri) (*will buy*)

Form	Pronunciation	English
أنا سأشتري	*an*.ā sa.'ash.*ta*.rī	I will buy
أنتَ ستشتري	*an*.ta sa.tash.*ta*.rī	You will buy (M)
أنتِ ستشترين	*an*.ti sa.tash.ta.*rīn*	You will buy (F)
هو سيشتري	*hu*.wa sa.yash.*ta*.rī	He will buy
هي ستشتري	*hi*.ya sa.tash.*ta*.rī	She will buy
نحن سنشتري	*naḥ*.nu sa.nash.*ta*.rī	We will buy
أنتم ستشترون	*an*.tum sa.tash.ta.*rūn*	You will buy (MP)
أنتنّ ستشترينّ	an.*tun*.na sa.tash.ta.*rī*.na	You will buy (FP)
هم سيشترون	hum sa.yash.ta.*rūn*	They will buy (MP)
هنّ سيشترينّ	*hun*.na sa.yash.ta.*rī*.na	They will buy (FP)
أنتما ستشتريان	an.*tu*.mā sa.tash.ta.ri.*yān*	You will buy (dual/M/F)
هما سيشتريان	*hu*.mā sa.yash.ta.ri.*yān*	They will buy (dual/MP)
هما ستشتريان	*hu*.mā sa.tash.ta.ri.*yān*	They will buy (dual/F)

روزسى (sa.ya.*zū*.ru) (*will visit*)

Form	Pronunciation	English
أنا سأزور	*a*.nā sa.'*a*.*zū*.ru	I will visit
أنتَ ستزور	*an*.ta sa.ta.*zū*.ru	You will visit (M)
أنتِ ستزورين	*an*.ti sa.ta.zū.*rī*.na	You will visit (F)
هو سيزور	*hu*.wa sa.ya.*zū*.ru	He will visit
هي ستزور	*hi*.ya sa.ta.*zū*.ru	She will visit
نحن سنزور	*naḥ*.nu sa.na.*zū*.ru	We will visit

Form	Pronunciation	English
أنتم ستزورون	*an*.tum sa.ta.zū.*rū*.na	You will visit (MP)
أنتن ستزرن	an.*tun*.na sa.ta.*zur*.na	You will visit (FP)
هم سيزورون	hum sa.ya.zū.*rū*.na	They will visit (MP)
هن سيزرن	*hun*.na sa.ya.*zur*.na	They will visit (FP)
أنتما ستزوران	an.*tu*.mā sa.ta.zū.*rā*.ni	You will visit (dual/M/F)
هما سيزوران	*hu*.mā sa.ya.zū.*rā*.ni	They will visit (dual/M)
هما ستزوران	*hu*.mā sa.ta.zū.*rā*.ni	They will visit (dual/F)

Appendix C

Answer Key

Here are all the answers to the Fun & Games quizzes.

Chapter 2: Taking a Closer Look at the Arabic Alphabet

1. c, 2. f, 3. j, 4. a, 5. i, 6. b, 7. d, 8. e, 9. h, 10. g

Chapter 3: Tackling Basic Arabic Grammar

1. أنتَ
2. نحن
3. هنّ
4. أنتِ
5. هو
6. أنتم

Chapter 4: Getting Started with Basic Expressions

1. i, 2. d, 3. f and h, 4. a, 5. j, 6. e, 7. c, 8. b, 9. h and f, 10. g

Chapter 5: Getting Your Numbers, Dates, and Measurements Straight

A. شتاء
B. صيف
C. ربيع
D. خريف

Chapter 6: At the Office and Around the House

1. حمّام (bathroom)
2. غرفة النوم (bedroom)
3. غرفة الطعام (dining room)
4. مطبخ (kitchen)
5. غرفة المعيشة (living room)

Chapter 7: Getting to Know You: Making Small Talk

1. أب
2. أم
3. أخت
4. جدّة

Chapter 8: Asking Directions and Finding Your Way

1. طف إلى اليمين. D.
2. هل يمكن أن تعيد من فضلك؟ A.
3. اذهبي إلى الغرب. E.
4. الفندق قريب. B.
5. البناية العاشرة. C.

A. Please repeat that. 2.
B. The hotel is close. 4.
C. It's the tenth building. 5.
D. Turn right. 1.
E. Go west. 3.

Chapter 9: Taking Care of Business and Telecommuting

1. متى سترجع؟ (When will she be back?) E.
2. هل عندك وقت فراغ؟ (Do you have free time?) B.
3. هل هو هنا؟ (Is he here?) A.
4. كيف الحال؟ (How are you doing?) D.
5. ما اسمك؟ (What's your name?) C.

A. 3 نعم. دقيقة من فضلك.

B. 2 لا. أنا مشغول.

C. 5 اسمي سعاد.

D. 4 الحمد لله, شكراً.

E. 1 سترجع بعد ساعة.

Chapter 10: This is Delicious! Eating In and Dining Out

1. الزبدة
2. بيض
3. جبن
4. حليب
5. خبز

Chapter 11: Going Shopping

A. حزام

B. بلوزة

C. تنورة

D. سروال

E. قميص

F. جورب

G. ربط عنق

H. حذاء

Chapter 12: Hitting the Town

A. الساعة الخامسة والنصف (as.*sā*.'āh al.*khā*.mi.sah wan.*niṣf*)

B. الساعة الثامنة إلا ربع (as.*sā*.'ah ath.*thā*.mi.nah *il*.lá rub')

C. الساعة التاسعة صباحاً (as.*sā*.'ah at.*tā*.si.'ah ṣa.*bā*.ḥan)

D. الساعة الثانية والنصف بعد الظهر (as.*sā*.'ah ath.*thā*.ni.yah wan.*niṣf ba'*.da aẓ.*ẓuhr*)

E. الساعة السادسة والربع صباحاً (as.*sā*.'ah as.*sā*.di.sah war.*rub'* ṣa.*bā*.ḥan)

Chapter 13: Enjoying Yourself: Recreation, Music, and the Outdoors

1. كرة السلة basketball
2. قيثارة guitar
3. سباحة swimming
4. رسم drawing
5. شطرنج chess
6. تنس tennis
7. شعر poetry

Chapter 14: Planning a Trip

A. قميص
B. فرشاة أسنان
C. جاكيت
D. قبعة
E. صندل
F. نظارات الشمس
G. حذاء

Chapter 15: Dealing with Money in a Foreign Land

1. C, 2. A, 3. D, 4. E, 5. B

Chapter 16: Getting Around: Planes, Trains, and Automobiles

1. سيارة
2. طائرة
3. قطار
4. حافلة
5. سفينة

Chapter 17: Finding a Place to Stay

1. فاتورة الهاتف C.
2. هل عندك رسائل لي؟ A.
3. مكتب الاستقبال D.
4. مرافق E.
5. متى وقت المغادرة؟ B.

A. Are there any messages for me? 2.
B. When is the checkout time? 5.
C. Telephone bill 1.
D. Reception desk 3.
E. Amenities 4.

Chapter 18: Handling Emergencies

1. شعر
2. رأس
3. عينان
4. فم
5. وجه
6. كتف
7. ذراع
8. صدر
9. يد
10. ركبة
11. قدم

Index

A

-a suffix, 29, 50
a- prefix, 53
Aatabou, Najat (singer), 312
abjad (writing system), 16
accessories, 175, 228
address, terms of, 64, 83–84
adjectives
  common, 29–31
  comparative form, 167–168
  defined, 28
  definite, 36, 40, 42
  feminine form, 30–31
  identifying, 29–31
  indefinite, 36, 38, 40, 42
  irregular, 32
  masculine form, 30–31
  multiple, 37, 38, 41
  noun interactions, 35–37
airplanes. *See also* transportation
  boarding, 259–260
  making reservations, 252
  registering at airport, 256
  Talkin' the Talk dialogue, 252–254
  terminology, 259
  Words to Know blackboard, 254
airport
  customs, 261–264
  exchange desk, 245
  immigration, 261–264
  registering at, 256
  Talkin' the Talk dialogue, 257–258
  Words to Know blackboard, 258–259
Ajram, Nancy (singer), 312
ALA (American Library Association), 16–17
ALA-LC Romanization Scheme, 16
al.'a.ra.biy.yah (news), 309
al-Atrash, Farid (singer), 312
al.baab.com (website), 311
aljazeera.net (website), 311
al.ja.zi.rah (news), 309
Allah, reference to, 62
alphabet, 9–14
al- prefix, 33, 35, 36, 61, 164, 180, 274
ambassador, 232, 304
American Library Association (ALA), 16–17
-a.ni suffix, 53
answer key, Fun & Games, 355–359
apostrophe, 17, 274
appetizers, 150
application form (bank), 240
appointments, business, 129
Arabic
  Egyptian, 2
  English word origins, 8–9
  expressions, 315–319
  Gulf Arabic, 2
  Koranic, 2
  learning quickly, 309–313
  Levantine, 2
  Modern Standard Arabic (MSA), 1, 2
  movies, 312–313
  music, 211, 311–312
  newspapers, 310–311
  North African, 2
  number of speakers, 1
  proverbs, 321–324
  regional dialects, 2
  scholars, 188
  script, 15, 17–25
  songs, 312
  speaking like natives, 14
  streaming services, 311
  structure of, 315
  television, 309–310
  transcription, 16–17
  transliteration, 2–3, 18–25
Arabic-English mini-dictionary, 327–333
arabicpod101.com (website), 310
Arabic-speaking friends, 312
Aramaic, 16
"to arrive" verb, 260–261
articles
  common, 34–35
  definite, 33, 34–35, 42
  exceptions to rule, 33
  indefinite, 33
  rule, 33
Asian currencies, 247
asking
  for directions, 114
  how someone is, 61–62
  for items, 163–166
  What's your name?, 64
  What time is it?, 180
  Where are you from?, 66
  "where" questions, 112–113
-a.ta suffix, 50
athletics, 204–208
ATMs, using, 244–245
-at suffix, 50
Australian currency, 247
auxiliary verbs, 288–289

B

bank
- account, opening, 236
- ATMs, 244–245
- contact info, 239–240
- deposits, 244
- forms, 240
- Fun & Games activity, 250
- going to, 235–236
- identification, 239
- Talkin' the Talk dialogue, 237–238, 240–242
- terminologies, 236
- withdrawals, 244
- Words to Know blackboard, 239, 242

bathroom items, 92

BBC Arabic streaming service, 311

beach
- going to, 208–210
- Talkin' the Talk dialogue, 209
- Words to Know blackboard, 210

"to be" sentences, 43–47

beverages, 151–152

"to be" verb, 37

bills
- hotels, 292
- restaurants, 154

body parts, 300–302

breakfast. *See also* meals
- as basic meal, 137
- fruits, 143
- items, 138
- ordering, 141–142
- Talkin' the Talk dialogue, 139–140, 141–142
- Words to Know blackboard, 140, 142

bus. *See also* transportation
- taking, 268–269
- Talkin' the Talk dialogue, 269–270
- terminologies, 269

business and telecommunications
- email communications, 113–115
- Google Translate, 134
- leaving messages, 131–133
- phone conversations, 124–133
- phone numbers, 124, 131
- social plans, 127

business appointments, making, 129

"to buy" verb, 173–174, 348, 350, 352

C

calendar
- days of the week, 76
- Gregorian, 77, 224
- Islamic, 77–78
- lunar, 77

cardinals, 120, 185, 224–225

check-in, hotel, 289–290

check-out, hotel, 291–292

clocks, 200

clothes
- accessories, 175, 228
- colors, 176
- finding, 159–160
- Fun & Games activity, 177
- packing for trips, 227–228
- shopping for, 174–176
- sizes, 175
- types of, 174

colleagues, interacting with, 83–84

colors, 32, 176

command form, 87–88, 118

common nouns, 28–29

common prepositions, 39–41

comparative adjectives, 167–168

comparative sentences
- with demonstratives, 168
- examples of, 168
- superlatives compared with, 169

comparing merchandise, 166–168

condiments, 144

congratulations! (expression), 318

consonants, 9, 12–14, 47–50, 55, 161, 189, 260

consul, 232, 304

consulates, 232, 304

contact info, 239–240

country names, 66–67, 218–219

co-workers, 83–84

currencies
- Asian, 247
- Australian, 247
- European, 247
- exchange, 245–248
- exchanging, 245
- Middle Eastern, 246
- North American, 246
- questions and answers, 247–248
- restrictions, 265
- Talkin' the Talk dialogue, 248–249
- types of, 246–247
- Words to Know blackboard, 249

cursive, 12

customs
- questions, 261–262
- speaking with, 264
- Talkin' the Talk dialogue, 265
- Words to Know blackboard, 266

Cyrillic languages, 17

D

dammah (dominant vowel)
common verbs, 53–54
defined, 11
double, 12
feminine singular nouns, 279
long, 12–13
subjunctive form and, 288
dammah vowel, 10–11
days, 76
definite adjectives, 36, 40, 42
definite articles, 33, 34–35, 42
definite nouns, 34–35, 36, 38, 40, 42
definite phrases, 36–37
demonstratives
comparative sentences with, 168
defined, 41
with definite noun/definite adjective, 42–43
with definite noun/indefinite adjective, 42
list of, 163
plural, 41
singular, 41
departments (companies), 82–83
deposits, 244
derivative form (numbers), 75
derivatives (vowels), 11
desserts, 151
dialects, regional, 2
dictionary
Arabic-English, 327–333
English-Arabic, 334–340
using, 310
difficult letters, 14
dining out
"to eat" verb, 53, 147–148, 342–343, 346–347
experience, 150
learning Arabic quickly, 313
length of meal, 150
menus, 150–152
paying bill, 154
placing order, 151
Talkin' the Talk dialogue, 151
tipping, 154
"to eat" verb, 147–148
Words to Know blackboard, 154
dining table items, 149
dinner
as basic meal, 137
at home, 148
time for, 148
diphthong, 11
diphthongs. *See also* vowels
directions
asking for, 114
asking for repeat of, 116–117
command forms, 118
directions, asking how to get to hotel, 118–119
Fun & Games activity, 122
Talkin' the Talk dialogue, 116–117, 118–119, 144–115
Words to Know blackboard, 117–118, 119–120
direct object pronouns, 279–280
"to do", 201–203
doctors, locating, 300
dominant vowel, 10–11, 53–54
double vowels, 10
"to do" verb, 202–203, 255–256
DVD, 313

E

eating out
experience, 150
learning Arabic quickly, 313
menus, 150–152
paying bill, 154
placing order, 151
Talkin' the Talk dialogue, 151
"to eat" verb, 147–148
"to eat" verb, 53, 147–148, 342–343, 346–347
ectaco.com (website), 310
Egyptian dialect, 2
El-Atrache, Farid (singer), 312
e-mail
etiquette, 134
sending in Arabic, 134
sending in English, 134
staying in touch by, 108–109
terminology, 134
translation, 134
embassies, 232, 304
emergencies
asking for help, 295–296
lending a hand, 298–299
medical help, 300–303
phrases, 296
Talkin' the Talk dialogue, 299–300
words, 296
English-Arabic mini-dictionary, 334–340
enunciation, 14
-er suffix, 166
European currencies, 247
excellent! (expression), 316
expressions, 55–57
Arabic favorite, 315–319
to be delivered, 319
congratulations!, 318
countries and nationalities, 65–66
excellent!, 316
Fun & Games activity, 71
God be exalted, 319
with God's permission, 318
God willing, 317
goodbye, 61
with health, 318
hello greeting, 60–61

T

U

V

W

Y

Z

About the Author

Amine Bouchentouf is a native English, Arabic, and French speaker born and raised in Casablanca, Morocco. Amine has been teaching Arabic and lecturing about relations between the United States and the Arab world in his spare time for more than 15 years and has offered classes and seminars for students at Middlebury College, the Council on Foreign Relations, and various schools across the United States. He runs and maintains the website `www.al-baab.com` (which means "gateway" in Arabic).

Amine published his first book, *Arabic: A Complete Course* (Random House), soon after graduating college in order to help an international audience understand Arabic language and culture. He has written *Arabic For Dummies,* 3rd Edition in order to reach an even wider audience with the aim of fostering better relations through education.

He holds a degree in Economics from Middlebury and has extensive experience in the arena of international investing. He is a registered investment advisor and is a member of the National Association of Securities Dealers. Amine is also the author of *Investing in Commodities For Dummies* (John Wiley & Sons, Inc.).

Amine is an avid traveler and has visited more than 15 countries across the Middle East, Europe, and North and South America. Aside from his interest in languages, business, and travel, Amine enjoys biking, rollerblading, playing guitar, chess, and golf.

Dedication

This book is dedicated to my greatest and most steadfast supporters — my family. To my mother for her infinite and unwavering support, and to my sister, Myriam, for her enthusiasm and passion — you are my greatest inspirations.

To my father and grandfather, may you rest in peace, thank you for instilling in me such a deep respect and awareness of my roots and culture. I am honored to be part of the Bouchentouf family.

And to my late grandmother, thanks for always believing in me.

Author's Acknowledgments

This book would not have been possible without the guidance and input from the wonderful folks at Wiley. It has been a great pleasure to work with a team that adheres to the highest standards of professionalism.

I would like to thank everyone who has supported me throughout this writing period. I would not have been able to do this without your precious support.

Publisher's Acknowledgments

Executive Editor: Lindsay Sandman Lefevere

Editorial Project Manager and Development Editor: Christina N. Guthrie

Copy Editor: Christine Pingleton

Technical Editors: Heather Sweetser and Abdullah Serag

Production Editor: Siddique Shaik

Illustrator: Elizabeth Kurtzman

Cover Photos: nicolamargaret/iStockphoto